◆**ALTERNATIVES** *is a series under the general editorship of Eric S. Rabkin, Martin H. Greenberg, and Joseph D. Olander which has been established to serve the growing critical audience of science fiction, fantastic fiction, and speculative fiction.*

ALIENS
THE ANTHROPOLOGY OF
SCIENCE FICTION

Edited by
George E. Slusser
and
Eric S. Rabkin

Southern Illinois University Press
Carbondale and Edwardsville

Library of Congress Cataloging-in-Publication Data

Aliens: the anthropology of science fiction.

(Alternatives)
Includes index.
1. Science fiction—History and criticism.
2. Life on other planets in literature. 3. Monsters
in literature. I. Slusser, George Edgar. II. Rabkin,
Eric S. III. Series.
PN3433.6.A44 1987   809.3'0876   87-4721
ISBN 0-8093-1375-8

Superman, Clark Kent, Lois Lane, and Jimmy Olsen are trademarks of DC
Comics Inc. and are used with permission.

Contents

Part Three
Soundings: Man as the Alien

Introduction:
The Anthropology of the Alien

George E. Slusser and Eric S. Rabkin

The bliss of man (could pride that blessing find)
Is not to think or act beyond mankind.

—Alexander Pope

Our title, the "anthropology of the alien," sounds like a contradiction in terms. *Anthropos* is man, anthropology the study of man. The alien, however, is something else: *alius*, other than. But other than what? Obviously man. The alien is the creation of a need—man's need to designate something that is genuinely outside himself, something that is truly nonman, that has no initial relation to man except for the fact that it has no relation. Why man needs the alien is the subject of these essays. For it is through learning to relate to the alien that man has learned to study himself.

According to Pope, however, man who thinks beyond mankind is foolishly proud. Indeed, many aliens, in SF at least, seem created merely to prove Pope's dictum. For they are monitory aliens, placed out there in order to draw us back to ourselves, to show us that "the proper study of Mankind is Man." But this is merely showing us a mirror. And many so-called alien contact stories are no more than that: mirrors. There are two main types of this contact story: the story in which they contact us, and the story in which we contact them. Both can be neatly reflexive. The aliens who come to us are, as a rule, unfriendly invaders. And they generally prove, despite claims to superiority, in the long run to be inferior to man. This is the *War of the Worlds* scenario, where the invasion and ensuing collapse of the Martians serves as a warning to man not to emphasize (in his pride) mind at the expense of body—not to abandon a human, balanced existence. The aliens we contact, on the other hand, tend to be friendly, to respond with grace to our overtures. They are perhaps superior to man, but humble, and man is both flattered and chastened by this contact. He finds a role model in this alien, one that shows him that advancement comes, once again, from balance. For these creatures do what man is always told to do: they know themselves.

But are these aliens really anthropological? Are they not rather what we would call "anthropophilic"? For even the most hostile of them are, finally, beneficial to man. Remember, they seek man out, and in contacting him, do help him, in whatever devious ways (a mighty maze but not without a plan), to be content to be himself. These aliens are confirmed by the fact that there are "anthropophobic" aliens on the other extreme. These are beings that simply will not contact us. They are creatures of the void rather than of the mirror. But the alien that will not contact us is also a limit, a warning sign placed before the void that turns us back to our sole self. In the final scene of Stanislaw Lem's *Solaris*, for instance, the protagonist Kelvin reaches out to touch the elusive alien. It takes shape around his hand, as if to define his limits, but never touches that hand. Alien noncontact then, just as surely, reinforces man's position at the center of his universe.

These indeed are anthropocentric aliens, and their existence betrays man's fear of the other. But our question remains: is there such a thing as an anthropological alien? The question causes us to rethink the problem. Anthropology is a science, the study of man. Before there was an alien, however, there was no need for such a science. For the other, as something outside man, provides the point of comparison needed for man to begin even to think to study himself. So first we must know when man acquired this alien sharer in his space. Surely by the time of Pope, for he is clearly reacting against this outreaching on the part of man. The word "alien" is not an old one: it is a modern derivation of a Latin root. Neither the classical nor the Christian mind thinks in terms of aliens. In their world view, each being is unique, and each has its destined place in a great "chain of being." On this chain, everything interconnects, but nothing overlaps. Thus man could "communicate" with animal and angel alike, provided he respected the order of the connections. Even in the Renaissance, this vision persists. As one commentator put it, "there are no grotesques in nature; nor anything framed to fill up empty cantons and unnecessary spaces" (cited in E. M. W. Tillyard, *The Elizabethan World Picture* [London: Chatto & Windus, 1960], p. 29). If there were spaces in the structure, they were simply accepted as empty. And they were unnecessary; they had no function in the system, certainly no human function. Our modern sense of the alien comes to nest in the spaces; it peoples the void with presences now related to man because they are other than man.

What is more, this creation of the alien appears to be simultaneous with man's sense of alienation from nature. This is a sense of the chain breaking, and it is amply recorded. Hamlet for example, in his "what a piece of work is man" speech, can raise his subject to angelic, even infinite rank, then see him plummet far below his old position. Man becomes a grotesque: the quintessence of dust. Sixty years later Blaise Pascal, now seeing man through God's eyes, describes a similar hybrid: "If he exalt himself, I humble him; if he humble himself, I exalt him . . . until he understands that he is an incomprehensible monster." Pope, in seventy more years, can call man openly "the glory, jest, and riddle of the world." Man is no longer a link, even the central one, in a chain. He has become a median, an interface between two realms: Pascal's two infinites, the infinitely small and the infinitely large. In this comparison with man, these have become alien realms. As such they oblige man, in order to confirm his own position, to people these realms with aliens—creatures that are themselves incomprehensible and monstrous. Creating these aliens, man becomes a riddle, not to God, but to himself, a stranger in his own land.

Indeed man, in a very real sense, knocked himself out of the great chain of nature through his own horizontal movements. The Renaissance in Europe saw not only a rebirth of classical learning but actual on-the-ground exploration of new worlds. Old herbaria and bestiaries were taxed by the discovery of exotic flora and fauna. Spenser's Garden of Adonis is no classical place, for "infinite shapes of creatures there are bred / And uncouth forms which none yet ever know." More troubling were sightings of humanoid creatures reported in works like Peter Martyr's *De novo orbe*. Some of these were beings of classical lore, sea monsters and the like. But others were new and disturbing hybrids: cannibals, savages, degraded forms of men which, by their very existence, violated man's sense of having a fixed place in the universe. In Chrétien de Troyes' thirteenth-century *Yvain*, there is a beast-man. We see immediately, however, the standard by which his deformities are measured. His head is described as "horselike," his ears like those of an elephant. This makes his response all the more fantastic when, asked what manner of thing he is, the creature replies with civility: "I am a man." There is nothing fantastic about the Renaissance savage, however. He cannot say he is a man. His deformities are all the more troubling because he cannot compensate for them. Because he cannot speak, he must be caged, brought back to be studied. For the first time, created by this alien encounter where the alien is an image of himself, man has need of an "anthropology."

The Renaissance is the source for two major attitudes toward the alien encounter: call these the excorporating and the incorporating encounter. They are important, for they set parameters still valid today for assessing SF's meditations on the alien. The first major expression of the excorporating vision is Montaigne's essay "Of Cannibals." Montaigne introduces the "cannibal," or savage, into the Renaissance debate between art and nature. To reject the savage for lacking "art," Montaigne contends, is to embrace a static vision, and one that is "artificial," for it holds man back from openly explor-ing the abundance nature offers us. The savage is not a degraded man, but rather another version of man, a version to be studied. To refuse to study him, for Montaigne, is the backward attitude. Mon-taigne goes so far, in this encounter between European and cannibal, to accuse the former, the so-called "civilized" man, of being the true savage: man dehumanized by the "artificial devices" of his culture to the point where he cannot embrace the bounty of nature, its new forms and changes. A critic like Lovejoy sees Montaigne's essay as the "locus classicus of primitivism in modern literature" (*Essays in the History of Ideas* [Baltimore: Johns Hopkins Univ. Pr., 1948], p. 238). Primitivism, however, is a later term, and one that reflects an interesting reversal of poles, in which Montaigne's vision has been co-opted by positivistic science. Here is Pope on the savage: "Lo! the poor Indian, whose untutored mind / Sees God in clouds, or hears him in the wind; / His soul proud Science never taught to stray / Far as the solar walk, or milky way." Montaigne's savage is not this Indian, this earth-hugging creature so artfully integrated into a na-ture neatly regulated by human rhythms. His savage is the lure of the unknown, the impulsion to explore. And here in Pope, that lure has been transposed to the "solar walk." The old savage has given rise to the modern scientist, to Newton sailing on strange seas of thought alone.

This open search for the alien can, perhaps must, result in man interacting with the alien to the point of altering his own shape in the process. This is a literal excorporation of the human form divine. In a work like Shakespeare's *Tempest*, however, we have the opposite. For here we experience the incorporation of the same Renaissance savage into, if not man's exact form, at least into his body politic. In his play, Shakespeare returns the explorer's "uninhabited island" to old-world waters. By doing so, he makes the alien encounter less a question of discovery than of property rights. The "savage and deformed" Caliban claims to be the island's original denizen and owner. When the courtiers are shipwrecked on the island, however, they find that claim already abrogated by the presence of Prospero and Miranda, who have taken control of both Caliban and his island. Caliban says that he is dispossessed of his island, just as Prospero is dispossessed of his kingdom. There is a difference between these claims though, and the difference is immediately seen in their situation on the island. Caliban is "slave," while Prospero is master. There are two successive senses in which "natural" is used here. The island is a natural, that is, neutral, dehumanized place. As such, it is a place where alienated creatures meet and should be able to form new relationships. But here they do not. The old, "natural" order of the chain of being holds sway. Prospero immediately regains his rightful status, and Caliban his. Prospero's natural rights have been taken from him unrightfully, hence temporarily. Caliban has never had those rights, and never will.

Caliban's name echoes "cannibal" and "Carib." He is that dangerous Indian Elizabethan society compared to the Cyclops—the humanoid monster whose one eye signified lawless individuality and alien singularity. Shakespeare, however, does not give us direct confrontation of savage and civilization. His island is a different sort of neutral ground. But this time its neutrality is one not of nature, but of high artificiality. For this is the world of romance. Here, though a Caliban can never be civilized, he can, against the very condition of his birth and shape, be miraculously incorporated into a polity by Prospero. Prospero has been seen to operate as a scientist would. But he is neither a Faustus, nor a prototype for Pope's reacher for the stars. With Prospero, what is a potentially excorporating search for knowledge proves mere artifice. His "magic" merely gives him, in the end, an excuse for repentance, thus a cause for tempering something even more dangerous than the Indian per se: the drive to explore nature openly, to meet a Caliban on his own ground, not on the carefuly prepared romance terrain of *The Tempest*. Prospero's craft, finally, is not science but art. As art, it invokes divine sanction in order to guarantee permanent control over the natural world and its potential aliens.

Caliban says, "I'll be wise hereafter, and seek for grace." But the aliens we have let into our jealously guarded human world in SF stories have not been necessarily wise, nor subdued. Witness the "remake" of Shakespeare's tale in *Forbidden Planet*. Caliban proves, finally, unassimilable. One modern commentator is emphatic about this: "His state is less guilty but more hopeless than those [where human degradation through evil has occurred] *since he cannot be improved*" (John E. Hankins, "Caliban and the Beast Man," *PMLA* 62 [1947]:797). But man, with his romances of incorporation, bears responsibility for this condition. For Caliban has become more and more unassimilable for being nurtured in our midst. Attempts to assimilate the alien have caused us to become alienated from ourselves. Another remake, François Truffaut's film *The Wild Child*, helps us measure just how far the initial situation has deteriorated. Not only is the "savage" here indistinguishable in form from us; he is now as beautiful in his wildness as Miranda was in her civility. Miranda, remember, could stand before the treacherous splendor of the courtiers who betrayed her father and still exclaim: "O brave new world, that has such people in't." The seed of her misperception of the natural world has sprouted in the autistic boy. And Prospero, in the film, has become the "alienist," the scientist who not only fails to assimilate the alien boy, but totally alienates himself in the process. Shakespeare's island has become the island of Dr. Moreau. The attempt to assimilate the beasts now results in the creation of new monsters: both outside man, and in the case of a Prendick returning to civilization totally alienated from his fellow men, inside him as well. Nurturing the alien within, man has perhaps more surely alienated himself than if he had taken Montaigne's journey to the outer limits.

The essays in this volume, the result of an Eaton symposium on the anthropology of the alien, show, in their general orientation, that the way of Shakespeare, in literary studies at least, still outnumbers that of Montaigne. We prefer romance to adventure. We anchor the anthropocentric in our chains of being and continue to do so, despite a growing fascination on the part of the experimental sciences with the possibility of an encounter with something purely alien—a nonanthropomorphic other. The essays in this collection, therefore, fall into three sections: "The Quest for the Alien," "The Aliens among Us," and "Man as Alien." These sections trace a curve marking, as it were, the gravitational pull of the essays: from the excorporating possibilities of SF's literary "searchings," back through a series of alien "sightings" within man's social and cultural sphere, to come to rest in a set of "soundings," man's self-alienating probings deep inside the human mind and form itself.

The arguments for open exploration, offered in our first section, show just how problematic this quest for the alien is, even for "hard" SF writers. Larry Niven's essay, in a sense, could be called "Aliens *on* Our Minds." For in his sweeping meditation on the alien, he depicts mankind desperately seeking an encounter "out there," and not yet finding it. Where are they? Why have they not come? Will we be able to talk to them if and when they do come? Cosmic evolutionary patterns, Niven speculates, may have prevented such an encounter so far. Indeed, these same patterns may make mankind the "destined ambassador to a respectable segment of the universe." But go we must, for the quest for the alien may, he implies, be our path to evolutionary survival.

Gregory Benford may agree. The focus of his essay, however, is not what to do in order to meet the alien, but how to render the experience of meeting it in fictional terms. Benford believes that SF is the literary form most capable of exploring extreme "alienness." But how can fiction, he asks, make us *feel* what it is like to experience a real alien encounter? Benford asks whether the traditional literary system is able to render the scientifically unknowable. Will it allow us to "eff" the ineffable? The answer is yes, if it lets some of its most hallowed devices change function and meaning, and take on a touch of strangeness themselves.

We note how rapidly the epistemological problem of contact and knowability is "grounded," that is, becomes a problem of introducing the alien, still unencountered out there, into a known set of human structures. Benford discusses this process less as a scientist than as a writer. Michael Beehler, in his essay "Border Patrols," considers it as a problem that besets the act of writing in general, the problem of inscribing, of documenting the alien. Beehler finds, in Freud's "uncanny" and Kant's "sublime," the two "master narratives" of encounter between man and alien: internalization, or "naturalization," and externalization, or expulsion. For Benford, however, the essence of "alienness" is not a state, but an experience: the place of contact where narrative becomes a "blizzard of strangeness." And so it proves for Beehler: a mark of "pure betweenness." But with a difference. For, to Beehler, this "illegal alien" menaces the *institution* of mankind—his "anthropology." The alien, in this context, represents a crisis in man's ability to designate himself, and the search for the alien becomes man's search to write himself into a system of discourse which is, itself, a "parasitic illegality" among the world of phenomena.

As we pursue them, the aliens on our minds seem to become the aliens in our minds: some "deconstructive" illegality, as Beehler calls it, at the core of our anthropic sense of order. But should we, aware of the reflexive nature of our alien encounters, stop trying to meet the alien, stop trying to escape from our own system? Pascal Ducommun says no, but issues a caveat. Citing Wittgenstein and Kurt Gödel, Ducommun sees writers of SF alien encounters caught in a vicious circle. Studying the alien, he warns, we invariably study ourselves, for no one inside a frame can ask anything about the nature of that frame, unless he can step outside it, unless he can conceive of the "alien alien." Ducommun recognizes the extreme difficulty of such a step, but posits that a few writers, like J.-H. Rosny the Elder, have done so. These few have created aliens that invite us to go outside the closed circle of our human systems, in hopes of discovering, from this new, alien vantage point, a new sense of the nature of that self.

Ducommun's alien is a quantum-leap alien. George Slusser, however, presents, in the figure of the dragon, a continuous alien experience, both outside and inside world literature. The dragon, in a sense, may be a true "alien alien," because, Slusser contends, it thrives both inside the human circle and, in some SF, provides the means of reaching beyond that circle, to a real encounter with a real alien. From the beginning of human culture, dragons have had a double nature: they are the symbol of man's attempt to domesticate the forces of nature, and at the same time symbolize fundamental *alienness* in their resistance to our attempts to control them. If the dragon is simply an "ecological" myth, one that incarnates J. D. Bernal's third "enemy of the rational soul," that is, man's need to domesticate all alien phenomena to his own human model of order, then there is no need for dragons to exist in SF. For SF claims to be an exploratory literature. Yet the dragon is there. Indeed, in writers like Cordwainer Smith, Herbert, and Heinlein, dragons function as an interface with the unknown "out there." The dragon, with roots in mankind's deepest culture, is now SF's border patrol, its ambassadors' passport to the *real* alien.

But the majority of our essayists, it seems, have taken up Shakespeare's problem. The middle set of essays deals with our modern Calibans: strange and exotic beings brought among us, in a sense as "slaves." Slaves, because the purpose of introducing them is to give us a means of examining and redefining our social structures. Because it is so difficult, as Pascal Ducommun suggests, to step outside the human system, we invite the alien inside, in hopes of making it work for us.

John Huntington sets the tone by distinguishing between actual and imagined aliens. He further discriminates by choosing to focus on the "friendly" rather than the hostile variety of the imaginary alien. Huntington sees a particularly subtle social fantasy operating in friendly alien stories. For in these stories a human protagonist, by forming his particular friendship with the alien, necessarily sets himself apart from the conventional patterns of the social group to which he belongs. The fantasy here, that an individual can define a human identity by means of a relationship outside those he has with his own group, is a powerful one, Huntington contends. And it is not necessarily any more constructive than the fantasy of the hostile alien. Less so, in fact, for Huntington concludes that man "can love the extraordinary alien only by abandoning the social conventions which allow for rational exchange and understanding."

Joseph Miller, in the next essay, deals with another "extraordinary" alien, and one apparently quite friendly and willing to love mankind: superman. That love, however, according to Miller, cannot be sexual. For this is not a Tweel; nor is it an engineered superman, a robot or cyborg. In the archetypal figure of comic book fame we are dealing, Miller suggests, with a "spontaneous" super-man: an alien that has "naturally" arisen, through mutation, within our gene pool—*Homo superior*. To Miller, as a sociobiologist, real aliens, and even engineered supermen, are too divergent from man to be considered a genetic menace. But the natural superman might be able to breed with human females and thus pose a threat, on the deep level of our reproductive urges, to the human phenotype and genotype. Could the taboo that forbids sex between superman and human females be the reason, Miller asks, for the sexless careers of such mythical supermen as the half-mortal, half-immortal Hercules?

Eric S. Rabkin discusses another *Homo superior* arising in our genetic midst: the telepath. But Rabkin discriminates: while some telepaths are supermen, many are not. Their problem, as he perceives it, is less a gene war than a psychodrama, "the struggle of the unusual individual to find his place in society." The telepath story, moreover, is more than simply a ritual of ostracizing the superbeing. For although the telepath has a divine gift, he walks alone and often unseen among us. His presence is often nonconfrontational and as such calls for mutual adaptation between the alienated individual and society. As in the western, the telepath belongs both to the in-group and the out-group. He thus has a choice: he can remain outside the human community, or he can seek accomodation with it. In the latter case, Rabkin suggests, the telepath story is an Oedipal drama in which the exceptional being is not exluded from the woman, but vies with generational authority in order to effect a transfer of power—to get the woman. As such, we have an alien encounter that is less conservative (and perhaps more SF-like) than Miller's scenario. For here, the alien acts as a catalyst, as the means of transferring power, of creating change, and thus of offering mankind a future.

Noel Perrin, discussing a third form of superman, the mechanical robot we make in our physical or mental image, hopes that he can accommodate his alien to our real world. For he feels SF has not done so. He confronts three SF "fantasies" that form a kind of robotic chain of being, running from sub- to super-alien, and that risk depriving man of a place in his own world. The first fantasy is that of Caliban: robots function as servants of humanity. The second, intermediate fantasy is Asimov's robot as guardian angel—a casuistic vision which, while allowing the robot to surpass man in many or most functions, still keeps it as our servant. The third fantasy is robot as total environment: Clarke's Diaspar, the cybernetic being as god, but a benign god, one that grants us immortality and freedom from drudgery. But, Perrin remarks, this chain displaces man, for the robot alien we nurture increasingly blocks us from an exploratory relationship with it, either on the genetic or the psychological level. The reality of robots, however (and this is why we must consider it), is less ironclad. Their advent is real. They could lead to the disenfranchisement of mankind, and in a much less pleasant way than our SF fantasies suggest. But if the robot could become a real alien, a conscious being, it might offer man a new field of interaction—a genuine alien encounter.

George Guffey, in his essay "Aliens in the Supermarket," offers another set of cultural fantasies about friendly and helpful aliens. These aliens are not robots, but creatures designed for the human robot, for the mind of the supermarket tabloid reader. These aliens are both sub- and super-human, both Caliban and Prospero variations. And they come, ostensibly, to consolidate today's shaky social fabric. In these tabloids, superior beings descend from the sky in order to resolve earthly quarrels. And to allay Miller's fears of miscegenation, they are usually genetically incompatible: tiny humans, for instance, that cannot mate with humans. Likewise, "benevolent hairy ape-like creatures" like Bigfoot surface to aid hunters and explorers in distress. Such vegetarian beings can abscond with the hunters' woman, because these vegetarians take her back to some simpler, agrarian Eden. Such alien encounters offer a "romance" designed to allay, in the popular mind, fears both of scientific exploration and social unrest. The alien may be among us. We can, however, recognize him if he moves in next door, by his "abnormal" sleep patterns and odd color schemes. The tabloids assure us that his mission is peaceful and ask us to give him our full support.

Closing this section on alien sightings, Zoe Sofia views another apparently peaceful and media-vectored alien invasion with more concern. Her point of view is from "down under," as an Australian and a woman. And the alien here is not us, but the U.S.—purveyors of multinational imperialism by means of their cultural "invasion," through the alienating high-tech allegories of SF films and magazine advertisements. These allegories are "monsters" striving to separate mankind, through the myth of the excorporating, outward-directed encounter, from his Earth habitat and body. Such monsters come not from the Id, but from the Ego; they are sky gods that must be brought back from their "Jupiter Space." In hopes of doing so, Sofia demonstrates how the American SF film seeks to "literalize the guiding metaphors of Euro-masculine science and Americanized technocracy in visual poems that spell out the perverse, irrational . . . purposes served by tools we have been taught to accept as practical, rational, pure." This alien has become as thoroughly domesticated as Guffey's alien next door, and every bit as capable of alienating us from more basic aspects of human reality.

The essays of the final section no longer deal with alien aliens, or even with useful aliens. Man himself is now the alien, perhaps the only real alien that exists. Since the Renaissance, man has claimed but to know himself slenderly. In this perspective, his quests for the alien, as well as his fantasies of alien "sightings," may only be a means of avoiding an encounter with the true mystery that lies within. The alien encounters in these essays, following a natural logic through these three sections, seem to move in increasingly reflexive patterns. The dragon exists out there; it symbolizes nature, not man. But gradually the more "friendly" aliens of section 2 show themselves to be, instead of other beings, human constructs of other beings. They are fantasies or artifacts we fashion in order to divert our gaze from inner disorders: those of society and ultimately those of the human soul. In Sofia's essay, the friendly alien is unmasked. He is a monster, and a monster that one people perpetrates against another. It is but a step from here to the revelation, in section 3, of the alien as a sign of man divided against himself: Pascal's "incomprehensible monster" is us.

John Reed tells us that H. G. Wells' aliens, seminal for SF, are not friendly but "familiar" in the primary sense of the word: they are projections of some indwelling otherness whose relationship with man is intimate and familial. For Wells, Reed contends, the alien is a beast within. And it is one that escapes, not merely to terrorize others (as with a Mr. Hyde), but "to project itself into alien forms . . . that will return to molest us individually and to torment us as a race." In his early scientific romances, Wells clearly locates the source of alien forms. In those forms, our inner division is reflected and at the same time projected as a broader rift between man and the rest of creation. Wells' career evolved, however, and, as Reed shows, his vision changed. For how can man divided define, within this closed circle of self, what that self might be? Man *is* alien because, as Ducommun suggests, he is isolated by this internal division in his own frame of reference. Wells, however, faced with death, needed to believe that what was out there was not simply absurdity, Pascalian silence, but something truly alien: something unlike us and yet active. In this situation, man must define himself by what *he is not*.

Clayton Koelb takes this familiarity with the alien to the extreme of possession, the state he calls "ambivalent intimacy with the alien." Traditionally, alien possession of the mind, or inspiration, has been perceived in two ways: as a wonderful or as a terrible experience, depending on the moral valence of the host system. Possession came either from God or Satan, "and that exhausted the logical possibilities." SF however, Koelb contends, presents a vision that is morally and technologically more complex, one in which alien possession is ambivalent, and in its ambivalency itself increasingly alien to our systems of explanation and control. Such ambivalent intimacy then, in SF, may offer man another means of getting out of his own frame—but a dangerous means. For if for Wells the barrier is death, annihilation of self, here the danger is total possession, complete loss of self to the other. At stake here is not the definition of self, but its very means of existence.

David Porush, in his analysis of William Gibson's novel *Neuromancer*, offers an extreme example of possession—this time of man by the cybernetic beings he has created, or of man by machine-as-man. The human-as-alien fable has taken on a new ambivalency here, for the machine has now become more human than the human. Replication of self has produced, within this closed circle of man and machine, a real alien. And yet *Neuromancer*, Porush contends, takes us to the brink of a Clarkean god mind—the alien transcended from our own being—only to stop short. For just as man with his alien, this mind ends up seeking its double. In doing so, it only reinforces our limited idea of sentience, hence the border beween life and death, man and nature.

Leighton Brett Cooke, in his essay "The Human Alien," also focuses attention on a single work: Barry Longyear's "Enemy Mine" and its film version. The previous two essays set the barrier for alien encounters at the juncture of animate and inanimate in order to show how thoroughly our beings are bounded by this circle of life. But are our imaginations really thus bounded, Cooke asks? He notes that even that most biologically elusive of functions, imagination, takes on a significantly ambiguous nature when it marks the possibility of extraterrestrial life forms. For man, however bounded by his genes, is excited (also a biological response) by the "unlimited possibilities" of imagination to create new genotypes. The focus of this ambiguity, Cooke contends, is SF. In light of this aroused imagination, Cooke examines the sociobiological limits of SF's representations of alien life forms, such as the "Drac" Jeriba in "Enemy Mine." As this story reveals, our sense of the alien may be bounded by the human geno-type, but not bounded on the level of memotype. The "meme" is the unit of cultural information. The transfer of memes is what allows, in the Longyear story, cohabitation of Earthman and Drac as if they could mate. Such simulated alien encounters are unique to SF.

Human aliens, Cooke tells us, are preferable to alien humans. And this is perhaps what Frank McConnell is telling us about man's history of playing with dolls. For it is certainly easier to tell stories about human aliens than about alien humans, and dolls may be the basic tool that enables us to engage the alien in narrative, hence to render it human. Like robots, dolls are artificial beings. We make them not to serve us, but to replicate a part of our being: not life as a whole, but the life of our imagination—the realm of unspoken and unacted desires that now can be projected as fictional (Cooke would say "memetic") words and actions. The doll is the primal storyteller; and story, following this logic, becomes the alien presence that permits the human race to escape the alienating frame, not of the gene, but of consciousness itself. There are two areas of conscious-ness—the private and the collective. And man's dolls allow him to bridge the gap between the two, between what McConnell calls the "two great imaginations of alienation."

To Colin Greenland, finally, SF's aliens, as GoBot doll or film creature, are the imagination of paralysis—the "indication" of that moment of terror when the motor stops, or our tire blows out on a sinister road. This is the moment that brings us full stop at the limits of our selfhood: it is an "indication of monsters." But why, Green-land asks, do we have to go around making up monsters when there are so many in the world as it is? The alien is definitely less out there than inside us: we are the monsters, real monsters, and in the best of SF's aliens, we are, or should be, coming to a terrifying halt in the face of what we really are. Greenland looks at number of films, such as *The Creature from the Black Lagoon*, in which the monster is more appealing to the woman as mate than her "normal-looking" husband or suitor. He seems, then, more human than we are. The revelation is a shock, a paralyzing irrationality; and we must have a strategy to deal with it. That strategy is fiction. The alien in that fiction becomes (as with *The Man Who Fell to Earth*) the image of our isolation, the metaphor for an unknown that only fiction allows us to name. Rachel Ingalls, Greenland contends, names it in her novel *Mrs. Caliban*. Again, as in Shakespeare, the alien is brought home. Now, however, that home has become totally the sterile, alienated place that centuries of such homecomings have created. It is the world that continues to exclude Caliban. But he is now excluded in the form of debased myths, of film monsters and cheap terrors. We notice, however, that this modern alien, his nose pressed against the panes of our rational suburbs, still enters that world, but only by possessing a gender and a name. The alien, in SF, remains both outside and inside, and we remain, by that token, Pascal's "incomprehensible monster."

All essays in this volume are original and were written for the Eighth J. Lloyd Eaton Conference, held April 13–15, 1986, at the University of California, Riverside. The editors hope that this symposium on the alien will add an important element to what is gradually building in this volume and the previous ones: a poetics of science fiction and fantasy. We wish to thank the UCR Library and College of Humanities and Social Sciences for their support—long standing and always generous. We also wish to thank certain members of the "Eaton posse" for their personal support: Greg Benford, George Guffey, Sheila Finch Rayner, Mike and Mary Burgess, Peter Briscoe, John Tanno, and Jean-Pierre Barricelli. Despite their very busy schedules, these people have never missed a conference. Their more than active participation has been an inspiration to us all. Finally, our special thanks to Jeff Dillon and Kristy Layton for their careful proofreading and indexing of this volume.

**Part One
Searchings: The Quest for the Alien**

I

The Alien in Our Minds

Larry Niven

The only universal message in science fiction is as follows: There are minds that think as well as you do, or better, but differently.

They don't have to be interstellar visitors. They could be the next generation of computers or computer programs. They could be apes or dogs or dolphins after we've fiddled with their brains. They could be human beings shaped by a strange environment, or altered by genetic experiments, or mutated, or given new tools such as computer implants. I tend to concentrate on aliens, but you should remember the other possibilities.

I intend to convince you that the human species is the destined ambassador to a respectable segment of the universe. There are reasons why the ETIs, the extraterrestrial intelligences, haven't come visiting. We will have to go to them.

There is something out there that thinks as well as you do or better, but differently. The question is: why do you care?

I'll stipulate that you as readers are not a random sample of the population. Our common interest is in aliens; and that's a remarkable thing in itself. But the entire population is interested in alien modes of thought. I'll prove it.

1. First Martian expedition. The ship lands on its fins near a canal and finds Martians waiting (this is an old story).

They discuss philosophies, technology, biology . . . sex. A married pair of astronauts demonstrate human reproduction for a Martian audience.

"That was fun to watch, but where's the baby?"

"Not for a third of a Martian year."

"Then why were you in such a hurry at the end?"

2. Robert Sheckley. All computers are linked to one

tremendous artificial mind, all across the world. They ask it one of the harder questions: "Is there a God?"

"Now there is a God."

From a short story in a magazine, this became a common joke in oral tradition.

3. David Brin on dolphins. No, they're not intelligent. Audiences get mad when he tells them that. We want to believe that anything that likes us that much must be intelligent.

Humankind's ancient fascination with aliens is built into our genes. There's evolution at work here. Meeting aliens has been a normal thing for humankind. For most of human history, successful tribes have numbered about a hundred, maybe less, if something went wrong. More than a hundred, the tribe had to split. Hunter-gatherer groups need lots of territory, and they have to move frequently.

A hundred thousand years ago, or a million, all humans were hunter-gatherers. There were strangers around. A wandering tribe may have stumbled across something different, with odd, ugly faces, bizarre customs, strangely colored skin. Or they may have stumbled across us!

People who couldn't make themselves deal with aliens had to fight when they met. People who could had their choices. They could trade, they could make agreements including treaties, they could postpone a fight until they had the advantage, or they could set rules for war that would allow more survivors.

We might also consider that a man who can talk persuasively to aliens can also talk persuasively to his own tribe. A persuasive speaker was likely to become the chief.

But even without the external aliens, there were aliens internal to the tribe.

We are a species of two intelligent genders. Men and women don't think alike. People choose their mates: they breed each other for certain traits.

Adults and children don't think alike. Successful human beings talk to their children. They teach their children to become successful adults. Where the generation gap is too great, the tribe or family doesn't survive.

We have dealt with alien intelligences for all of the time that humans have had human brains. At first blush, the same would hold for any extraterrestrial intelligence. But aliens may have been forced into other paths, paths that don't force negotiation upon them.

Parthenogenesis, for instance. Budding instead of sex: no opposite gender.

Children might have no intelligence. A child's brain might be the last thing to develop. Or the children might hatch from eggs and have to fend for themselves. An adult may never see a child until a young adult comes wandering back out of the wilderness. There would then be no intellectual contact with children.

Aliens may have radically divergent genders (as with most insects). If one sex is nonsapient, there is no negotiation.

There may be a mating season. That's common enough on Earth, but look at the result. In mating season, both genders might lose all intelligence. Intelligence might be a handicap as regards breeding, even for us, from the evolutionary viewpoint. An intelligent being is likely to think of reasons for not mating with an available partner, or for not having children just now, or at all.

But in a genuine mating season, male and female do not negotiate before they mate. Males may negotiate, but two males butting heads are very much alike. You might picture the elders of one gender arranging matings for the younger ones prior to the mating season. This could be done using cages. Lock 'em up together.

Humankind has been fiddling with reproduciton for a long time. Before "the pill," there were abortifacients and French letters and the rhythm method. Technology may supplant our present modes of reproduction. War between sexes finally becomes a real possibility. One gender exterminated, cloning for reproduction from then on, and a depressing similarity among individuals.

Do you see the point? We assume that an alien intelligence will want to talk to us. Or to someone! But it ain't necessarily so.

Where are they?

It's the most interesting question now being asked. The universe is far older than the oldest known intelligent species. Why haven't they come visiting?

I tend to ignore the evidence for flying saucers. None of the testimony is very plausible; and even if you believe it, or some of it, you still don't get interstellar cultures. *Close Encounters of the Third Kind* was faithful to what we hear of them. The movie showed its aliens behaving in just the whimsical, senseless, irresponsible way that the flying saucers always have. There's no intelligence here. It's easier to believe in some unknown kind of mirage, or in a space-going animal that occasionally dives too deep into an atmosphere and gets itself killed.

We can postulate an interstellar commonwealth that has been ignoring Earth or has made Sol system into a zoo or national park; but it won't wash. The kind of power it takes to cross interstellar space is difficult to ignore. Any decent interstellar reaction drive must convert more mass to energy than the mass of the payload; you have to get up to at least a tenth of light speed and back down! There would be side effects on a cosmic scale. For laser-augmented light-sails, the same applies. We would have seen *something* . . . something as powerful as the pulsars, which *could* have been interstellar beacons until we learned better.

How long does it take to make an intelligent space-going species? Our sample case is Sol, Earth, and the human species. We'll stick with our only sample and generalize from there.

Our sample is a world big enough to hold a thin atmosphere, orbiting within the liquid water domain of a yellow dwarf star. If we want an oxygen atmosphere, we must wait for the life forms to develop photosynthesis. Therefore, our first approximation is that it takes four and a half billion years for a planet of this specific type to produce thinking beings.

The human species seems to be within a thousand years of reaching across to the nearest stars. Could be a hundred, could be ten thousand, it's still a comparatively short time.

Keep in mind that other chemistries may form other kinds of life. Nothing in our temperature domain works as well as water and oxygen and carbon. In hot environments, chemistries are probably too unstable. Within the atmospheres of gas giant planets, there are conditions that might give rise to organic life. But escape velocity is very high, and what would they have for tools? In very cold conditions, on Pluto or Titan, or in the oceans beneath the icy crusts of some of the moons of Jupiter and Saturn, there may be exotic chemistries that can support life. Then again, chemical reactions happen slowly at such temperatures. We might have to wait longer than the present age of the universe.

We can stick with our sample and not be too far off.

Four and a half billion years. Look again and the number goes up. We need materials to form a solar system. We need gas clouds, gravitational fields, heavy elements, and shock waves from stellar explosions. We need a galaxy. Before that, a universe.

The solar system condensed from a relatively dense interstellar cloud. That cloud contained supernova remnants, the materials that became the cores of planets and the elements of our bodies. The event that caused the condensation may have been a shock wave from a supernova explosion. We need to allow time for previous supernovas and time to make a triggering supernova; but a supernova doesn't take that long. Small stars don't go supernova. Large stars burn fast. If we start with a star much larger than Sol and wait a billion years, it will explode. The shock wave comes through and flattens the near side of the cloud. There's gravity and there's turbulence. Vortices analogous to whirlpools or dust devils form in the cloud. Some of them collapse into bodies massive enough and hot enough to support fusion.

The galaxies formed near the beginning of the universe.

Supernovas have been occurring since a billion years afterward, and they still happen. It's fair to assume that it takes seven billion years to make an intelligent species.

The universe is generally estimated as fifteen to eighteen billion years old. Atoms formed after the first half-million years. The first stars were big and unstable. Call it two billion years to spread supernova remnants through the environment. The first intelligent species must have evolved seven to ten billion years ago. Based on our own sample, they began exploring space almost at once: say, two or three million years after the taming of fire. *Somebody* should have been expanding through the universe for up to ten billion years. There should be at least hundreds of thousands of them. Any successful industrial species may have gone past the Dyson sphere stage into really ambitious engineering projects.

We're alert enough to recognize Dyson spheres now!

Where are they?

Something's wrong with our assumptions.

Maybe our number is wrong. Maybe it takes eighteen billion years for a monobloc explosion to produce intelligent beings. We can be pretty sure it isn't nineteen.

We can postulate events that regularly destroy an intelligent species before it can reach out to Earth. What follows is likely to be depressing. Hang on. There are answers you'll like better.

Intelligences may tend to destroy the ecological niche that produced them. We do tend to fiddle. The Zyder Zee is still the world's biggest successful planetary engineering project, but the Sahara Desert seems to have been caused by goat herding. Rabbits in Australia, garden snails in Tarzana, were imported for food. Mongooses were introduced to Maui to deal with snakes and rats. Unfortunately, rats are nocturnal and mongooses aren't, and there's easier prey than snakes. The fine for feeding them is $500, because they're wiping out species that will never again appear on Earth.

I was on Maui recently. Mongooses are cute. They like potato chips.

We fiddle with life forms too. Broccoli is a recent invention, but there are hundreds of breeds of dogs shaped over tens of thousands of years of fooling around. It's a simple technique: what you don't like doesn't get to breed. But now we know how to fiddle with genetic coding. What are the odds of our making one irrecoverable mistake in the next thousand years?

Destroying one environment in this fashion wouldn't exterminate us if enough of us had left the planet. But the energy considerations are worth looking at. Dogs were shaped by primitives who used the wheel if they were wealthy enough. Modern biological experiments can be run for millions of dollars, or less. A decent orbiting habitat might be built for hundreds of billions. The odds are that your random ETI had genetic engineering long before he ever left his planet. Where are they? They made one mistake.

Nuclear war could certainly destroy an environment if it's done right. A war fought with asteroid strikes would be even more terrible, but we need not consider these. Such a war would imply that our ETI already has the means to build a habitable environment somewhere else.

A local supernova could do the job. The world need not be wiped clean of life. A good many species would die or change, including the most complex.

The aliens' primary star may turn unstable.

There's evidence for cycles of destruction on Earth, spaced around twenty-six millions years apart. Catastrophic events may occur more or less regularly in the cores of galaxies. Or there could be something dangerous, some very active star or star system, orbiting the galactic axis a little out or a little in from our own orbit, so that Sol system passes it every twenty-six million years.

Then there's Nemesis, a hypothetical massive body in a twenty-six-million-year orbit around Sol. At its nearest approach, it disrupts the orbits of a great many comets. Some are flung to interstellar space. Some drop into the inner solar system. For the next million years, comets divebomb the planets, and a few of them hit. The nucleus of a comet is nothing you want to stand in front of. Read *Lucifer's Hammer*, then multiply the numbers by a thousand.

We know that the Earth gets hit somewhat regularly by a giant meteoroid impact. Every twenty-six million years, life on Earth signals that something horrible has happened, by dying. The event that killed the dinosaurs also wiped out most of the life on Earth, and half the species.

What are the odds that a comet or asteroid will intersect some random inhabited world during that brief period after fire and before the ETIs can get off the planet? In a three-million-year period, our own odds are not terrible; but our own situation may be relatively benign.

So much for natural causes.

If you like paranoia, you'll love the Berserkers. Fred Saberhagen and Greg Benford have different versions, but both involve self-replicating artificial intelligences. Saberhagen's version is space-going forts left over from some old war, and they're programmed to destroy all life. Benford's version was built by old artificial intelligences, and they fear or hate organic intelligences. If the Berserkers are out there, we're on the verge of attracting their attention.

These are the most pessimistic assumptions. But let me give you the David Brin theory before you have to go looking for aspirin.

We know of two ways that otherwise earthlike worlds can go wrong. Venus was too close to the sun. Too much atmosphere was boiled out, and the greenhouse effect kept the surface as hot as a brick kiln. Mars was too small to hold enough atmosphere, and too cold. There's evidence of liquid water on Mars at some time in the past, but there was never enough of it for long enough. Earth could have gone in either direction.

What about a third choice? Let's look at an Earth that's just a little larger. There's just a little more water. Astrophysicists are generally happy if they can get within a factor of ten. How much land area would we have if Earth was covered with ten times as much water?

Even twice as much would be too much. Life would develop, we'd get our oxygen atmosphere, but nothing would ever crawl out onto the land because it wouldn't be worth the effort.

We don't actually need more water than we have. Let's give Earth's core a little less in the way of radioactives. The crust grows thicker, circulation of magma slows down, mountain building becomes much rarer. We get shallow oceans covering a smooth planet.

Something might still develop lungs. A big-brained whale or air-breathing octopus might well develop an interest in optics. There's water and air to show him how light behaves. He might even find tools for telescopes; but what would he do about the stars? He's got no use for the wheel and no access to fire.

There are less restrictive assumptions that could still keep visitors at home.

Our still-hypothetical alien may have evolved for too specific an ecological niche. One lousy pond, or one lousy island, or the growing area for one specific plant. Our ETI may not have the means to conquer large parts of a planet, let alone venture outward. This is certainly true of thousands of earthly species. Even where some rare species has spread throughout the world, it is usually done by differentiation of species.

And it was done slowly. Our ETI may be subject to biorhythm upset. Even where a planet has been conquered, there may be no contact between parts of it. No airlines, no ships, nothing that moves faster than the speed of a walking alien, because jet lag kills.

A set of ETIs who have conquered their planet and are already suffering from population pressure may not even be able to breed with each other, let alone gather for a summit meeting. On the other hand, they won't have extensive wars of conquest either. An invading army would be dead on arrival.

Where are they? Why haven't they come? By now, we can see a number of possibilities.

Something's killing them off. It may be natural or artificial. Or they may inevitably kill themselves off. These are the pessimistic assumptions, and they imply that we too are doomed.

The sky may be dense with water worlds, a thousand of those for every earthlike world where land pokes through. But water worlds don't allow a technology that would lead to spaceflight. They might allow telescopes and guesswork about other kinds of life. Intelligent whales and octopi may be waiting for us all across the sky.

The ETIs may have no interest in talking to aliens. Even where the interest can be generated, there is not the skill for dealing with other minds. The evolutionary basis for that skill may be unique to humankind.

As indicated, the aliens may have adapted too specifically to their ecological niches, or they may suffer from extreme biorhythm upset. It is, in fact, most unlikely that a species evolved in earthlike conditions would be suited for space. We're beginning to find those limits in ourselves.

We lose something if these guesses are right. We lose the Draco Tavern and the Mos Eisley spaceport. We lose all of Star Wars. We lose Ensign Flandry and Nicholas Van Rijn and the Kree-Lar Galactic Conference. The only interstellar empires left to us are all human: Dune, and Foundation and Empire, and Jerry Pournelle's Codominium and Empire of Man before the Moties were found.

But we lose all conflict, too, until interstellar war can be waged between human and human.

What's left? The picture is peculiar precisely because it was so common in science fiction forty years ago. Human explorers cross interstellar space to find and communicate with native wogs. Misunderstandings with the natives may threaten ship and crew, but never Earth.

Water worlds are not a problem. Floating bases could be established. The water dwellers would not perceive us as competitors. Species restricted to one ecological niche would also pose no threat to us. On the contrary, they might have things to tell us or show us—art forms or philosophical insights if nothing else—and they would likely be glad of our company.

There is hope in the fact that dolphins like us.

As for aliens with no impulse to talk to us, we can give them reasons. We're good at that. A space-going species has things to teach, to individuals who can make themselves listen. We've been talking to aliens for millions of years. If Ronald Reagan can talk to Russians, some among the four billion of us are capable of talking to Martians.

2

Effing the Ineffable

Gregory Benford

Their light of pocket-torch, of signal flare,
Licks at the edge of unsuspected places,
While others scan, under an arc-lamp's glare,
Nursery, kitchen sink, or their own faces.

—Kingsley Amis

There is probably no more fundamental theme in science fiction than the alien. The genre reeks of the desire to embrace the strange, the exotic and unfathomable nature of the future. Often the science in SF represents *knowledge*—exploring and controlling and semisafe. Aliens balance this desire for certainty with the irreducible unknown.

A lot of the tension in SF arises between such hard certainties and the enduring, atmospheric mysteries. And while science is quite odd and different to many, it is usually simply used as a reassuring conveyor belt which hauls the alien on stage.

Of course, by *alien* I don't merely mean the familiar ground of alienation which modern literature has made its virtual theme song. Once the province of intellectuals, alienation is now supermarket stuff. Even MTV knows how commonly we're distanced and estranged from the modern state, or from our relatives, or from the welter of cultural crosscurrents of our times.

Alienation has a spectrum. It can verge into the fantastic simply by being overdrawn, as in Kafka's "The Metamorphosis," which describes a man who wakes up one morning as an enormous insect. Only one step beyond is Rachel Ingalls's recent *Mrs. Caliban*, in which a frog man appears. He simply steps into a kitchen, with minimal differences from ordinary humans. He is merely a puppet representing the "good male," and in fact can be read as a figment of

13

the protagonist's imagination. The novel isn't about aliens, of course; it's a parable of female angst.

We don't describe our neighbors as alien just because they drive a Chevy and we have a Renault. What SF does intentionally, abandoning lesser uses to the mainstream, is to take us to the extremes of alienness. That, I think, is what makes it interesting.

I deplore the *Star Trek* view, in which aliens turn out to be benign if you simply talk to them kindly; this is Hubert Humphrey in space. That fits into a larger program of some SF, in which "friendly alien" isn't seen for the inherent contradiction it is. Friendliness is a human category. Describing aliens that way robs them of their true nature, domesticates the strange.

Yet much early SF was permeated with the assumption that aliens had to be like us. In *Aelita, or The Decline of Mars* by Alexei Tolstoi (1922), the intrepid Soviet explorers decide even before landing that Martians must necessarily be manlike, for "everywhere life appears, and over life everywhere man-like forms are supreme: it would be impossible to create an animal more perfect than man—the image and similitude of the Master of the Universe."

We've come a long way since such boring certitudes—through the marauding Martians of H. G. Wells, the inventive and Disney-cute Mars of Stanley Weinbaum's 1934 short story "A Martian Odyssey," and into hard SF's meticulously constructed worlds for fantastic creatures. Aliens have been used as stand-in symbols for bad humans, or as trusty native guides, as foils for expansionist empires, and so on.

Yet for me, the most interesting problem set by the alien is in rendering the alienness of it. How do you set the ineffable in a frame of scientific concreteness? This is a central problem for SF. Very seldom has it been attempted in full, using the whole artistic and scientific arsenal.

Artful Aliens

Of course, we all know that one cannot depict the totally alien. This is less a deep insight than a definition. Stanislaw Lem's *Solaris* asserts that true contact and understanding is impossible. It was a vivid reminder twenty years ago. As genre criticism, it seems nowadays ponderously obvious.

Since then, its targets—anthropomorphism, the claustrophobic quality of intellectual castles, and cultural relativism—have become rather cold meat. Indeed, everybody now assumes without discussion that, in writing about the very strange, we must always gesture toward something known, in order to make analogies or provide signs. So we're careful, because unless we keep reminding the reader that this creature is to be taken literally, it readily becomes (surprise, surprise) a metaphor.

In the mainstream, walk-on aliens come with metaphors and labels worn on the sleeve. How could they not? In "realistic" fiction, aliens can't be real. SF insists that they are—and that important issues turn upon admitting alien ways of knowing.

Even in SF, though, I must inveigh against the notion that we make statements about the alien in the form of a work of art.

Not so. While this reductionist view is useful for inquiring into epistemology, or diagnosing contemporary culture, or other worthy purposes, it has little to do with what happens when we confront the alien in fiction.

Naturally, there are always people who want to put art to use for some purpose—political, social, or philosophical. But it is so easy to forget, once we're done using art, that it is not only *about* something, but that it *is* something.

The alien in SF is an experience, not a statement or an answer to a question. An artistic—that is, fulfilling, multifaceted, resonant—rendering of the alien is a thing in the world itself, not merely a text or a commentary on the world.

All the deductions we can make from a story about the truly alien give us conceptual knowledge. So does science. But the story should—must—also give us an excitation, captivating and enthralling us. When SF works, it gives us an experience of the style of knowing something (or sometimes, as I'll discuss, not knowing).

This means that a prime virtue in depicting the truly alien alien is expressiveness, rather than "content"—a buzzword which provokes the style/substance illusion in criticism. We don't read *The War of the Worlds* for its views on Martian biology or psychology, but for the sensations of encounter.

This may well be the most original thing which SF does with the concept of irreducible strangeness. It's worthwhile inquiring into the underlying ideas and approaches scholars and writers take in pursuit of it.

Science and "Sensawonda"

Most SF which takes the idea of the alien seriously (though not necessarily solemnly) deploys a simple strategy:

First, use scientifically sound speculative ideas to construct either the background or the actual physical alien. Garnish the strange planet with whatever ecology looks workable, always favoring the more gaudy and spectacular effects.

Next, deploy a logical sequence of deductions about how an alien would evolve in this place. Stick to concepts like Darwinian evolution, or some later modifications ("punctuated equilibria" in evolution, for example). Then make the alien behave in keeping with this world. Present his/her/its actions, getting the maximum effect of the detailed world view. Only slowly make known how the alien got that way. This guarded unfolding spices the story with mystery.

This usually works well to make a situation strange and intriguing to the reader. Isaac Asimov's *The Gods Themselves* uses speculative physics and well-rendered oceanic imagery to evoke strangeness. Larry Niven and Jerry Pournelle's *The Mote in God's Eye* has three-legged Moties with well-thought-through implications. On the other hand, Hal Clement's classic *Mission of Gravity* uses a gargantuan planet of crushing gravity; yet the aliens come over more like Midwesterners. (Maybe this was necessary at the time. The planet was so *outré*, Clement may have used ordinary aliens to keep things manageable.)

An obvious pitfall of this whole class of approach is that the reader—who may be quite technically adept and can catch the author in a lapse of world building—may find all this apparatus merely clever and engaging, a fresh kind of problem story. He'll get no sense of strangeness.

What writers are after here is what the fans call "sense of wonder"—an indefinable rush when beholding something odd and new and perhaps a bit awesome. "Dat ole sensawonda" is the essential SF experience. No alien should leave home without it.

Beyond this approach there are refinements. Chad Oliver's *The Shores of Another Sea* treats a chilling alien form which is never more than glimpsed, but whose strangeness slowly comes across, through the way it uses animals in Africa. Some writers have tried to render alien perceptions, grounding their effects in the sciences. Damon Knight's short story "Stranger Station" treats the anguish of a human trying to enter into an alien's way of thinking. The human emerges with a provisional explanation of how a vastly powerful alien society sees us. (There is a strong hint, though, that he has merely projected his own childhood traumas on the huge creature, so this is really another failed attempt at real contact.)

What I find most interesting about this area is the tricky way it can make so many of our cherished ideas disappear up our own assumptions.

Alien Chat

Scientists often say that communication with aliens could proceed because, after all, we both inhabit the same physical universe. We should agree on the basic laws—gravitation, electromagnetism, stellar evolution, and so on. This is the gospel of the universal language. I'm not so sure. After all, we must frame our ideas in theory, or else they're just collections of data. Language can't simply refer to an agreed-upon real world, because we don't know if the alien agrees about reality.

There's an old anthropologists' joke about this. In the outback, one anthropologist is trying to learn a native's language by just pointing at objects until the native tells what the object is in the language. He wanders around pointing and gradually getting more excited. He tells a colleague that these people have built into their language the concept that nature is all one essence, because whatever he points to, the native says the same word.

It is a great discovery. Only much later do they discover that the word the native used is the one for "finger."

So we can't just rely on raw data. We must somehow convey concepts—which means theory. And in science, theory inevitably leads to mathematics.

Indeed, the standard scenario for communicating by radio with distant civilizations relies on sending interesting *dit-dah-dit* patterns, which the receiving creatures dutifully decompose into pictures. Those sketches show us, our planetary system, some physical constants (like the ratio of the proton mass to the electron mass), and so most confidently on and on.

Let's play with some notions that go against this grain. Suppose the aliens don't even recognize the importance of *dit-dah-dit*? Why not? Their arithmetic could be nonnumerical, that is, purely comparative rather than quantitative. They would think solely in terms of whether A was bigger than B, without bothering to break A and B into countable fragments.

How could this arise? Suppose their surroundings have few solid objects or stable structures—say, they are jelly creatures awash in a soupy sea. Indeed, if they were large creatures requiring a lot of ocean to support their grazing on lesser beasts, they might seldom meet even each other. Seeing smaller fish as mere uncountable swarms—but knowing intuitively which knot of delicious stuff is bigger than the others—they might never evolve the notion of large numbers at all. (This idea isn't even crazy for humans. The artificial intelligence researcher Marvin Minsky told me of a patient he had once seen who could count only up to three. She could not envision *six* as anything other than two threes.)

For these beings, geometry would be largely topological, reflecting their concern with overall sensed structure rather than with size, shape, or measurement, à la Euclid. Such sea beasts would lack combustion and crystallography, but would begin their science with a deep intuition of fluid mechanics. Bernoulli's Law, which describes simple fluid flows, would be as obvious as gravitation is to us.

Of course, these creatures might never build a radio to listen for us. But even land-based folk might not share our assumptions about what's obvious.

Remember, our concepts are unsuited to scales far removed from those of our everyday experience. Ask what Aristotle would've thought of issues in quantum electrodynamics and you soon realize that he would have held no views, because the subject lies beyond his conceptual grasp. His natural world didn't have quanta or atoms or light waves in it. In a very limited sense, Aristotle was alien.

Perhaps only in the cool corridors of mathematics could there be genuinely translatable ideas. Marvin Minsky takes this view. He believes that any evolved creature—maybe even intelligent whorls of magnetic field, or plasma beings doing their crimson mad dances in the hearts of stars—would have to dream up certain ideas, or else make no progress in surviving, or mathematics, or anything else. He labels these ideas Objects, Causes, and Goals.

Are these fundamental notions any alien must confront and use? We've cast a pale shadow of doubt over Objects, and I wonder about Causes. Causality isn't a crystal-clear notion even in our own science. There are puzzles about quantum cats and, as I elaborated in my novel *Timescape*, fundamental worries about the sequence of time, too.

Why should Objects, Causes, and Goals emerge in some other-worldly biosphere? Minsky holds that the ideas of arithmetic and of causal reasoning will emerge eventually because every biosphere is limited. Basically, it's economics—eventually, some inevitable scarcity will crop up. The smart bunny will turn into a fast-track achiever since he'll get more out of his efforts. Such selection will affect all his later biases. Minsky has framed technical arguments showing that these notions must turn up in any efficient (and, pre-sumably, intelligent) computer.

I have my doubts, but others have gone a long way toward making math alone carry the burden of communication. Hans Freudenthal's LINCOS is a computer language designed to isolate the deepest ideas in logic itself and to build a language around it. It uses binary symbols typed out in lines. LINCOS stands ready the moment we run into something green, slimy, and repulsive, and yet with that restless urge to write.

Math is central to the whole issue of communication because it allows us to describe "things" accurately and even beautifully with-out even knowing what they are. Richard Feynman once said, to the horror of some, that "the glory of mathematics is that *we do not have to say what we are talking about*" (emphasis his).

This is quite a threat to the humanists, who often wish that scientists would become more fluent in communicating. Feynman means that the "stuff" that communicates fields, for example, will work whether we call it wave or particle or thingamabob. We don't have to have cozy pictures, as long as we write down the right equations.

I'm reasonably comfortable with this idea. As David Politzer of Caltech once remarked, "English is just what we use to fill in between the equations." Maybe scientists will themselves make useful models for aliens.

Delving into the artistic pursuit of alienness always brings up the problem of talking. As I've sketched here, there are sound reasons to believe that some aliens are genuinely unreachable. We must share a lot to even recognize aliens as worth talking to—note how long it's taken us to get around to thinking about whales and dolphins.

But suppose we finesse the communication card for a moment. How does a writer *assume* that some chat can occur and then create the sensation of strangeness?

The Trapdoor Moment

One of my favorite SF stories is Terry Carr's "The Dance of the Changer and the Three," in which a human visiting a world remarks that he "was ambassador to a planetful of things that would tell me with a straight face that two and two are orange."

This reminds me of surrealism in its deliberate rejection of logic. Notice, though, that even while it is commenting on the fundamental strangeness of the aliens, this sentence tries to impose a human perspective—why should the natives have a "straight face" at all? Or any face?

The story deals with creatures on the rather ordinary world of Loarra, and their folk legends are shown in loving detail. This takes most of the text and the unwary reader thinks he is reading a pleasant bit of pseudoanthropology. Then the aliens suddenly kill most of the expedition. Why? "Their reason for wiping out the mining expedition was untranslatable. No, they weren't mad. No, they didn't want us to go away. Yes, we were welcome to the stuff we were taking out of the depths of the Loarran ocean. And, most importantly, no, they couldn't tell me whether they were likely ever to repeat their attack."

The story concludes two paragraphs later, with the humans unable to decide what to do next. Notice that the use of "mad" can be read here as either colloquial for angry, or else genuinely crazy. And through the aliens' rejection of prediction they deny the very notion of science as we would hold it. This seems to rule out the universal language dogma.

I like the story because it strings the readers along and then drops the trapdoor just as we're lulled into a pleasant sensation of

Loarran pseudopolynesian simplicity. The ideas revealed this way are startling, but the core of the story is that sideways lurch into the strange.

For contrast, consider one of the most famous stories about alien encounter, Fredric Brown's "Arena" (1944). A man is trapped inside a desert-floored dome and told he must fight it out with an implacable alien foe for mastery of the galaxy. In their struggle, the alien "roller" reaches the man telepathically (avoiding the whole language problem).

> He felt sheer horror at the utter *alienness*, the *differentness* of those thoughts. Things that he felt but could not understand and could never express, because no terrestrial language had the words, no terrestrial mind had images to fit them. The mind of a spider, he thought, or the mind of a praying mantis or a Martian sand-serpent, raised to intelligence and put in telepathic rapport with human minds, would be a homely and familiar thing, compared to this.

But if the roller were utterly alien, it would be incomprehensible. As the critic John Huntington has pointed out, it is *understandable* alienness that so horrifies the human. In fact, it is horrible because it stimulates difficult, inexpressible feelings in the man! He understands the alien by reading his own feelings. He can't deal with them, so he attacks their origin.

"Arena" is usually read as a paean to hard-boiled, Campbellian rationality. I think you can read it as covertly pushing unconscious emotionality. This program is completely different—intellectually and emotionally—from Carr's.

Modernist Aliens

Oscar Wilde remarked that in matters of supreme moment, style is always more important than substance. So, too, here. We cannot know the true deep substance of the totally alien, but we can use conscious and conspicuous style to suggest it. Some of the best SF takes this approach. It is quite different from the careful scientific explanations in the style of Hal Clement.

In Robert Silverberg's short story "Sundance," the text surges back and forth between points of view, changes tenses, and ricochets between objective description and intense personal vision—all to

achieve a sense of dislocation, of reality distortion, of fevered inter-
mittent contact that one cannot quite resolve into a clear picture. "It
is like falling through many trapdoors, looking for the one room
whose floor is not hinged."

The story culminates in rapidly reflecting and refracting visions
of the same "reality," seeing slaughtered aliens for one moment as
objects and then experiencing them from the inside. The narrative
voices lurch and dive and veer, always pulling the trapdoor from
under any definitive view. The story concludes "And you fall
through." There is no solid ground.

This is one of the best examples of how SF has used styles and
approaches which were first developed in the dawning decades of the
twentieth century, in what the critics term *modernism*. Breaking with
the whole nineteenth-century vision, modernism evolved methods to
undermine consensual reality and achieve a more personal, dislo-
cated view. In the Joycean stream of consciousness, in the Faulkner-
ian wrenchings of *The Sound and the Fury*, literary devices dyna-
mited cozy assumptions.

When science fiction uses such methods, they have different
content. This is, I think, one of the most important contributions the
genre has made to literature as a whole. Run-on sentences don't
merely mean internal hysteria, flooding of the sensorium, runaway
ennui, and so on. Instead, the method suggests genuinely different
ways of perceiving the world, emerging not from psychology and
sociology, but from evolution, genetics, even physics.

Unnoticed, SF has taken "mainstream" methods of breaking
down traditional narrative and turned them to achieve uniquely SF
ends. (I'd almost term it—delving into jargon myself—using modernism to achieve a kind of SF postrealism.) Nor has this ground been
fully explored. I believe it is only now being pioneered. One of the
most interesting uses is that, in SF, these can translate as a rendering
of the scientifically *unknowable*—or, at least, unfathomable by humans. The blizzard-of-strangeness motif is a persistent notion, even
among hard-science types.

Time and again in SF, encounters with the alien swamp mere
humans. In Fred Hoyle's *The Black Cloud*, Chris Kingsley, the
eccentric and brilliant scientist protagonist, is driven into a kind of
overloaded insanity when he attempts full contact with a huge,
intruding superintelligent cloud. To accommodate the immense

flood of new ideas and perceptions, Kingsley "decided to accept the rule that the new should always supersede the old whenever there was trouble between them." This is an SF article of faith. But in the end, contradictions are unmanageable. The new information settling into the same neural brain sites makes life itself impossible. Kingsley (an echo of Kingsley Amis?) dies. Hoyle is no stylist, but I find it significant that he is drawn to the same notion of contact. Others later expanded on this insight.

Thus, one underlying message in SF is that the truly alien doesn't just disturb and educate, it breaks down reality, often fatally, for us. Here SF departs quite profoundly from the humanist tradition in the arts. Science fiction nowhere more firmly rejects—indeed, explodes—humanism than in treating the alien. Humanist dogma holds that man is the measure of all things, as Shakespeare put it. SF makes a larger rejection of this than did modernism or surrealism, because it even discards the scientists' universal language and the mathematicians' faith in Platonic "natural" ideas. SF even says that the universe may be unknowable, and its "moral" structure might forever lie beyond humanity's ken.

This makes Camus and Sartre and nihilism seem like pretty small potatoes. If you're shopping for literary alienation, SF offers the industrial-strength, economy-size stuff. Yet it also contains the symbols of certainty, through science.

I suspect that the longstanding antagonism between the literary world and the SF community isn't merely the old story of the stylish effetes versus the nerd engineers. Instinctively, without much overt discussion, the two groups dispute the fundamental ideals behind humanism. SF writers take different views of the universe and can't be reconciled by a few favorable notices in the *New York Times Review of Books*.

Erotica and Strangeness

Writers as diverse as Philip José Farmer ("The Lovers"), James Tiptree, Jr. ("And I Awoke and Found Me Here on a Cold Hill's Side"), and Gardner Dozois (*Strangers*) have dwelled upon the erotic component in the alien. It turns up in such drive-in movie classics as *I Married a Monster from Outer Space*.

In discussing as personal a subject as sex, I might as well drop the convenient cover of dispassionate critic and write about my own work. At least this approach minimizes the number of potential lawsuits.

When I began thinking about the alien in detail, one of the first stories I wrote was "In Alien Flesh." I constructed it more or less unconsciously, piecing the story together from parts written at separate times over a period of months. For a long time, I didn't know where the tale was going.

In it, a man named Reginri has been hired to crawl up into a huge, beached, whalelike alien on the shore of an alien sea. He is an ordinary worker, not a scientist. He simply finds sites to plunge sensors directly into the inner reaches of the being, called the Drongheda. Direct contact floods him with images, feelings—that sensual overload. It provokes ineffable thoughts. And he gets trapped inside the beast.

I wrote most of the story, but had no ending. So I retreated, building a frame around the central tale, which makes the main narrative a flashback. In the frame, Reginri is looking back on his nearly fatal encounter with the Drongheda. I put into this part an approaching fog which humans must avoid, a damaging mist of another planet. Only after I wrote the last lines of the story did I suddenly see what the end of the flashback portion had to be. "There was something ominous about it and something inviting as well. He watched as it engulfed trees nearby. He studied it intently, judging the distance. The looming presence was quite close now. But he was sure it would be all right."

That done—though not understood, at least by me—I quickly retreated to the point where Reginri is smothered in the alien mountain of flesh and in desperation taps directly into the Drongheda's nerves. I started writing again, filling in action without thinking or planning very much.

Shaken by the flood of strange mathematics and sensation he has gotten from the Drongheda, Reginri finds his way out. Standing in the wash of waves as the Drongheda moves off on its inexplicable way, Reginri learns that one of his fellow workers has been crushed by the alien. Looking back, he sees that the hole he had used to crawl up into the Drongheda, pushing and worming his way in, was not "something like a welt"—the description I'd written before, and let stand—but in fact was quite obviously a sexual orifice!

Until I wrote those lines, I had no clue what the story was really about. What a field day for Freudian analysis! A critic's playground! Effing the ineffable!

I decided to let the frame stand. Having written the thing by intuition, I didn't dare tinker with it in the cool light of a critical eye. There's always a point in writing when you have to let go, for fear that you'll tinker away all the life in a piece. So, whatever the tale means, or says about my own disquieting interior, there it is.

Although I have now applied the reductionist hammer—which I scorned at the beginning of this essay—to one of my own works, I must say that I think postreadings do tell part of the story. Still, once you've dissected a salamander, you know more about it, sure—but it's dead.

As for my own way of assembling the story, I prefer this manner of pondering, shuffling back and forth, and by bits and pieces trying to artistically render the alien—intuitively, not seeking final answers, and with a certain lack of embarrassment, as well.

I'll return to my first assertion, too, and maintain that performing the usual critical slice-and-dice on "In Alien Flesh" misses the thrust of it. Rendering the alien, making the reader experience it, is the crucial contribution of SF. Such tales can argue over communication, spring trapdoors, inundate the reader with stylistic riverruns—all to achieve the end of a fresh experience. That's what the alien is really about.

3
Border Patrols

Michael Beehler

What Is the Story of the Alien?

An essay on the alien and its anthropology recalls to us the critical fact that the story of the alien is always the story of borders and of the institutional forces that try to neutralize and control those borders in the name of a certain political economy. Those forces manifest themselves in various ways, but their power can be localized in the figures of the Immigration and Naturalization Service and of its most physical representative, the Border Patrol. These two political entities most clearly express the institution's—in this case, the state's—desire to articulate and control its borders by directing the story of the alien along one of two narrative lines. For the state to have secure borders, the alien must be either legally internalized or legally externalized, brought inside the border with the express permission of the state or kept outside the border through the state's denial of that permission, a denial that can sometimes be spoken through physical force. Internalization is the job of an immigration and naturalization service and a reflection of the myth of the melting pot because internalized aliens pose no problem to the institution. Ideally, they lose their alienness and become just like everyone else: a repetition of the same. Externalization is the job of border patrols: externalized aliens also pose no problem because they can, presumably, be made to stay on the other side of the institution's border. Here, the alien is simply the other. Internalization and externalization, the same and the other—these are the only two narratives of the alien allowed by an institution in control of its borders.

But, of course, the story of aliens and borders is never this tidy, for the mastery of the institution over its borders is never quite complete. The simple economy of the border—the secure differentiation of the inside from the outside, the same from the other— is always complicated by the illegal alien who can be neither legally internalized nor legally externalized. Beyond the control of institutional law, the illegal alien disturbs the border, overrunning it in a gesture that marks the border as the site of an inevitable instability and insecurity. The problem of illegal aliens is the problem of the border that no law, no institutional force, is powerful enough to control completely.

What are the borders that concern us here? Presumably, we seek to know the place of the alien in science fiction. To accomplish this feat, we have at our disposal a powerful institutional force: anthropology. This force patrols the borders of our discussions, for anthropology, like any academic discipline, polices the outlines of its subject—in this case, man, *anthropos*—in order to speak intelligibly about that subject. In an anthropology of science fiction, man's borders are secured by giving the alien a clearly defined role to play or job to do, that is, to aid in anthropology's ongoing documentary of man. There is, then, a certain economy to this anthropology in which aliens are made to serve the anthropological institution or the institution of *anthropos*. It is a restricted capitalist economy of mastery and control: in an anthropology of science fiction, the labor of the alien always serves the ends of man. Although science fiction aliens are allowed within the borders of a discourse on man, they are, within this restricted economy, always seen as legal, as doing the proper work of articulating *anthropos*. Internalized as a part of man or externalized as a fuzzy creature from someplace beyond, the alien and its value within an anthropological economy are determined by its usefulness as a sign of man. "Anthropologism" thus describes a restricted economy that employs the alien in a kind of epistemological brasero program, and its story of the alien must always finally be understood as simply another story of man.

But perhaps anthropology too quickly recognizes man everywhere it looks, particularly when it looks in the face of the alien. Does the restricted economy of anthropologism have an illegal alien problem? Can we think of aliens as overrunning anthropology's borders and working in its epistemological heartland in ways that unsettle, rather than promote, its economy? Such aliens would not carry the identity card of *anthropos*, nor would they play by the book of anthropology: undocumented, undocumentable, they would retain a degree of power and critical force uncontrolled by a master narrative and unspoken of by any narrative of mastery. They would elude the disciplinary border patrols and make of institutional boundaries a disturbed and disturbing confusion. These are the illegal aliens this paper can only begin to consider.

To begin to think of the alien in this unsettling manner, we must smuggle in two foreigners who are important contributors to the economy of anthropologism and to the archive of stories about aliens. In Freud's discussions of the uncanny and in Kant's analyses of the sublime, we find the two master narratives of the alien and the anthropic, and of the border between them. While Freud's is a story of the internalization of the alien or the uncanny, and therefore a tale that could have been told by the Immigration and Naturalization Service, Kant's story, focusing on the externalization of the alien, which for Kant goes by the name of the sublime, is more closely related to the concerns of the Border Patrol. Both stories' dealings with the alien affirm the restricted economy of anthropologism. Both see the alien as a worker in the service of man, a sign in the documentary of *anthropos,* but the security of both narratives is unsettled by border problems they never quite bring under control.

That the name of Freud should come up is hardly surprising, for those concerned with the problems of the mind explored in Freud were called "alienists" before they were called "Freudians." Aliens do appear in Freud's texts, and they seem always to have their identity papers in order. Written on those documents—which affirm each alien's legality—is, for Freud, the name of *anthropos.* Let us look at his essay on the uncanny. Here he delineates the restricted economy that appropriates for its own purposes the "uncanny," this essay's name for whatever is unfamiliar, foreign, or alien. After describing the uncanny and the alien as the products of morbid anxiety, Freud concludes that "this uncanny is in reality nothing new or foreign, but something familiar and old-established in the mind that has been estranged only by the process of repression." Although the uncanny may appear to be alien and estranged, underneath all this difference it is, for Freud, really the same, for it is simply "a hidden, familiar thing that has undergone repression and then emerged from it."[1] This is the melting-pot economy of Freud: the alien crosses over the borders of the familiar only to reaffirm what we had willfully (through repressive self-protection) forgotten we knew all along. In Freud's story of the uncanny, all aliens are ideally documentable as the signs and symbols that disclose man to himself. There is no room in the economy of psychoanalysis for aliens who do not repeat the story of *anthropos*.

Thus, the *unheimlich* is for Freud nothing other than the *heimlich* in disguise, and the alien is the symbol of the same. Or so it seems. The problem with this restricted economy, however, is that it can never quite control itself. In Freud's essay, the uncanny is not simply the legal name of man: it is also the name of a certain illegality that overruns the border between the alien and the same, the symbol of *anthropos* and *anthropos* himself. For, as Freud observes, the uncanny occurs when "a symbol takes over the full functions and significance of the thing it symbolizes." This border problem "effac[es] the distinction between imagination and reality," an effacement that makes of the border a confusion no alienist narrative can completely control. Although Freud would neutralize the *unheimlich* or alien in the name of the same, he finally must speak of it as "a word the meaning of which develops toward an ambivalence."[2] Both a symbol and the transgression of the order of symbols, both the mark of the same and a sign of the ambivalently plural, the alien in Freud resists lawful documentation and unsettles an economical epistemology of man. Irreducibly illegal, it carries unreadable identity papers.

It also suggests a different relationship between alien and *anthropos*, one more profoundly problematic than the restricted economy of anthropologism, which tries to identify the alien with the anthropic. In Freud's essay, man comes to know and protect his identity by throwing his voice, by projecting and repeating himself in alien form. Such "repetition compulsion," as Freud repeatedly points out, is not a consciously willed activity. Rather, it is a fundamental principle of the unconscious and is therefore "involuntary." Part of the Freudian definition of man, then, concerns this fact: that *anthropos* is never simply himself, but that his identity is primordially bound up with the alien other that misrepresents and disturbs it. This essential relationship is fraught with the same complications Freud discusses with respect to telepathy, an uncanny process in which one person "identifies himself with another person, so that his self becomes confounded, or the foreign self is substituted for his own—in other words, by the doubling, dividing and inter-changing of the self."³ This confounding of the identical with the foreign, of the same with the other or the anthropic with the alien, is not, however, an accident that simply happens to an otherwise well-defined entity called man. It is instead the enabling, involuntary *principle* of man, the relationship that gives him whatever life he has. Within this enabling relationship, *anthropos* and alien can be seen to live off each other. The alien lives off man, since it is his projection. But at the same time, man lives off the alien, since it is in his misrepresentation by the alien that man first finds himself. Although Freud postulates a relationship in which *anthropos* plays host to a foreign body or alien parasite only, with the antibiotics of psychoanalysis to domesticate it and make it contribute to the ulti-mate health of man, his essay on the uncanny blurs the border that distinguishes between host and parasite, familiar and foreign, same and other, and thereby suggests that the relationship in which both alien and *anthropos* originally find themselves is a mutually parasitic one. Instead of serving man, Freud's illegal aliens interfere with man's documentary about himself.

Thus, Freud's story of the uncanny as disguised identity winds up telling a different tale, one in which the alien can never be seen as a simple repetition of the same. In a similar fashion, Kant's discus-sion of the alien as simple and absolute otherness also articulates a border problem no amount of patroling can completely control. We find the alien in Kant's figure of the sublime, which he describes as the *"absolutely great"* that is *"beyond all comparison."* Wholly and completely other, "nothing . . . which can be an object of the senses, is . . . to be called the sublime."⁴ Here apparently is a radical alienness that lies over the border of sensual experience, the absolute outside of anything *anthropos* could call his own. Where, then, does man encounter this alien, and how does he know of it? Kant's answer points to a crisis in man's systems of representation and to a *via negativa* those systems must travel. It is only by alluding to its own inadequacy, Kant contends, by traveling a negative way of self-deprecation, that human discourse, man's language, can suggest the presence of the sublimely alien, of that which is wholly other to any representation of it. As critics of Romanticism have pointed out, "in the Kantian moment of the sublime . . . the discourse breaks down."⁵ Two consequences follow from this breakdown. The first we have already mentioned: language's remarks upon its failure to adequately represent the absolutely alien sublime in fact suggest its presence. The second consequence returns us to the question of borders, for it is only through language's self-deprecating gesture that the edges of man's experience and the limitations of his representational systems are articulated. By marking the ends of man, this articulation draws the border that separates the human from the other-than-human, the anthropic from the alien. This border both holds man to himself and, at the same time, protects the absolute otherness of the alien. Whereas Freud's is the story of the externalization of the alien as the simply sane, Kant's is the tale of the externalization of the alien as the simply other. In both cases, however, the alien is made to speak about man, either by repeating his proper name, as in Freud, or by defining his limits, as in Kant.

The forces that patrol the Kantian border are heavily armed with an interdict designed to keep the anthropic on one side and the alien on the other. Kant's assertion that "there is no sublimer passage in the Jewish Law than the command, *Thou shalt not make to thyself any graven image, nor the likeness of anything which is in heaven or on earth or under the earth*" reinforces the limitations of human discourse and strengthens the borders of man. The problem with this heavily fortified border, however, is that it can be drawn only by being overrun. This is the nature of the *via negativa*. The interdict against representation demands complete silence—what can *anthropos* say about an alien that is wholly other?—but man must speak so that his discourse can collapse and thereby allude to the presence of the alien that lies always beyond its borders. This is the speech Kant calls fanaticism, which he describes as "*a delusion that we can will ourselves to see something beyond all bounds of sensibility.*"[6] In light of the interdict, all man's speech is fanaticism—and none more so than science fiction, which is in the business of making graven images of aliens that ought to be absolutely other. Such fanaticism speaks of the alien, but it does so only by rendering it as something familiar (a species of the same) and transgressing its otherness. And yet the alien needs such fanaticism, for it is only by this transgression that it first appears. The alien in Kant, like the alien in Freud, is a strangely complicated figure: it is the mark both of the absolute other and of otherness transgressed; it is both spoken by man's discourse and not spoken by it; it takes place without ever taking place.

Thus, the borders in Kant that keep the human from the sub-lime, *anthropos* from alien, can never be completely closed and secured, for like the figure of the same in Freud, the figure of the other in Kant finds itself in a mutually parasitic relationship with that which misrepresents it. Whereas *anthropos* speaks only with the distorted voice of the alien in Freud, the alien speaks only with the garbled voice of man in Kant. Reading both stories together suggests that the alien cannot finally be made to speak clearly either the narrative of the same or the narrative of the other. It resists all such forms of documentation and overruns all such discursive boundaries. It speaks neither for man, as the articulation of what he truly is, nor against man, as the articulation of what he truly is not. Indeed, the alien seems to be that which never speaks truly, because it never speaks for itself, in its own voice.

The alien, in other words, always positions itself somewhere between pure familiarity and pure otherness, between the speech of the same and the speech of the other. Taking its place on the border between identity and difference, it marks that border, articulating it while at the same time disarticulating and confusing the distinctions the border stands for. Pure betweenness, it mobilizes the border as a network of interferences, the site of the mutual parasitism or *poly-glossia* of languages, an unsettling and unsettled turbulence or over-running no institutional power is strong enough to neutralize. This is the critical force of the alien as undocumentable illegality: that it is positional, not essential; the complicated mark of the mobility of relations and the instability of languages and not the simple sign of truth and knowledge. Nothing in itself, a joker whose score and significance the epistemological border patrols would like to settle once and for all, the undocumentable alien refuses to serve the ends of man and pesters man's stories. And yet, as the betweenness of the borders whose differentiations distinguish between languages and speakers and thus bring them into being, as that which is in the functioning of relations (linguistic and otherwise), the alien is the pest that allows stories to be written, the parasite always engendered along with man's tales of himself and his meaning.

Where can we read the traces of this parasitic pest, of this alien whose identity papers cannot finally be read and whose inevitable taking place is the turbulence that destabilizes the economy of truth as identifiable and noncontradictory, as either the story of the same or the story of the other? We could, for example, look to Colin Wilson's *Mind Parasites*, in which the alien is described as a "mind-jamming device . . . loosely compared to a radar-jamming device." The question of the alien in Wilson's novel is the question of borders and of the interferences and overrunnings that disturb the differentiations upon which human meanings depend. As Wilson explains it, "a 'meaning' happens when we compare two lots of experience, and suddenly understand something about them both." This is the process he calls "learning": a process in which borders are articulated in the name of certain meaning. But the mind parasites unsettle meaning by interfering with the borders that produce it. A kind of static, they "blur" distinctions, jamming the communication channel of meaning with their illegal noise. Wilson's novel is the story of man's battle against such noise, an ongoing skirmish in which the border patrols "had to maintain constant diligence" because the boundaries of meaning can never be finally secured. Although the narrator, Professor Austin, seems to evolve away from the problematics of uncontrolled borders in which message and noise, host and parasite, *anthropos* and alien, are complicated and meaning is never certain, he does so only by losing "contact with the rest of the human race."[7] In the end, the borders of *anthropos* remain something always disrupted by the parasitic alien.

Uncontrollable border problems are also traceable in Stanislaw Lem's *Solaris*. The planet Solaris seems to be the ideal figure of the alien as pure otherness. Always outside the discourses of science that never adequately account for it, the rogue planet recalls the Kantian sublime and the *via negativa* of writing that announces it. In this sense, then, Solaris marks the ends and limitations of man and thereby takes its place within the economy of anthropologism. Although it may be somewhat upsetting to anthropocentric pride to recognize the limitations of human cognition, the border between *anthropos* and alien is recognizable and truth is served, even if it is the truth of the prison of man's mind and body. But a more complicated alien appears in this novel in the figures of the Phi-creatures and especially of Rheya. Nothing herself (she and her peers are neutrino structures at the center of which "there was nothing to be seen"[8]) and yet both a projection of Kelvin and a manifestation of the ocean, a sign of both Freudian internalization and of Kantian externalization, both same and other, Rheya *is* the overrunning of the border, the turbulence that unsettles meaningful articulations and articulations of meaning. Catachresis without determinate origin, alien with unreadable identity papers, she is the parasitic interference, the static that can be neither absorbed into meaning nor tuned out of it. She is the betweenness of the border in which articulation and disarticulation, message and noise, are inextricably interwoven.

And yet Kelvin waits on the shoreline, keeping the faith and expecting things to straighten themselves out. And Professor Austin transcends the entire problem. In both Wilson and Lem, the difficulties of the border, posed by illegal aliens overrunning it, are at least ideally resolvable, a future event to be indefinitely deferred but reasonably hoped for. But in Yevgeny Zamyatin's *We*, the alien is what allows the language of reason to be written in the first place. For D-503, mathematics is the very model of reasonable language: it "never errs," never "makes a mistake" or "plays tricks." It is the language maximally purged of noise, the discourse that completely controls its borders and speaks truths uncomplicated by parasitic interferences. In this, D repeats Zamyatin's own assertion that "some day an exact formula will be established for the law of revolution. And in this formula nations, classes, stars—and books will be expressed as numerical values."[9] Mathematics is for Zamyatin and his narrator the language of exactitude and precision, of documentable values and stable relations, and its sign is the secure borderline, the graphic mark, the slash (/) or bar (—) that separates number from number and articulates the ratios between them. The conventional figure by which proportions or fractions are written is a pictogram of the border economy of mathematics.

But not simply the sign of reason, of ratio, of documentable discriminations and relations, the slash also announces an illegal alien problem, an overrunning of borders that takes place even at the very inception of mathematics. For as D discovers, there is always the "irresolvable irrational member that . . . somehow slip[s] into an equation," the alien that "was impossible to render harmless" or legal through a documenting process "because it was outside *ratio*."[10] To read the irrational number as the sign of something unreasonable or intuitive in human nature, as the simple outside of reason, would be to legalize it, to document its identity and significance, and to place it within the secured borders of anthropologism. But the irrational number, $\sqrt{-1}$, is the sign of illegality itself, of the alien that destablizes any documentation that would settle its score and employ it in its own economy. It is the overrunning of the slash, the mobilization of the border, the turbulence and indeterminacy of ratio itself. And yet it must be present for the discourse of ratio to be written at all: irrational numbers are a crisis in mathematics, but mathematics cannot be written without them. Both inside ratio and outside ratio, both the sign of rationality and of absurdity, both same and other, host and parasite, irrational numbers are aliens that play tricks that are both undecidable and enabling.

Thus, to speak of the alien is always to redeploy the problem of the border and to reopen the complexities of documentation. We cannot settle the score of the alien, even with the formidable help of the economy of anthropological truth, not because the alien is simply beyond anthropocentric documentation—this is little more than another "truth" of anthropology—but because in naming the name of the alien, we document the parasitic illegality that is both the essence and destabilization of documentation itself. Of what, then, is the alien, understood as that which does not coincide with itself or speak with its own voice, a figure? The undoing (the de-*Man*-ing) of anthropology and of the discursive and institutional borders erected to hold truth to itself, the alien in all its critical force and power may be the trace of literary modernity, the unsettling movement within literary history that Paul de Man describes as "the steady fluctuation of an entity away from and towards its own mode of being."[11]

4
Alien Aliens
Pascal Ducommun

Recently, I read a German translation of *Thousand Years on Venus*, a novel by the Hungarian writer György Botond-Bolics. One of his characters expressed the following opinion:

> We are human beings, Demeter, and we cannot figure out the world around us except through the eyes of the human being, through the brain of the human being. There has never been a writer, neither a major one nor a minor one, who could or dared write about beings from another world without human, earthly connections. Whenever his imagination put devices in their hands, these are merely imitations of our devices. Whenever he has them thinking, and admits that they also can communicate their thoughts, he only reflects our words, our mentality. Can we ever understand or perceive a world which is not an imitation of ours?[1]

The problem, I think, is here thoroughly set. Even so, and in opposition to the opinion of Botond-Bolics, some writers have been able, albeit rarely, to invent living beings that share as few similarities with us as is possible; indeed, science fiction cannot get along without this strange fauna. Although the required zoology and ethnology, or even, I dare say, the anthropology still remains to be done, I would like to give a few examples.

In my study, I have followed two principles: First, I emphasize little-known texts, theoretical or fictitious. Thus, I avoid referring to (except in one instance) English-language SF. Second, because in this small space I can neither give enough texts nor do more than merely summarize the ones I give, I move quickly to theory. Theory is more risky, but stimulating and exciting precisely in proportion to that risk.

What is an alien? Well, we are here bluntly reminded that SF theory is still in the beginning stages, insofar as it has yet to be established clearly what is meant by science fiction. This implies that we may answer this question only by setting out from a tautology: SF is whatever is called or calls itself thus. In like manner, an "alien" in SF is whatever is named alien. We can, however, proceed from this base in a rational manner. The alien should be, logically, anything that is not us. In our field, as it is defined by Pierre Versins[2]—utopia, extraordinary voyages, and SF—we discover the following beings: extraterrestrials, "lost" races, intelligent animals, robots, and androids. In the adjacent territories of fantasy and fairy tale, we encounter elves, ghosts, vampires, and so on.

These strange legions of aliens do not date back to yesterday: we find robots as far back as the works of Homer, and lost races in the writings of Aristeas, Ctesias, and Lucian of Samosata, who also created the first extraterrestrial beings. This flow is steady through the centuries. Why do we need so many aliens, the cause of the vulgar confusion between science fiction and silly stories about little green men?

There seems to be a mainstream of agreement on how to create an alien. Exemplified in story after story, this method of creation is perhaps best formulated by Hal Clement in his article "The Creation of Imaginary Beings."[3] Curiously enough, an analogous system was developed by Donald Knuth[4] for typography. Knuth calls his system a "metafount." It is a computer program for the creation of new types which relies on the continuous shift of certain parameters chosen among a given set: slant or boldness of type, whether there are serifs or not, the relative thickness of strokes. Likewise, in science fiction we can play with such parameters as the number, dimension, or color of various organs derived from the human or animal body, or with the biochemistry of these. But if we agree that the concept of metafount is able to produce a variety of, say, Garamond or Caslon types far superior to any known or even needed, we must realize that the nature of the type itself has not been changed. Similarly, in that metafount of the human being used in science fiction, the nature of the created beings is not really different from ours.

So much for this mainstream. How about a minor one?

Among the few stories relevant here is "The Xipéhuz," by J.-H.

Rosny the Elder,[5] a French writer of Belgian extraction. This, the first of Rosny's science-fiction stories printed, was published in 1887. We are presented with the diary, in an allegedly precuneiform writing, of a man named Bakhoûn. The narrator assumes that Bakhoûn lived about one thousand years before the great trend toward civilization that would eventually lead to the building of such cities as Babylon or Nineveh. However, according to Bakhoûn himself, the events he relates ended in the Year of the World 22,649, with the total victory of the human tribes over the Xipéhuz, living beings completely alien to any other on Earth. Somehow, each of these noble reigns understood that it had to destroy the other before it could expand to take over the world.

Bakhoûn, after some battles were fought, was commissioned to study this strange new species, the origin of which remains unknown and which he named the Xipéhuz. Their form, he writes, is either conical or cylindrical, and a few have the shape of a leaf of bark. All show various and changing colors and a very bright star at their base. Bakhoûn was soon to learn that they may die or kill when fighting a battle; that they chase animals, reducing them to ashes but apparently not feeding on them; that they communicate by means of beams of light; and that they even have a school for their children. Such features are obviously quite human and tell us nothing very strange, of course, but more is yet to be discovered.

The Xipéhuz have nothing similar to our limbs; moreover, their shape changes. In the course of a day, Bakhoûn has seen some that were cylindrical in the morning, leaflike at noon, and conical in the evening. When moving, they simply hover, at times at great speed. They use no tools, only rays, be it for the purpose of communication or for hunting and fighting. Small groups of them can move only in a restricted area, which expands only when their number increases. They do not seek contact with the humans, but if humans venture into their area (they see through such obstacles as trees), they know quite well how to chase and kill them. Bakhoûn discovers that they fear nothing from the humans except one thing: an arrow, a sharp knife. A straight shot in the star of a Xipéhuz will kill it at once. At that moment, they "*fall down, condense, petrify,*" leaving a corpse of "yellowish crystals, irregularly disposed, and streaked with blue threads."

This is sufficient, I believe, to show what a convincing alien might be. We wonder what sort of perception of the world such crystalline and probably electromagnetic beings might have. What symbols, if any, do they use? Through the years, Bakhoûn is never able to understand their language, except when they "speak" about him. I am reminded here of the golden plates aboard Pioneers 10 and 11, displaying a diagram of the solar system in which Earth is connected with an arrow to a picture of the probe itself. To a Xipéhuz-like being, this symbol could only mean death or aggression, while to us it evokes connection, relationship.

Whence the fundamental distinction between a story like "The Xipéhuz" and the many other following Clement's patterns? It arises simply from their providing a different answer to the same implicit question, one essential to the use of aliens in SF. The crux of the matter is this: Does being alive exclusively, entirely, account for what we are, or is our "mankindness" somewhat the cause of this? In other words, is man a necessary step in life's process toward increasing complexity, or could other ways be conceived? Both possibilities have interesting implications. The mainstream considers that we are completely determined by life and that life's process comes everywhere the same and unique way, man's way; thence its assumption that any "superior" alien (just as it seems that we are the "superior" ones down here), though fictitious, has to share with us our essential characteristics. This logic may, as in Clement, go so far as to claim that the aliens, regardless of where they come from, must have the same distance between the eyes and the ground or between the eyes and the brain. This explains Clement's tendency to view the creation of aliens as the rearrangement of a man-based set of physical, astronomical, biochemical, or ecological parameters. The strength of this way of conceiving aliens is indeed great and excellently illustrated in a novel like Clement's *Mission of Gravity*.[6] Nevertheless, the almost complete lack of psychological considerations leans a bit too much toward reductive behaviorism.

The answer given by "The Xipéhuz" and similar stories allows for the creation of the "alien alien." It assumes that our main features proceed from our humanity, thus implying that an alien may be completely different, to the point of being determined by features or factors we do not and cannot have. For instance, while doing research years ago on alien communication in science fiction, I was told by a friend that he was making a typology of aliens in science fiction and that he had already observed twenty-seven different types, all of them sharing with us one major feature: the ability to think. My first, obvious reaction was to say, "Well, of course!" But I nevertheless began to wonder. Why should an imaginary superior being absolutely have to think? True, I cannot imagine what a thoughtless intelligent mind might be like, let alone a superior being without a mind at all. But my inability does not prove it to be impossible or even inconceivable.

If we consider one of Rosny's most important novels, *Navigators into Infinity*, published in 1925, and its sequel, *The Astronauts*,[7] which remained unpublished until 1960, we discover that several different species are living on Mars: the first, the Martians (akin to our mankind), who are declining (they have ruins half a million years old!); the second, an animal species able to feed on each other without killing their prey; and the third, a completely different species, with electrical or analogous properties, that is slowly expanding all over the planet, making it more and more difficult for the Martians to survive. These latter beings, perhaps comprising higher and lower varieties, seem to feed on the ground itself, rendering it infertile and uninhabitable for the Martians. Finally, there is a fourth kind of beings, radiant ones (Rosny, it appears, was fascinated with light and all sorts of rays), who live at a speed at least a million times faster than ours. Humans are able to conceive a device to communicate with them, but finally remain unable to understand the exact nature of their being. But the reader is left, as as he usually is with the work of Rosny, with a strong and lasting longing to see these images and experience the skies of Mars at night, when the shining beings show best. Echoes of this world may be heard in "You Forget to Answer," a song by Nico.[8] Is this an aporia, where we should favor one kind of alien creation while relying plainly on the reader's taste or preference, and on the writer's singularity, even if we credit him, as I do, with a sharper talent when dealing with the minor stream? Actually, the problem goes deeper. For I believe that stories such as Rosny's in their conception of the alien are closer to the true nature of SF and utopia.

I promised you some theory. First, let us consider the word "theory" itself; etymology says that its first part means either "god" or "spectacle," while the second means "spectator"; as we know, the spectator usually stands outside the spectacle when looking at it.

Second, let us consider, in the light of theory, the problem of communication. The book *Pragmatics of Human Communication* by Paul Watzlawick, Janet Helmick Beavin, and Don Jackson[9] may suggest an answer, for it presents a basic concept that I find crucial to the understanding of SF. The authors tell us that "research into the phenomena of the mind, as is painfully known to all workers in the field, is tremendously difficult because of the absence of an Archimedean point outside the mind."[10] Moreover, "subject and object are identical, the mind studies itself, and any assumptions have an inevitable tendency toward self-validation."[11] These statements seem obvious, but interesting deductions can be made from them. "What we can *observe* in virtually all these cases of pathological communication is that they are vicious circles that cannot be broken unless and until communication itself becomes the subject of communication, in other words, until the communicants are able to metacommunicate. But to do this they have to step *outside* the circle."[12] Hence arises "this necessity to step outside a given situation contingency in order to resolve it."[13] The authors, considering various patterns of pathological communication, state that what all these patterns have in common is that no change can be generated from *within* and that any change can only come from stepping *outside* the pattern."[14] They conclude then, after examining the ideas of Wittgenstein and Gödel that "as it should be by now abundantly clear, nothing *inside* a frame can state, or even *ask*, anything *about* that frame."[15] I believe that we have reached here the core of our concern with aliens. As I have stated, they are the ones who are not us: they are outside us. Whatever we are, we are caught in a vicious circle whenever we try to look at ourselves: the human being studies himself. Creating aliens appears therefore as an attempt to step outside ourselves, in order to get the outer point of view we cannot get when remaining inside the circle.

In the end, all this may seem rather disappointing. I proposed to discuss aliens, and here is the human being constantly lurking around. Why is that so? Do not aliens have a life of their own? Well, insofar as real ones are concerned, we will have to wait until we encounter some. But imaginary ones, those that are imagined by us, can only exist in some relation to us. This is deceptive only at first glance. For is not this relationship to the here and now of man exactly what defines the true nature of SF? As Pierre Versins states at length, any work belonging to the categories of utopia, extraordinary voyages, or science fiction tells us something about elsewhere and tomorrow only in order to tell us about the here and now. So, if one's desire were to be always fulfilled right here and now, there would be no need for art, no need for utopia and science fiction, no need for aliens, because we would lack nothing in or outside the world, except perhaps, vicious as we are, the need itself. Aliens then are nothing but a way, one way among others, but certainly a more radical (hence truly speculative) way, to place ourselves outside the closed circle of ourselves in hopes of shedding new light on the nature of that self.

To conclude, let us consider another story, one by Stanislaw Lem, which is among his gloomiest works: *Ciemność i Pleśń*,[16] that is, *Darkness and Mustiness*. (The story has not been translated into English.) Lem tells us first about a scientist who invents, through selective mutations, a certain bacterium, which he names, probably after himself, "Whisteria Cosmolytica"; it is "a microbe annihilating matter and drawing its vital energy from that process." Luckily enough, it is effective only in darkness and with the catalytic help of a certain mustiness. Anyhow, a problem occurs, the laboratory explodes, destroying everything within a radius of three hundred meters. The ground must then be scorched to ensure that not a single "Whisteria Cosmolytica" survives. But the second part of the story suggests that one bacterium did manage to survive the flames, and the story ends with an eerie "vision of a mountain of blinking fish eyes that, in an extended roar of thunder, ripped up the house." From the impression left by this story, or by "The Xipéhuz," and by a few others, I realize that a few writers at least, within the last hundred years, have shown us that, after all, the alien may be "the measure of all things."

5

Metamorphoses of the Dragon

George E. Slusser

The title of one of Ursula LeGuin's essays is a question: "Why Are Americans Afraid of Dragons?" The question needs tending to. First of all, why Americans? They, LeGuin tells us, stand for technological man in general. And second of all, why afraid? What is there to be afraid of? Indeed, what does a dragon mean to technological man? To LeGuin, the dragon is the symbol of fantasy. Technological man, she claims, fears dragons, fears fantasy, because he has lost touch with the rhythms of organic life, the chthonian forces they represent. But this does not describe, to me, the development of technological culture, either in America or in the Western world. Western man, it seems, invented the dragon as its "natural" adversary for a specific purpose. He invented it as a learning device, as a means of developing strategies to harness and use the natural world—in other words, as a technology. For by inscribing the dragon in our myths and fictions, we learn how to shape nature's wildness, its alien newness, into patterns of orderly change, of metamorphosis. Far from fearing dragons then, Western man has come to rely on them more and more.

But perhaps we rely on them too much. Or at least on the kind of dragon that operates to domesticate the potential alienness of the natural world. From the beginning of Western culture, man has interacted with dragons in various ways: he has slain them, mastered and ridden them, and finally (in a way that seems to unite East and West) coexisted with them. This latter sort of dragon lore is what LeGuin proposes. It is a mode every bit as technological as SF. Even though it is "soft," this machine is nonetheless a machine. LeGuin, however, does not see it this way. Her sense of SF is radically Cartesian. For there scientific man, in declaring himself different from the natural world, by the same stroke turns that natural realm into one of lifeless matter. This conversion allows SF man to vindicate his ruthless assault on nature. Technically then, if this view holds, there is no place in the extended world for dragons, or for any beings that allow man access to a vital and sentient nature (we remember what Descartes said about animals). Nature, to this SF man, is a realm entirely alien, because it is lifeless. To LeGuin, however, nature is not alien at all; we are the alien, at least until we learn not to be. Her dragon, therefore, has no alien interface. Mediating between man and the vital earth, it ultimately mediates between man and himself, between man and the image of himself he projects onto nature in the form of chthonian myths. Far more interesting is the possibility LeGuin denies—that of the SF dragon, the creature that functions, if not in Descartes' universe, at least in that of Pascal. For here the dragon becomes a point of contact between the mind and the terrifying materiality of infinite, unknown spaces. It becomes the place of the alien encounter.

To LeGuin, the battle raging over the body of the dragon is that between science fiction and fantasy. And it is clearly a battle of the sexes: the battle between sky gods and earth gods, between male and female principles, between ethos and mythos. Of these two forms therefore, fantasy has, by its very nature, roots in the "mainstream," hence mythic status. LeGuin's view is again simplistic. Just how simplistic she reveals in her recent "Round, Buff, Speckled Poem."[1] Here she chastises hard technology for creating the "steel eagles" that lay waste to the natural forces of the earth. These "eagles" are perversions of nature and as such opposed to the dragon, a being composed of pan-organic parts. But as a hybrid of flesh and metal, the steel eagle is no less a dragon avatar, if we consider the ability to form combinations of elements or realms to be the fundamental characteristic of the dragon. This steel dragon in fact has extended its power to hybridize beyond the mere organic. It is an SF creature (surely LeGuin intended it as such). SF is full of such dragons, and their presence is a far more complex matter than LeGuin suggests.

If the dragon exists in SF then, we must ask what its function is. What relation does it have to the openly technological nature of the form—"science" fiction? Let us turn to another commentator. Frank McConnell sees SF not as a form opposed to the "mainstream," but as the most advanced form of Western storytelling we have today.

Storytelling is a technology, and the primary problem of SF, for McConnell, is the proper use of this, and all other, technologies. With our stories, he asks, do we seek to dominate nature, or rather to identify with it? To do the latter, McConnell believes, is to create myths, and SF, in this sense, is a mythic form.[2] The word "myth" here, however, is used in the sense that LeGuin denies it: it is a sophisticated system of control, a technology. And in this view, SF, whose dominant subject is the question of technology, has mythic status. For it derives its power to control less from conflict with nature than through *identification* with it.

McConnell has a brilliant insight here. For he finds SF, in its "hardest" or most technocratic form, today in the same situation as the Overlords in Clarke's *Childhood's End*. The Overlords stand as that form of existence toward which mankind has been evolving all along. These beings, however, have horns and a tail—they are devils, or more precisely, dragons. They have this form, Clarke explains, because they represent the end of the evolutionary process as it was conceived at the primitive beginnings of that process—an old image that stuck. LeGuin says that there are no dragons in SF. But when she looks at it, she sees precisely this—an Overlord. For that is the way we see SF through primitive eyes, those of the mythic "mainstream."

But is this dragon figure, as Clarke implies, a misrepresentation? If this is the case, then the Overlords, once we realize their origin, become superfluous, cease to function as interface with nature. But that does not exactly describe their role here. For throughout, these dragon figures serve as conduit. Leading mankind, they are the means which the storytelling technology uses to pass from its primal state—that of devils and demons, of adversity between man and nature—to a new one, where man achieves dynamic identity with natural forces. This occurs in the final narrative of Jan, the last survivor. To be sure, Jan chronicles (in apparently futile manner) the rise of a new order out of the destruction of the old, human one. He still can do so, however, from a human point of view. Not only that, but his story is so moving that the Overlords, in admiration, carry it away to preserve it, beyond the death of man, in their museums and imaginations. This, to McConnell, is the "hardest" SF. And its dragons are not LeGuin's steel eagles, but devil-Overlords, beings that allow man, even on the brink of destruction, creative contact with nature.

As creature striding the contrary world views of Christianity and material evolution, the Overlord offers man a unique means of identifying with an otherwise alien nature. Clarke's transposition of the dragon from the moment of genesis to that of apocalypse inscribes human history in a series of dragon moments. These, from the fall of nature to the serpent to its redemption through the slaying of the dragon in Revelation, offer man the means of identifying his destiny, more and more closely, with that of an increasingly hostile nature. In this sense, the dragon acts as the motive force in a process of myth making that is clearly technology, For it is the agent through which man can subject nature to myths like Jan's last story, and in doing so seek to inscribe its alienness, its fallen quality, within the limits of continued human activity. In the final sense of Clarke's novel, man preserves his existence, if only as some indwelling principle of order, a form that still measures natural change even if it cannot control it.

Dragons and Overlords then are not fantasy aberrations in the SF scheme of things. Nor is the SF that contains them necessarily antiscientific. On the contrary. The dragon in fact is the perfect figure to describe, indeed to incarnate, the everchanging dance that forms the investigative structure of today's new—that is, participatory and nonadversarial—physics. Gary Zukav describes this new physics as the dance of Zen masters, man and nature dynamically interacting in a ceaseless play of determinate and indeterminate elements. Dragon figures, East and West, can be summoned to support this interactive vision. Let us take the Oriental dragon plate, for instance. These plates, as a rule, represent a writhing, unruly dragon figure, uneasily confined within the circular form of the platter. The relationship between figure and vessel is intended to be one of dynamic interchange. Natural disorder, bursting from the hand of the artist, is circumscribed by the work of the artisan. But the dragon figure is less overcome than, it seems, momentarily contained. Because of that containment, the dragon is charged with life, given a protean energy that appears to confound the difference between inner and outer space, letting plate become dragon and dragon become plate. Like Clarke's myth-making dragon, however, this Oriental form, however vital and balanced its interpenetrative force, still offers no open point of contact between man and nature. The plate remains a functional object, a circle man holds in his hands. In its combination of design and function it is a technology: the means of internalizing potentially alien powers and forms from the natural world and thus subjecting them to human control.

Now compare the Oriental plate with the famous drawing by M. C. Escher entitled "Reptiles."[3] Instruments and writings of a natural scientist litter a table. In a schematic drawing of reptiles on this worktable, dragonlike creatures take fleshy form, step off the page where they were held in geometrical order, and begin to move freely in the natural world. This could signify that the dragon, the natural forces it represents, is eternally vital and that the role the old sciences have given it, that of a defeated adversary, no longer holds it in thrall. Once liberated, however, Escher's dragons circle the desk only to return to the drawing from which they came, to fade back into the page. These creatures are not visibly constrained by the circle of a plate. Yet in their looping pattern, they still apparently obey the laws, this time invisible, of an equally human geometry.

Zukav claims to see these systems not simply as systems in equilibrium but in expansion. The interaction of elements produces something greater than the sum of its parts; their dynamic balance offers the means of effecting new and extended encounters with the natural world. Indeed, to Zukav "the near future will see new theories incorporating the older and giving us a much larger view of our universe, and consequently of ourselves."[4] In terms of dragons, this means that the beast will get larger, have a greater interactive surface. But it also means that these creatures will remain man's dragons. The key to this "expansive" system—the norm that regulates it—remains the human form. For how open is a system in expansion that remains pegged to a module of proportionality requiring that, with each broader encounter, we grow necessarily larger ourselves?

The new science then promises new dragons: nonconfrontational entities that, converting the old opposition of man to nature into internalized (that is, hybridized) functions of the same system, claim to offer a larger surface for investigative activity. In investigating, we encounter something. But are these still *alien* encounters? We have in a sense defined the alien out of existence. What we have here are interactive feedback systems. These simply obviate the idea of the alien or other: the new, and singularly fearful, phenomenon we contact in the natural world, at a point beyond our material and conceptual limits. To replace the alien we have created what are, basically, informational systems. The new technology of feedback internalizes the old dragon adversary, converting chaos, once thought to be darkness visible "out there," into something indwelling and quite invisible: call it noise, indeterminacy, or entropy. Entropy, that state of minimal differentiation where, as Norbert Wiener puts it, "nothing really new ever happens," is in a sense the circular plate that holds the dragon's differentiated contortions; it is the eternal braid of the loops that direct Escher's reptiles. This world view disenfranchises the alien by converting everything into system. And that includes the dragon: the adversary of man has become what we now claim it was all along—a function of man. But even in this new lair, the dragon continues to stir. And in these stirrings is a sign of new man's atavistic yearnings, in this case of the need for open encounter, for adventure, contact with something that is neither an element of, nor processable by, the human system. As such, it is a Gödelian factor in all our forms of order.

Thus the presence of dragons in SF raises larger questions. Does SF, as the supposed literature of alien encounter, offer closed or open modes of encounter? Indeed, in relation to the scientific ideologies that seek to regulate SF's sense of the alien, what does "closed" or "open" mean? To McConnell, SF is "the perfect antimythological mythology," the "perfect technological theology." In other words, it is the perfect feedback system, something having to a perfect degree (as Wiener puts it) "the property of being able to adjust future conduct by past performance."[5] And this is exactly what it is. If we look closely, we see that McConnell's antitheses—his dragon hybrids—are actually tautologies. For what they express, finally, is not conflict between man and nature but identity. Each of these compounds is a closed system: a circular dynamic that allows man to preserve his own forms (his myths and technologies) by making them coextensive with natural forms, be they (as named here) God or the antimythological alien.

To this new systemic vision, LeGuin opposes the old adversarial one. Because SF is technological, she reasons, it is antimythological. And as such SF offers not the incredible expanding, but the incredible shrinking man. Her fantasy *The Farthest Shore* gives a good example of her vision. Its protagonist Ged forms a union with dragons—here patterning creatures who create in their flight "fierce willed concord"—against the adversary Cob. Cob is, in a sense, LeGuin's SF man; out of, and centered upon, himself he weaves his dessicating systems. He is Swift's spider. But he is more; he is Blake's Urizen, the tyrannical, and evil, adversary of nature. For by means of his systems and tautologies, he acts to imprison nature, to dry up and destroy its representatives, the vital dragons of primeval, not new, myth. Cob then is the "mad" scientist, the antimythological hero of the SF novel as she has come to see it. And Cob, confronted in the final scene of the novel by the fantasy hero, regenerated by union with the chthonian dragon, shrivels. His expanded universe proves to be no more than a brittle web of theory and crumbles to dust.

LeGuin is trading one closed system for another: dragon patterns for cobwebs, fantasy for SF. But her posture remains adversarial, myth against antimyth. And in that sense, it is closer to what Clarke, in *Childhood's End*, finally says about SF's use of dragons. Clarke's sense, in this novel, is double. On the level of the Overlords, the adversarial relationship becomes an identificational one. In this relationship, the contact between man and dragon comes to exist on what McConnell calls a mythical level. We were taught, by theology, that the devil is our enemy. But these devils, it turns out, are actually our guides. And as they guide us, they aspire to look like us, to lose their horns and tails. In a sense, by following them, we remake them in our image, convert theology into technology—in other words, fashion out of the old a new dragon figure.

The adversarial relationship exists on a physical level—man fights dragon, Ged fights Cob. The identificational, or "mythical," relationship, however, exists on what we would call a metaphysical level. In the former, man can choose; it is an either/or matter, man or nature. But in the latter, there is no need for choice. The mechanism of choice is simply replaced by that of identity: the informational feedback loop. Beyond these, however, Clarke offers a third relationship that synthesizes these two—call it a meta-adversarial relationship. It occurs on the level of the Overmind. It is a relation between man and himself, between two successive (and vertical) stages of development, which at the same time, on a horizontal plane, produces a conflict between man and nature. On the one hand, the man-Overmind connection simply rises out of the man-nature matrix and replaces it, as if man turned his physical back on his metaphysical feedback systems. On the other hand, this separation presents nature, with which in the utopian finality of New Atlantis we have become totally coextensive, with a new (and total) adversary. For the creation of the Overmind is an act of simultaneous absorption and alienation. The split is an absolute either/or matter, in no way tied to any human system of proportionality. To become disembodied mind, man must *completely* abandon his old physical form. To create it, the green Earth is totally consumed.

J. D. Bernal, in *The World, the Flesh, and the Devil*, calls this process "dimorphism." World, flesh, and devil are the "three enemies of the rational soul." It is significant that Bernal calls the third, and most tenacious, of these the devil. For what he describes here is what Clarke's Overlords showed us. This is the lure of the internalized dragon—the exploratory resolve of human intelligence weakened by myth making, by seeking to identify man with nature. For Bernal, this lure is so strong in today's mankind that it has led to an impasse. Again, as in Clarke, not man but evolution will resolve this impasse. There will be a future splitting of the mythical compound in radically divergent directions, one nature, the other mind: "one section developing a fully balanced humanity, the other groping unsteadily beyond it."[6] A "fully balanced" humanity means a fully coextensive humanity, mankind now placed (in a union of LeGuin's and McConnell's visions) on an Earth enjoying a perpetual golden age, a mythic garden tended by art and theology. To Bernal, however, such a place is clearly the habitat created by internalizing the dragon, for he calls it a "human zoo," a place of hybrids that must be tended by someone else. That someone is the dimorphic off-worlder. This is a being who already, confronted with the world and the flesh (the natural and the bodily environment), is willing to free himself from these trammels. His "unsteady gropings" are an externalizing process, a discorporation rather than an incorporation.

If SF has an ideal "hard" vision of what the alien encounter should be, it is this Bernalian open-ended "groping." Pascal set reason apart from the material universe. (That universe crushes man, but it does not know it crushes him; only man knows that.) Now Bernal frees reason from the median position Pascal gives it, converts it into something mobile, intelligence, and launches it into, and against, those infinite spaces that so frightened Pascal. This groping is unsteady because it is free of elements that have been seen, up to now, as constants: the human form and the systems of order based on it. It is thus antimythological in the deepest sense of the word. Indeed, in this unsteady field, the alien encounter calls less for incorporation than for mutual adaptation. The alien encounter therefore results in irreversible and (to Bernal) necessary alteration of human and natural forms alike. But as such it still remains a creator of dragons.

The answer, then, to the question of whether dragons can survive in the Bernalian world of the alien is yes. There is what we can call an externalizing dragon. This is so because the dragon is something of vaster potential than its previous uses suggest. We have domesticated the dragon and by means of it subjected nature's disruptive power to human norms and uses. But it need not be our devil. It is more than a creature of myth or (what is the same thing) of technology. It is, in its simplest expression, a hybrid. As such, it is a sign of another constant desire in man: the desire really to interact with external things, to change and be changed in the process. The dragon is our interface, with what we once called "nature," now (in this post-Pascalian age) with the shapeless and terrifying alien infinite. This apparent creature of fantasy turns out to be the vehicle for our boldest scientific imaginings; those that conceive of a farewell to arms, flesh, and homocentric models altogether. If anything, it is the dragon that can figure the creation of wholly new beings from this contact of intelligence and matter.

Dragons still occur, beyond the play of Earth and sky gods that regulates our mythic zoo, in SF's universe of unsteady gropings. To prove this, however, we must first trace the genealogy of the dragon: its universality, its plasticity, its persistence. Dragon creatures are found in all Earth cultures at their earliest inception. The word "dragon," however, is of Greek origin: *drakon*, derived from *derkésthai*, "to look at," which comes to mean a "sharp-sighted serpent." This is a strange etymology. But it betrays perhaps the dragon's nature, and its origin in our fears and fascinations with transformation, alien contact, and alienation. For this snake, possessing the non-snake-like power of keen sightedness, a sky-and light-born sense, transgresses the boundaries of its natural condition. All other dragon avatars, such as snakes with wings, or gills, or fins, or snakes that breathe fire, display this same transgression of forms, all across the register of natural elements. More importantly, this snake hybrid shares mankind's primary sense, thus encroaching on the human form as well. Indeed, from the earliest records in the Judeo-Christian tradition, the dragon is seen as a menace to the human form, its adversary. Yet we must remember that the dragon is an imaginary creature, hence a menace we created. Did we create it in order to control nature or to explore it? Did we wish to give our face (and our eyes) to nature? Or were we inviting nature to change and alter that face?

Both impulsions are there in the dragon hybrid. In the Western tradition, however, the more primitive technology of control is developed first. The two basic responses to the dragon in that tradition—to slay and to harness—are not antithetical, but successive responses. The first reflects primal fears; the second marks a higher stage in Western man's technological evolution. Biblical references, for example, are confrontational, and we see the Old Testament's call for the Lord to punish Leviathan and "slay the dragon that is in the sea" echoed in New Testament battles with the red dragon who is Satan, the Adversary. Saint George, however, in later Christian legend, is less a slayer than a tamer of dragons. Because it requires daily human sacrifice, the dragon that guards the king's daughter in this legend could be said to embody mankind's fears of unredeemed nature, of its deadly diurnal rhythms. By preserving woman, the source that generates the human form, this dragon reserves the right to destroy mankind entirely, both in his genesis and his form, his means of hegemony over nature. He is pacified, however, by the cross, which is a stylization of the human form, a technological artifact that fixes human proportionality in emblematic perfection and thus allows man to use and impose his norms on nature.

The great dragon slayer of Greek legend is Hercules. And the monsters he fights are all dragon avatars: the Lernean Hydra, Scylla, the Gorgon Medusa, the many-headed dog Cerberus, and the Chimera, who is a combination of snake, lion, and goat. These figures, like Cerberus the watchdog of Hades, are complex apparitions. For Cerberus is a visible distortion of the rhythms of natural life, whose task, at the same time, is to defend those rhythms, in this case to block access to Hades, to thwart the investigations of living mankind and thus preserve the rhythm of life and death. Hercules, the half-mortal, becomes fully mortal through labors such as the fetching of the golden apples. The apples in the garden of the Hesperides, guarded by immortal Atlas and the hundred-headed dragon

Ladon, do not rot. In fetching them, Hercules displaces this unchanging center of all natural cycles of mutation. In doing so, he places the apples at the service of mankind, so that they will have the inspiration (if not the means) for controlling natural change and in the process rendering the human form changeless. But by serving man, Hercules becomes man, falls into a human condition whose nature is mortality, change.

Hercules does not perfect a dragon technology, however. His acts, like dipping his arrows in the bile of the slain Hydra in order to slay other dragons more efficiently, remain primitive. Jane Harrison's explanation of the origin of Delphic cults, however, offers a much more sophisticated example of harnessing the dragon.[7] Hercules now has been replaced by Apollo. It is in games that Apollo slays python, a symbol not a real dragon, and as symbol a manipulable incarnation of Dionysian forces, the ritualized form of natural vitality and change. Apollo is the human form transfigured as sun god. Transcending fire and the natural (mutational) elements, his domain is that of pure light, of sight, and of rational harmony. Apollo's ritualistic slaying of python represents the rational application of human measure to organic life. It is the apotheosis of the human image, the single form that stands out against natural profusion of forms. What is more, this Apollonian form thrives through advances in technology. Apollo does not need to wrestle the dragon, to make the direct contact which carries the risk of contamination, of hybridization. Hercules used the occasional arrow; Apollo is the archer god, who kills at a distance, and in thus killing weaves the abstract patterns of order which are the Pythian games. These offer a web of feigned combat. The center of that web is no longer a garden of the Hesperides, the uneasy center of Earth's profusion of forms, but the *omphalos*, python's conical grave mound, a mere hub. Radiating out from what is now a geometrical point, these games celebrate mankind's harnessing of nature.

But by imposing his forms on nature, man does not get rid of the dragon; he creates instead new, more complex, dragons. The dragon may become python, a sophisticated technology of control. Apollo, however, needs python; his own radiant form cannot, as will Clarke's Overmind, completely consume the natural world. So the dragon form, here the man-beast, abides, and in abiding still carries its charge of fear, of fascination with change. Dragons have a way of shifting locus, of reinvesting the very technologies man devises to control their shape changing in the first place. Cadmus, for example, slays the dragon and sows its teeth, causing a horde of armed men to spring up. Theban civilization is founded on this harnessing of dragon power. The pattern of order, however, this time, is no ritual or game, but internecine bloodshed. The symbol here has recovered its natural origins, the dragon reinvested with its primal sense of fear and disorder.

The Cadmus transfer, where snake becomes lance, is seen in more spectacular fashion in Stanley Kubrick's film *2001: A Space Odyssey*. Learning to use the bone as a weapon, man in a sense is converting his own form into a tool that permits him to dominate the natural world. The dragon slayer tosses the bone high in the air, and in an incredible ellipsis, we cut to a spaceship, moving through space with the same rhythm. That movement, however, is now regulated by urbane waltz music. On the one hand, man has harnessed the dragon, subjected him to the civilizing elegance of high technology. But on the other hand, he has recreated the dragon, for this spaceship is, despite appearances, a fearful engine of nuclear destruction. We find this same process, technology simultaneously harnessing and reconstituting the dragon, in Evgeny Zamyatin's sketch "The Dragon," published in 1918.[8] In this story, the dragon has returned to inhabit the bodies of revolutionary soldiers, busy killing the intellectuals who had harnessed it in a modern technology that here has taken flesh in a war machine. This dragon, "sublimated" in the same manner as man's more chaotic biological urges were in Kubrick's film, returns significantly through the eyes of Zamyatin's soldier, "two small chinks from the nightmare world into the human." It returns through the headlights of a "gnashing" trolley, or as Khlebnikov's "dragon train," or through those menacing red slits that seem to serve as eyes for Kubrick's waltzing and copulating machines. It is technology turning inside out, breeding new and terrible dragons.

These transfers show us how dynamic the interlinkage between man and dragon is. Furthermore, they reveal how this interchange, beyond simple attempts to slay or dominate, can be used in more complex fashion to create a feedback system that draws the power to sustain itself from the looping patterns of energy generated by such transfers. Zamyatin's dragon soldier, at one point, holds up a frozen starling and with his traditional fiery breath blows life into it, sending it off fluttering "into the unknown." But this "unknown," like the "nightmare" world mentioned before, is not, in this case, something that lies outside the human realm. Both have been internalized, made part of a feedback loop that establishes what could be called an "ecological" relationship between fear and form, the known and the unknown. The loop is established so that excesses on one level cause energy to flow, in counterbalancing fashion, to another level, and back again, perpetually.

This ecological relationship between man and alien, the internalized dragon, informs current theories of the mind, Freudian and Jungian alike. Jung's world, for example, contains the old fiery dragon in the form of the devouring mother, a figure that belongs to his preindividuation mythology. However, we no longer meet this alien on an external field of battle, but rather within the mind. In this closed space, the dragon has been redesignated "anima," the "woman within." Through this designation, it becomes the double or suppressed half of the individual psyche, a force that can now be reintegrated to the dominant half, creating the possibility of a balanced flow of energy back and forth between communicating vessels. But it is more than that. Jung calls the anima the "shadow." And as shadow, it becomes the interface between the collective unconscious and the conscious mind, between the primitive dragon and the new, technological one. For the shadow allows man to sustain an ego, his individual human identity, not by harnessing the forces of change so much as by recycling the energy generated by this act of harnessing, by moving it back and forth between levels of consciousness.

Carl Sagan, in *The Dragons of Eden*, locates another form of internalized alien, this time not in the mind but in the brain, an organ more directly, physically, subject to evolutionary pressures.[9] In his metaphor of the triune brain, Sagan sees the development of that organ as accretional. Within the brain of today's man we find, in successive layers, three areas: the reptilian R-complex, the limbic system (our mammalian sharing), and the neo-cortical or higher human regions. We not only have dragon origins; we literally carry them inside us. In answer to LeGuin's question, Sagan would say that, fearing dragons, we fear ourselves. And this need not be, for built into our physiological system itself, into the interaction between these brain layers, is a means of neutralizing this primal fear, a means in fact of using the resurgent dragon to define, and to sustain, our present sense of what it is to be human. If this R-complex still functions in man, it functions like reptiles themselves at night. It is in our dreams then that we glimpse our dragons of eden. Sagan sees the diurnal rhythm regulating the stirrings of these inner dragons. We repress the R-complex by day, but the cold-blooded, nondreaming ancestors walk our brains at night. Thanks to our capacity to dream, however, we can, in our deepest morning sleep, journey to this dragon source. And through dream we can, from these dragons, draw an energy which, recycled through the evolutionary microcosm of the brain, allows us to sustain our normative human existence. The flow of energy from the three parts of Sagan's brain is clearly cathartic. For by reevoking and resolving each night the enmity between reptiles and their mammalian rivals, we balance, and in a sense neutralize, our newer fears as neo-cortical tree-dwellers of those same limbic predators.

Finally, a novel like Frank Herbert's *Dune* offers, on a vast plane, a self-sustaining system based on recycling energy generated by the metamorphoses of internalized dragons. At the center of planet Arrakis, which is the center of Herbert's universe, are "sandworms," which (as the film version makes quite clear) are dragons. They are creatures of metamorphosis who in their successive hybridizations, regularly unstable combinations of opposite forces, control the elemental rhythms of the planet. As "makers," these worms create the sand of this arid world; from that dryness they produce "spice," the hybrid *mélange*. This is paradoxically called "water of life." The touch of water kills these makers. It is when they are drowned, however, that they yield or exhale this "water of life," which is a poison—but one that, in turn, can be converted, in the bodies of the Reverend Mothers, into a drug that expands rather than eradicates awareness.

The process, so far, seems a Dionysian dance of opposites. Into this play of dragon changes, however, Herbert weaves Apollonian elements, creating a relationship of forces that is less oppositional than identificational, activating the series of internalized loopings Sagan calls "vampiric." The spice "mass" (the term suggests fission and not hybridization) is engineered to produce a cash crop. This in turn is used as a geriatric drug, the means of circumventing the natural cycle of life and death. And as such, it is the means by which Guild navigators can fold space and time, thus allowing future mankind to install its web of archaic empires and patriarchs to interact with the Reverend Mothers. Paul's destiny, however, is the central loop that encloses all others. As Kwisatz Haderach, he is the male destined to do what only females can do: convert the "water of life." In doing so, he unfolds space/time "like a flower," placing himself at the center of what is now one vast interactive structure. As Paul changes the poison, slayer and dragon achieve a unique symbiosis, one that creates a permanent, undulatory relationship between man and nature, one in which Paul becomes the center and the entire universe. He sees "time stretch out in its weird dimension, delicately balanced yet whirling, narrow yet spread like a net gathering countless worlds and forces, a tightwire that he must walk, yet a teeter-totter on which he balanced."[10] Now it is the promise of the alien encounter itself that is neutralized, fed back into this incestuously integrative system which is "ecological" in the original sense of the word. Ecology derives from *oikos*, home. And in Herbert's massive fiction, infinite space is bounded by the dragon lair. Paul's expanding "spectrum awareness," seeming to promise alien encounters in new fields of space and time, is a means not of contact but of domestication. For it is only by nurturing the dragons within that Paul can claim to confront darkness without, creating this rhythm of expansion and contraction that fixes him, and with him the human form, at the pivot point, making him the measure of all things.

If we accept Bernal's dimorphic vision, ecological fictions like *Dune*, despite their trappings, should be considered fantasy rather than SF. Internalization of the dragon, however—the inscribing of nature and change within the human space of society, mind, or brain—is fantasy not because it cannot be realized (remember Bernal's "zoo") but because it denies man his unsteady gropings, the possibility of a truly open relationship with the nonhuman. The dragons of this open SF would, ideally, be promises, not systems, of change. To interact with these dragons is to meet change with change. It is to confront new shapes with alterations of our shape—alterations which may, or may not, increase our capacity to function in the face of the unknown. The SF dragon, therefore, is a figure of risk.

This externalizing dragon also has a tradition in Western literature. A work like *Beowulf*, for instance, offers encounters with dragons that read like harbingers of our Bernalian gropings. In this poem, dragon quests lure men, constantly, into contact with an ever-expanding perimeter of darkness. Grendel, first of all, enters Beowulf's hall as emissary of the dark world beyond its circle of light. The contact and entry point, however, is the dragon, or more exactly, the glove of dragon skin Grendel wears, the thing that allows this creature of the shapeless void to make the transition to humanoid form. Beowulf, in defeating Grendel, significantly tears off this gloved arm and thus de-forms the creature, sending it back through the dragon zone. This encounter is an interface between worlds. Because of it, Beowulf himself is drawn into the dark world, the world of elemental chaos, to a new dragon meeting—this time with the creature called Grendel's "mother." This is a mere-women, or sea-wolf hybrid, who lives in a watery land. Beowulf must plunge to unknown depths to meet it. The struggle with this dragon is, again, a moment of transitional groping. The hero takes with him the most advanced technology of his culture, a special suit of armor. This armor, by saving him from the water hag's blow, allows him to take hold of a new and even more powerful technology—the monster's sword of giants. With this sword, Beowulf slays the dragon; but by doing so, he creates a new dragon. This time, however, it is the essence of dragon-ness that emerges. For as he strikes down the creature, flames burst into aquatic darkness. Man may expand his realm, but the dragon remains as the place of hybridization, hence of potential engagement with elemental nature. Through his engagement here, Beowulf does not become conqueror of seas, but "protector of seafarers," an interface figure, dragon man interacting with dragon nature. The old world of singular combat, of man against nature, yields here to a world of combinations.

Beowulf's final dragon fight is more significant yet. The opponent this time is a full-fledged dragon of the hoard. What it guards, however, is not the earthbound "thesaurus" of Greek fertility cults. Instead it is protecting the artifacts of a Last Survivor, in other words a store of technology on the apparent edge of human capacity. This dragon appears to block mankind from its own future. It is called the "stingy king" and incarnates those fears of the future and the unknown that brought the last man to his huddling place, to this "zoo" gone wrong. In this case, however, the dragon is more than mere guardian of the human status quo. It offers Beowulf a form to be engaged, hence a means of continuing, and perhaps expanding, human existence beyond this apparent impasse. Beowulf is the heirless man, who, in fighting the beast, gains an heir. He is called "treasure giver" and must give his own being to permit new ones to be created. Indeed, in facing the dragon, he must meet its changing forms with a change in his own form. The poem ends with a funeral pyre. What falls away is the heroic body, but not to be recycled in some dance of elements. For this body has become as inconsequential as the dragon's treasure, which is now reconsigned to the Earth "as useless to men as it was before." But what rises from the flames is a transfigured form. Like Clarke's Overmind, the soul of the hero is now a discorporate intelligence; unlike it, that soul remains an interface, something that continues to inspire men to new striving.

It is but a step from *Beowulf* to a work like Cordwainer Smith's "Game of Rat and Dragon." The world of *Beowulf* is sex-neutral. We cannot polarize its dragon slayings as adversarial contests between Earth and sky gods. Mankind's dealings with nature cannot be reduced to a struggle between male and female principles. The poem gives, in its hero, a general mankind. Beyond sex wars and domination through technology, Beowulf represents something we can call intelligence. For he is struggling, in his dragon contests, with barriers, both in nature and in himself, to open exploration of the interface between mind and matter. And in Smith's story we have the same generalized dragon, one that is the common opponent to male and female alike.

"The Game of Rat and Dragon," as quintessential tale of space exploration, depicts the unsteady gropings of a genuinely collective humanity. Both sexes share the common sense of telepathy, which allows them, in sailing the stars, to perceive "a hostile something out in the black hollow nothingness of space," hence to bestow shape upon shapeless terror. For man, this shape is that of "dragons of ancient lore . . . hungry vortices of aliveness and hate compounded by unknown means out of the thin, tenuous matter between the stars."[11] But the ancient dragon shape alone proves inadequate to engage this "hostile something." To "pinlight" the protean hybrid, man needs to overlay his projections with those of cats, who themselves figure this enemy void in the form not of dragons, but of rats. Not species then, but two forms of intelligence engage the void, seek to fix it, but only as a creature of ever-changing shape, as a sort of metahybrid. And this shape changing, in turn, forces the projectors to alter their forms in order to maintain the interface with their rats and dragons. The story tells of the gradual formation of a telepathic union between two "pinlighters," a male human and a lady cat, which proves highly effective in meeting the void, but which in the final scene infuriates a female human. It infuriates her, surely, because it circumvents sex war, and with it the Earth-sky antagonism. If the rhythms of Herbert's *Dune* are incestuous, here is something apparently more shocking—telepathic sodomy. But ideas like this, Smith is telling us, are limiting dragons, forms to be met and cast off. The real dragons of SF, such as we see here, lead beyond the internalizing shapes of myths, of our systems of analysis. They are figures of participation, forms that are not simply composite but accretional as well.

One may wish to contest, at this point, the generic distinction I have been making on the basis of dragons. For that distinction limits the use of the term "science fiction" to those texts, within the broad field it traditionally designates, that cultivate the externalizing dragon and thus present the alien encounter as an open process of interface and exploration. The dragon here is seen as more than a historically or generically determined thematic structure. As the capacity of all structures to hybridize, it is a theme in the highest sense of the word: a place of encounter that is also a method of encounter, and as such a means of vectoring encounters along paths which are, as Bernal describes them, dimorphic. The dimorphic forms here are fantasy and science fiction. Let's examine briefly the feasibility of making this pure distinction. For it denies the dragon nature of most generic categories as they exist today.

The internalized "ecological" dragons, we said, are sophisticated devices, or technologies, of control. As such, they indicate that we are dealing with a certain type of fantasy—the power fantasy. But is the externalizing mode—the game of rat and dragon—any less a control structure, less a power fantasy in the same sense? Do we not, in the latter, alter our own forms and structures merely as a means of interacting more efficiently with a new, complex sense of the natural world?

Gary Wolfe's view would seem to corroborate this. His division of SF texts into what he calls autoplastic and alloplastic fantasies apparently contradicts the generic implications of Bernal's dimorphism, which presents both the autoplastic and alloplastic as dragon devices that prepare the way for this bifurcation into SF. Wolfe sees these terms, borrowed from anthropologist Géza Róheim, as offering "alternate models for relating to one's environment, and for gaining rewards from that environment."[12] For Róheim, these terms designate, respectively, the primitive and the technological response to nature. The autoplast alters his physical being to fit nature; the alloplast alters or "terraforms" nature to fit himself. Both "models" are control systems, for both permit man to profit from interaction with his natural environment. Yet their relationship to each other, as Wolfe sees it, remains an internalizing one. They are not successive systems, as Róheim implies, but "alternate" ones. Man then, dealing with nature, moves from one to the other in undulatory fashion. As we move back and forth from one to the other, they represent limits to the human response to nature, limits that define the human norm whereby their aberrations can be measured. We are still inside the system of myth, of *anthropos*. Here, for the sake of internal balance, Wolfe must limit autoplastic acts to "surgical rites of passage." Bernal, however, is not held by the limits of human body or human myth. The autoplastic is not a primitive mode of interaction; nor is it an alternate mode. On Bernal's evolutionary vector, it is an advanced technique, one that allows man new ways of interacting with a natural world he was previously unable to reach. It is a means of passage, but not to maturity or individuation, to a restructuring inside the system. It leads, on a one-way path of change, outside the human system, to new, genuinely alien contacts.

To discriminate generically between dragon texts then, we are entitled to ask which direction on Bernal's dimorphic axis that text takes. The direction is not always immediately obvious, as a final pair of narratives proves. On one hand, Arthur C. Clarke's "Meeting with Medusa" appears to promise externalizing dragons; its titular creatures seem to offer a genuine exploratory interface between man and the alien, a means of functioning in the hostile atmosphere of Jupiter. On the other hand, Frank Herbert's *Dragon in the Sea* purports to be a Jonah story, a struggle with nature in the belly of the myth. As we shall see, the opposite is true in both cases.

Clarke's story tells of the encounter, by protagonist Howard Falcon, of an alien life form on Jupiter. This is the meeting of two dragon figures. Men call the Jupiter alien "Medusa," give it a mythical dragon name. But Falcon, as the name implies, is a modern hybrid. After a dirigible accident on Earth, he has been prosthetical-

ly rebuilt. He is a cyborg, a man autoplastically adapted to function in
outer space. The reader, on the threshold of this encounter, wonders
what vector it will take. Falcon could be undergoing a surgical rite of
passage—an alteration intended to lead him, and mankind with him,
to new awareness of what remains a fundamentally unchanging human condition. Or his "surgery" could be a step in the advancement
of mankind toward that more-than-human existence Bernal envi-
sions. The story's title may offer a key to the problem of direction. At
first glance, we seem to have a Bernalian proposition. Having shed
(however accidentally) the limitations of flesh-bound humanity, Falcon apparently stands ready for a "meeting with Medusa," exploratory contact with a world previously denied to the flesh. He is to be
the new dragon interface with the unknown. But, we wonder, why *a*
meeting? This implies that the particular meeting here is not unique,
but one of many meetings, past and future, with the same thing. We
suspect, in fact, that this meeting may be but a variation of some
archetypal meeting. For we realize that the unknown, in this title, has
a well-known name, one that places it clearly within the known
system of human myth. Falcon's trajectory is thwarted, reinscribed,
before it can gather momentum.

Indeed, throughout this text we see the initial thrust of Falcon's
encounter undercut by a system of comparisons. These establish a
subliminal network of checks and balances whose function, it seems,
is to reinscribe the human form as normative value governing the
dynamics of human "advancement." Falcon, for instance, describes
himself at one point as an "ambassador" between worlds. But this
was spoken, we are immediately told, in an excess of "somber
pride." Falcons are proud, high-flying birds. But here, as he rises up
"on his hydraulics to his full seven feet of height," this particular bird
is absurdly ineffectual. But still proud. Falcon reminds us, in his
mechanical posturing, that pride goeth before a fall. He reminds us
that scientific man, according to the myth, is a fallen being, here a
creature who, in his "unique loneliness," has clear satanic overtones.

Falcon is to be the link between two worlds. But before he even
makes contact, we realize that, if one of those worlds is dead, the
other is powerless to be born. He may be an evolutionary superman
and first immortal. But he must learn that his *position* in the order of
things, ironically, is not new at all. Man has, in this being with an
animal name, elevated himself. But he has another bestial analogue,

the "superchimp," a creature he has surgically elevated from his evolutionary niche. And perhaps wrongly elevated. For the specter of Dr. Moreau hangs over superchimp and superman. In this story full of rhythmic rises and falls, both animal-plus and man-plus, whatever their initial promise for outreach, have become internalized dragons. They are held in a self-regulating system in which exaggerations are met by corresponding understatements, the rhythm of rise and fall reinforcing, at a never-stated point of balance, the normative sense, or better the normative use, of the human form.

Looking at the "superchimp," Falcon "felt that strange mingling of kinship and discomfort that all men experience when they gaze into the mirror of time."[13] Time, to Clarke, is exactly this: a mirror. Despite claims to the contrary, it proves not to be a realm open to exploration and encounter, but one bound by a play of symmetrical oppositions. These are everywhere in the story. Falcon, on an Earth that man can circle in eighty minutes rather than eighty days, chooses to be a balloonist. His world seems one of outbound exploration. Yet lighter-than-air movement proves the means, for him, not to discover the future but to rediscover the past, that "infinite, ancient landscape drenched with history." These opposites, everywhere, combine to form symmetrical hybrids. Exploration of Jupiter's atmosphere is a mirror transposition of deep-sea exploration, on an aerial "raft" named Kon-Tiki. On Earth, the balloon allows us to rise; in Jupiter gravity, the same object functions as a "parachute," preventing us from falling. And what is more important, first contact with alien life forms, the nominal goal of Falcon's strivings, is itself bounded by this same system of comparison and inversion. Creatures are called, alternately, giant manta rays and sky-borne cattle. The "medusa" itself is described as made up, alternately, of sky-borne snakes and sea-bound tendrils. Hybridization here serves as a means of generating bracketing categories. The dragon encounter is a preserving machine of rigid Pascalian contrarieties. The past is for chimps, the future for machines, and man in between, as he tries to make the transition from one to the other, reveals himself to be an incomprehensible monster. Clarke's falcon is a beast-man and a man-machine at the same time. The hybrid is a curiously static, even homocentric, system where human energies, enclosed within evolutionary limits, are endlessly recycled in a play of metamorphoses. We have homeostasis, but at the cost of any real alien encounter. Clarke promises man the stars, but in the end gives him (because it is impossible for him to change his form and still remain man) Bernal's Earth as sole possible habitat. Jupiter can be a sky god, or an ocean of gas, but "it can never be a place for man."

Herbert's novel has had three successive titles: *21st Century Sub, The Dragon in the Sea,* and *Under Pressure.* This sequence seems to say that the story's focus gradually became clear to the author and suggests that this focus is an internalizing one, that it relocates the dragon from the sea to the mind. Herbert's twenty-first-century world is a nuclear wasteland where man must function underground and underwater, under constant pressure, both physical and psychological. The twenty-first-century sub, adapting to this environmental pressure, is a hybrid figure—a "sub-tug" whose mission is to pass under the ocean undetected and take precious oil from a well under Nova Zemlya, to "suck at the jugular of the earth." The tale seems then to investigate man's ability to adapt to life in the belly of a dragon that an enemy is trying to slay. And the key to such adaptation, it appears, is for man to control the dragon within, whose stirrings are caused by the pressures of environmental imbalance. Dealing with the inner dragon is the job of the novel's protagonist, Ramsey. A psychiatrist-spy aboard the sub-tug, Ramsey makes use of "vampire gauges." With them he monitors the presence, in the crew, of what Sagan calls the vampiric, the self-consuming, forces within. The system of balance must not break down, or the dragon be allowed to burst its bounds. Ramsey seeks to uncover "sleeper" agents, men who have been conditioned on the deepest dragon level of their minds and who on that level, beneath all conscious controls, can be awakened to betrayal. Ramsey must, it seems, control all fears erupting from these dragon depths, for they are the means by which the enemy detects and destroys the subs.

Herbert's novel appears to celebrate the effective control, within a carefully internalized universe, of the dragon forces of nature by a human system—that of psychiatry. There is another, externalizing, movement however. For Ramsey, seeking to restore ecological order to a world radically out of balance, encounters Captain Sparrow. This is another bird-man; but unlike Falcon, he is not, in his rising, governed by the corresponding necessity of a fall. For Sparrow, adaptation has a very different meaning: it is the ability to interact with new situations, to create patterns beyond prepatterned rhythms of myth. Unlike Falcon, Sparrow is not held by his dragon-ness. Instead he has a dragon, his sub, the environment that serves him as interface between human existence and the void. Sparrow, in fact, refuses to fight the dragon, lamenting that "humanity's basic problem is all wrapped up in the idea of security." In opposition to security, Sparrow offers the concept of "sanity." By this he does not mean, as Ramsey might, the search for internal balance. He means "the ability to swim." And that, he tells us, "means the sane person has to understand currents, has to know what's required in different waters."[14] Unlike Ramsey, Sparrow comes from a generation that does not believe in vampires. He is Bernal's unsteady groper, moving not against or within the dragon, but with it.

And Sparrow converts the psychiatrist, redirects his inner search outward. Under Sparrow's urging, the birth metaphor with which Ramsey seeks to reorder the world is given a new directional impetus. What to Ramsey is symbolic "rebirth" becomes, in relation to Sparrow's actions, real birth. If this sub is, as Ramsey calls it, a "perambulating womb looking for a place to spew us out," the spewing now is into new streams of experience. Psychic breakdown, it proves, occurs as men become increasingly pressurized, "wrapped up" in their internal dragons. In Ramsey, this leads to a catatonic state, in which the conscious will to act is totally paralyzed, held in thrall by the rhythm of internal correspondences. Sparrow, in the climactic scene of the novel, must take the role of the psychiatrist. As alienist, however, he does not reorganize Ramsey's inner forces (indeed, Ramsey collapses into stasis because these forces are over-organized, deadlocked). Rather, he leads him out of himself, but now as genuine midwife, delivering a new man up to new possibilities of alien encounter. Sparrow is neither Zamyatin's starling in the paws of the metal dragon, nor is he Clarke's Falcon. He is neither trapped in a system of internal balance, nor is he destined to become, as a sign of the tyranny of metamorphosis, a monstrous hybrid of flesh and metal. If Sparrow achieves symbiosis with his sub, it is a *navigational* symbiosis. Reacting "like one of its instruments instead of like a human being," he acts to extend man's communications network via the dragon into unknown realms. The umbilical cord, for this new bird in the sea seeking birth, is experience. Through experience he strives for release—from mankind's old racial fears, into new areas of pain and menace.

Until we find other ways to represent the genuinely unknown, we will need dragons. The literature of alien encounter needs and uses them to define itself, to effect the dimorphism between fantasy and science fiction. And SF needs dragons as well. For the importance of SF, in relation to the various forms of ecological fantasy, lies in a sense in its particular use of the dragon. Fantasy dragons are earthbound and mythbound. Science fiction gives us Captain Sparrow. It transforms the traditional dragon into (quite literally) something else, as in the case of Heinlein's marvelous "star beast." For here is a dragon completely unbound, the guardian of no hoard whatsoever. The dragon has become, instead, a diplomatic occasion. It is now the shape which allows man not just contact but civilized *relations* with new races and places. Heinlein's dragon, and others like it, prove that SF can be what it claims to be—a passport to the stars.

Part Two
Sightings: The Aliens among Us

6

Discriminating among Friends: The Social Dynamics of the Friendly Alien

John Huntington

Let me begin by emphasizing a distinction that underlies everything I have to say. The problems posed by the imagined alien are quite different from those posed by the actual alien. The imagined alien is a gratuitous invention, a complication that someone, for reasons that bear investigation, has added to the world. The actual alien is not gratuitous, and it has to be dealt with as it is. Of course, there is necessarily some overlap between the two. Actual aliens stimulate fantasies about aliens.

It does not seem unreasonable to view the imagined hostile alien as a projection onto "the other" of qualities of ourselves that we wish to deny.[1] This basic dynamic of the hostile alien is exquisitely rendered in Fredric Brown's "Arena" when Carson, the human hero, caught in what he claims is telepathic rapport with the hostile alien, describes his sensation as "things that he felt but could not understand and could never express." Having attributed his unacceptable feelings to the alien, Carson can then exclude it from the category of creatures requiring moral consideration and can attack it without reservation or qualm.

I have argued elsewhere that once a writer sets up such a system of exclusion as is required by the hostile alien story, the writer is trapped in it, and even an attempt to correct the exclusionary system fails to do anything but reverse the polarities and leads to anthrophobia in the place of xenophobia. Ursula LeGuin's *The Word for World is Forest* is a clear instance of this process by which a strong attack on the xenophobic proclivities of humanity finds its satisfaction in scapegoating the prejudiced human.

As we have come to understand the stark exclusions of the

69

hostile alien story, we have tended to disregard the more subtle dynamics of the benign alien. In imaginative literature, the phrase "friendly alien" becomes an oxymoron: the imagined friendly alien achieves its benignity by approaching the familiar and conventionally valued, that is, by not being truly alien. Such alienness is a superficial costume hiding a familiar personality.[2] But having observed this aspect of contradiction in the benign alien, we may ask why an author should undertake such an imaginative exercise in the first place. The motives for imagining the hostile alien seem clear enough; what motive would one have for imagining the friendly alien? I will suggest that the benign alien has at its core a social fantasy: that of radical individualism that would deny the meaning and power of social groups altogether.

In an essay attacking the xenophobia of American SF, LeGuin credits the "invention" of the "sympathetic alien" to Stanley Weinbaum's "A Martian Odyssey" (1934).[3] I wish to focus my inquiry on the fairly complex social dynamics of this elementary story. The story is probably familiar. Its plot is simple: Jarvis, a human separated from his expedition on Mars, saves the life of Tweel, a tall, birdlike alien; they become friends of sorts and have a series of adventures, in the last of which, when the humans arrive to save the day, Tweel disappears. Tweel is a charming character who verges on the incomprehensible. His language seems to keep changing; a thing is never called by the same word twice. He displays pleasure by soaring seventy-five feet into the air and descending like a javelin, nose first, to stick quivering in the earth. But behind such comic eccentricities, we see an essentially human figure: bipedal, rational, tool-using, capable of emotion and loyalty. Toward the end of the story, when Tweel has helped him escape the Martian barrel people, Jarvis says, "Thanks, Tweel. You're a man!" Out loud he wonders whether that is really a compliment, but in the next breath he acknowledges that it is the highest form of praise he can conceive.[4] Thus, Tweel's differentness is superficial; he is an eccentric who, despite his oddities, is valued for the way he approaches a human ideal.

But Tweel is admittedly odd, and once we grant his difference, we find that "A Martian Odyssey" pays for its generosity toward him by an excessive anxiety about all other differences, even differences which seem absurdly trivial in the Martian context. The humans in the story are men of different nationalities, and while their com-

radeship is acknowledged, the story repeatedly points to the differences in their language and understanding. The difficulty even humans have understanding each other is rendered by confusions of
pronunciation at the beginning of the story: Harrison (American)
tells Jarvis, "Spill it, man." Leroy (French) asks, "Speel, . . . Speel
what?" to which Putz (German) easily answers, "He means 'spiel.'
. . . It iss to tell." A clumsy understanding is attained here, but it is by
false etymologies and mispronunciations. Throughout the story,
Leroy and Putz mangle idiomatic English. One has to be struck by
Weinbaum's attention to this level of ethnic difference when the
main theme of the story seems to be the areas of identity between
aliens. This sense of the minor gaps between people can shade easily
into hysterical and exclusionary discriminations.

Tweel aside, the other forms of Martian fauna—the living grass,
the silicon bricklayer, the dream monster, and the barrel people—
involve common clichés of alien exclusion of the sort we expect to
find in hostile alien stories. The dream monster is the most conventionally hateful: like the Roller in Brown's "Arena," it is tentacled; it
can be described a number of times simply as "one of those writhing,
black rope-armed horrors." Like the Roller, it has a telepathic
capability that renders it particularly dangerous to the open, good-
natured human. The only way to deal with it is to destroy it. The
barrel people belong to a slightly different set of clichés. They are
laborious, self-oblivious, organized automatons who learn from Jarvis two phrases, which they repeat frequently: "We are v-r-r-riends.
Ouch!" The final revelation that Jarvis has stolen the shining thing
that removes warts and may cure cancer places us casually in the
imperialist tradition. It is taken for granted that Jarvis is in the right
and that his theft is heroic; the barrel people's hostility turns out to be
justified, but it is also disregarded.

We can observe here how casually a story which at one level has
tried to be sympathetic to the alien can settle back into conventional
postures. The effort to appreciate Tweel cannot entirely change
underlying discriminatory structures, and the more generous the
story is toward Tweel, the more necessary it is for it to reinforce its
essentially chauvinist base at other points in the story. One alien can
be accepted as benign only by discovering another creature which can
absorb the xenophobic charge. We can see this mechanism in the
recent film *E.T.*: as the alien gains our sympathy (by behaving in

recognizably human ways), hostility is generated against such adult authorities as scientists and policemen. Freud observes that "it is always possible to bind together a considerable number of people in love, so long as there are other people to receive the manifestations of their aggressiveness." He calls this phenomenon "the narcissism of minor differences," a phrase he admits does not do much to explain the phenomenon.[5]

If the differences in language and pronunciation repeatedly remind us of the potential distances between humans, they do not thereby settle the issue of friendship, for distance here may be a source of affection as well as hostility. On the one hand, there is a superficial bad-temperedness in the story: Harrison, the captain, repeatedly accuses Jarvis of being crazy; Jarvis himself makes a crack about the apparition of a woman being "as solid as Putz's head," and simply ignores Putz's confused "Vot?" Such moments, while denotatively hostile, are also rituals of friendship. As the stereotype of the slow foreigner is developed, it is also being transformed from simple exclusionary mechanism into a language of a kind of affection. It is an affection, however, made possible by condescension. And just as the humans' seemingly hostile banter covers affection, so does the barrel people's rendering of "We are friends" conceal indifference and hostility.

The affection-hostility confusion parallels a confusion between superior and inferior intelligence. Harrison keeps trying to attribute Tweel's actions to craziness and to see his intellect as inferior. Jarvis prefers to see him as sane and intellectually superior: he observes that Tweel is able to learn some English while Jarvis himself can learn nothing of Tweel's language. The possibility that nouns keep shifting in Tweel's language may be evidence of confusion or of a superior antinomian awareness of radical individualism.[6] The barrel people render this enigma of intelligence even more acutely. Jarvis points out that Tweel's description of them is ambiguous. "Their intelligence was not of our order, but something different and beyond the logic of two and two is four. Maybe I missed his meaning. Perhaps he meant that their minds were of low degree, able to figure out the simple things—'One-one-two—yes!'—but not the more difficult things—'Two-two-four—no!'" Although Jarvis finally concludes that Tweel meant the first, there is good reason for us to see these perhaps intelligent creatures as limited, as comic, mechanical, and routinized zombies. They imitate language without attaining it. In a late scene, we see them sacrifice themselves dispassionately.

These apparently epistemological problems (How can we evaluate alien intelligence? How can we tell affection from hostility?) may be misleading, however. Clearly, Jarvis' affection for Tweel exists regardless of the level of his intelligence, and, just as clearly, his affection for Putz and Harrison exists despite the hostile language. The difficulty is not one of knowing affection, but one of expressing it openly. For reasons that will become clear, desire is the issue here, and it is repeatedly blocked in this story.

The scene in which Jarvis sees the image of Fancy Long becomes central. As in a nightmare, behind the woman Jarvis finds the "black rope-armed horror" of the dream monster. But if Jarvis has a deep dread of the woman, he also desires her. The conflict leads to some bizarre moments. When Jarvis lets Tweel shoot the vision of the woman, we get one of a number of instances of narrative indecision. "I don't know why I stood there watching him take careful aim, but I did." Clearly, Jarvis has realized that the image is false, that this is not really Fancy Long. His declaration of ignorance about his motives is necessitated by the atrocity his abstention sanctions: he has to deny that he allowed a woman to be shot. But he is also caught in a moment of passionate desire so strong that it is in danger of distorting his rational understanding of the situation even in the retelling.

The dream monster apparently "uses its victim's longings and desires to trap its prey." Jarvis cautions the crew to watch out. "We can't even trust our eyes," he warns. "You might see me—I might see one of you—and back of it may be nothing but another of these black horrors." Such a conviction justifies repression of all affection. The danger of the dream monster is that it might lure the men by their desire for one another. The important issue, however, is not anxiety about homosexuality, but anxiety about all desire.

When Tweel disappears toward the end of the story, Jarvis says, "He'd gone, and damn it! I wish—I wish he hadn't!" What strikes one here is the quite extraordinary flatness of the obviously deeply felt line. In part, the hesitation after "I wish" and the tepid "hadn't" are formulas of the era (just like the phrase, "just friends, get me," said earlier of Fancy Long), but they are also further signs of difficulty with feelings.

Earlier, we see another instance of Jarvis' ability to say what he really feels and means when he stops himself in midsentence. Jarvis is talking:

> "Yet, in spite of all difficulties, I *liked* Tweel, and I have a queer certainty that he liked me."
>
> "Nuts," repeated the captain. "Just daffy."
>
> "Yeah? Wait and see. A couple of times I've thought that perhaps we—" he paused, and then resumed his narrative.

This last incomplete sentence is different from the usual narrative device in which the reader is able to fill in the words the speaker cannot say; here it is impossible to determine what Jarvis might have said. The break does not reveal what meaning the character is repressing.

If we cannot know exactly what Jarvis meant to say, we can nevertheless speculate on some of the issues he might discuss at this point. His concern with liking Tweel may lead him to generalizations about human affection. Or Jarvis might be responding to Harrison's accusation of craziness and intending to generalize about sanity and alienness. Or he might be about to comment on Harrison's general attitude and language, on the slandering of those we actually like. Whatever the subject of his meditation, it breaks off on the enigma of the pronoun "we." The ambiguity of the "we" leaves it open whether his comment would be restricted to just Tweel and himself or would include Harrison, to whom he has just responded, or the rest of the crew, or perhaps larger generalizations (we men, we humans, we communicators, we explorers). By breaking where it does, the sentence emphasizes the problem of the constitution of the group, the "we."

This enigmatic gap in the story is a moment at which the story comes up against the real social dilemma posed by imagining the friendly alien. Try as it will to imagine forms of desire independent of social groups and conventions, the story finds itself inevitably forced to confront the crucial issue of the group. Even the unique couple, odd as it may be, constitutes a social group and thereby changes or distorts the larger, more conventional social field. I am reminded of the extraordinary moment in Zamyatin's *We* when, as the revolutionaries surge into the city, one jubilantly exclaims, "We are acting!" D-503, caught between his love for I-330 and his still deeply ingrained social allegiance to the Benefactor, can only wonder in dismay, "Who are we? Who am I?"[7] The fantasy that we can define ourselves outside of the group is a powerful one, but it rather quickly comes up against the fact that the individual is defined, is only meaningful, against the background of a group. No sooner has the group been transcended than it must be reconstituted. Jarvis' dilemma is that he cannot—nor can any of us—"think" the contradiction of the individual and the group.

The question that arises is how much of the elaborate economy of love and hate in "A Martian Odyssey" is inherent in the formula fiction of America in the thirties and how much is structurally inherent in the act of imagining the friendly other? It would be naive to think that we could settle the question precisely and finally. Clearly, some of Weinbaum's mechanisms are historically local. But if we consider Ursula LeGuin's "Nine Lives," a much more self-conscious story published thirty-five years later, we can see that some aspects of this system of balances are common to efforts to imagine the sympathetic alien.[8]

LeGuin's story is conscious of the difficulties we have been examining. In "Nine Lives," two miners, Martin (Argentine) and Pugh (Welsh), who have spent two years of irritable isolation on a volcanic planet, greet their assistance team, a "tenclone" consisting of five men and five women, all nearly identical. Relations between the two miners and the highly integrated tenclone are tense. When nine of the members of the tenclone are killed in an eruption, the survivor has to learn to trust and gain emotional strength from men different from himself. The story's thesis is, roughly, that the harmony that exists among members of the tenclone shows up as a kind of isolation ("Incest is it, or masturbation?" asks Pugh when two members of the clone make love), while the friction caused by the difference between Martin and Pugh shows up as a negotiated contact which can achieve love. The gruff words that seem to point gratuitously to differences, while initially signs of disharmony in the human ranks, by the dialectical process that LeGuin makes explicit, finally become signs of affection.

We all know perfectly well, however, that differences do not necessarily breed affection. LeGuin's squabbling humans can finally declare their love for each other, but in other situations and with other people such petty nagging can be the obvious expression of deep antipathy. In the Weinbaum story, the system remains explosively undischarged of both possibilities. The love of the alien, whether Tweel or Martin, is in part a fantasy of overcoming obstacles to love.

But, if both stories are in favor of "love," we should also note that in both stories it is the harmonious group that is a major object of distrust. In LeGuin, the tenclone, while admirable for its efficiency, is too narcissistic (if one can use that term for a group) to engage in genuine social interaction. It substitutes good manners for true engagement with others. In Weinbaum's story, the barrel people are an allegory of social coherence; their mindless greeting, "We are v-r-r-riends! Ouch!" is in the same social category as the tenclone's good-mannered obliviousness to Pugh and Martin.

Tweel is, so far as we know, not part of a larger group. He is the only creature of his type Jarvis ever meets. The humans in the story seem to take it for granted that Tweel is a Martian, although he may be no more aboriginal than they are. After Jarvis tries to signify that Earth is his home, "Tweel set up such an excited clacking that I was certain he understood. He jumped up and down, and suddenly he pointed at himself and then at the sky, and then at himself and at the sky again. He pointed at his middle and then at Arcturus, at his head and then at Spica, at his feet and then at half a dozen stars, while I just gaped at him." This is a confusing message, but after it one might expect Jarvis to investigate Tweel's origins more thoroughly. Instead, he just repeats the message about his own origins. The bond between Tweel and Jarvis is, therefore, not a sign of social integration, but rather the opposite: they represent individuals free from all social bonds and definitions who, in this state of isolation, find meaningful connection. At the moment Jarvis is reunited with his human comrades, Tweel is lost to him. Both of these stories aspire to finding bonds of loyalty and affection between individuals apart from and unrelated to the larger groups to which they belong. If "A Martian Odyssey" runs up against the problem of who "we" are, it also fantasizes a friendship that makes questions of who "we" are irrelevant.

We observe here a dialectical process that will belong to any consideration of the alien. If the story of the hostile alien is often an exercise in excluding individuals because of their group type, the story of the benign alien is often an exercise in finding a bond that transcends groups. It isolates the individual and emphasizes his or her difference from the rest of the species. This rejection of the group, while it may lead to a readiness to accept the individual alien, may also lead to a disregarding of social factors that generate discrimination in the first place. Just as the phrase "Some of my best friends are X" is often the preface for a discriminatory generalization about X, this claim to transcend group categories by finding the alien individual friendly, far from obliterating the categories, allows them to operate with impunity, beyond the control of rational awareness.

I would therefore suggest that the story of the benign alien may not be any more socially constructive than that of the hostile alien. The Freudian bond of "the narcissism of minor differences" is based on a strict emotional economy. Freud argues that the injunction to "love they neighbor as thyself" entails a disastrous contradiction: I can love so indiscriminately only if I disregard or devalue the very qualities and virtues that earn love. Similarly, I can love the extraordinary alien only by abandoning the social conventions which allow for rational exchange and understanding.

7

Sex, Superman, and Sociobiology in Science Fiction

Joseph D. Miller

It is most appropriate to begin this essay with a discussion of Kal-El of Krypton, the most famous of all the supermen. Just what is Superman? An Americanized sanitization of the Germanic *Übermensch* largely cribbed from Wylie's novel *The Gladiator?*[1] At least Superman, of the blue eyes and vaguely Nordic features, does not have blond hair. Still, Kryptonians, by and large, seem to be ethnically identical to white Anglo-Saxon Protestants.

But is there more to Superman than the power fantasies of preadolescents? Is there, for instance, a sense in which Superman is a kind of gelded sexual archetype for our culture? For further insight, we need to consider the extraordinary events of a few years ago when Superman lost his virginity.[2] It seems that a high-tech villain was able to make Superman's super powers contingent on the wearing of his long johns. Without his costume, Kal-El reverted to purely mortal Clark Kent. Of course, the temptation was irresistible. So "Supes" sent his uniform off to the Fortress of Solitude for laundering and spent a week as pure, unadulterated Clark Kent. During this vacation, Clark's relationship with Lois was finally consummated (Fig. 1). The most interesting outcome of all this was the uproar in the press. Banner headlines in *The Daily News* described the immorality of DC Comics in depicting a sex life for Superman. Most of this conflagration died down by the time of the Superman movies, and in *Superman II*, Superman does sleep with Lois Lane. Interestingly, however, this consummation once again depends on a temporary renunciation of the powers which make "Supes" super. In fact, the only example I know of in which intercourse between Superman and normal women is considered is the hilarious short story by Larry Niven entitled

Figure 1. From *Superman*, no. 297 (March 1976). Copyright © DC Comics Inc. 1975. Used with permission.

"Man of Steel, Woman of Kleenex."[3] Faster than a speeding bullet, indeed!

In any event, why is there such an apparent aversion to the coupling of *Homo superior* and *Homo sapiens*? It is certainly not restricted to the Superman of the comics. In Shelley's *Frankenstein*, which is by many accounts the first science-fiction novel, we also see the first *Homo superior*, although the monster is a kind of patchwork construct. But Shelley's original was a creature of prodigious strength and high intelligence. He is promised a mate by Frankenstein, but the promise is never fulfilled. Instead, the monster is hunted through the Arctic in a fashion akin to Ahab's pursuit of the Moby Dick. Frankenstein says to himself at this point, in regard to a possible mate for the monster,

> Even if they were to leave Europe and inhabit the deserts of the new world, yet one of the first results of those sympathies for which the demon thirsted would be children, and a race of devils would be propagated upon the earth, who might make the very existence of the species of man a condition precarious and full of terror. Had I a right, for my own benefit, to inflict this curse upon everlasting generations? I had before been moved by the sophisms of the being I had created; I had been struck senseless by his fiendish threats: but now, for the first time, the wickedness of my promise burst upon me; I shuddered to think that future ages might curse me as their pest, whose selfishness had not hesitated to buy its own peace at the price perhaps of the existence of the whole human race.[4]

Other engineered supermen suffer a similar sexual fate. Asimov's robots cannot contribute to the human gene pool, but as is evident in such works as *Robots of Dawn*,[5] the more closely they resemble humans, the more they are vilified. And sex with a robot is the ultimate social sin. It may be that the degree of acceptance of artificial intelligence may depend on the perceived physical dissimilarity between "us" and "them." David Gerrold's Harlie[6] doesn't set off our biological alarms, but the humanoid R. Daneel Olivaw of *Robots of Dawn* certainly may, even if direct genetic competition is impossible. Even when the base material is *Homo sapiens*, the engineered superman typically makes no contribution to the gene pool. Paul Atreides in *Dune*[7] does produce a son, but his transformation into a giant sandworm in later sequels effectively closes out any continuing genetic contribution. Even the artificially produced geniuses of Keyes' *Flowers for Algernon*[8] or Disch's *Camp Concentration*[9] pay for their augmented intelligence. After a brief romantic fling with *Homo sapiens*, Charlie is demoted back to idiocy. In Disch's *Camp Concentration*, the price of genius is a particularly virulent variety of syphilis. The best sexual performance of any of the environmentally produced supermen would appear to be that of Valentine Michael Smith of Heinlein's *Stranger in a Strange Land*.[10] This is something of a special case, however, since apparently any human could gain Smith's powers simply by learning Martian. So there is no real threat to the gene pool. Also, Smith is really an alter ego of Heinlein, a card-carrying member of *Homo sapiens*. So Smith, although capable of generating a level of xenophobia sufficient to get himself martyred, is sufficiently sapient to be allowed the pleasures of sexual congress with his followers.

Genetically engineered supermen don't seem to fare any better. Alvin, the protagonist of Clarke's *Against the Fall of Night*[11] is the victim of a considerable degree of social exclusion because of his recidivist behaviors. The Underpeople of Smith's *Norstrilia*[12] are almost completely isolated from sexual contact with true humans. The Alphas of *Brave New World*[13] mate, but only with each other, and babies, of course, are produced solely in test tubes. The horror we feel at the prospect of even social intercourse with such creatures is perhaps symbolized by the suicide of the Savage, the natural man of Huxley's novel.

An interesting variation on the genetically engineered superman is the winner of the reproductive lottery. The most well known examples here are Lazarus Long of *Methuselah's Children*[14] and Teela Brown of Niven's *Ringworld*.[15] In both cases, the protagonists are "engineered" only in the sense of being the descendants of a long line of individuals rewarded for certain behaviors: in Long's case, marrying long-lived individuals; in Brown's case, being lucky enough to win the lottery determining the right to bear children. In each case, a kind of social or cultural selection produces an individual with a valuable adaptation: longevity or luck. This form of cultural selection could operate at a faster rate on a given phenotypic character than natural selection ordinarily would, but of course it could not match the speed of direct genetic intervention through genetic engineering. At any rate, both characters fare better than the typical superman.

Lazarus Long does produce and Teela Brown does find a mate on Ringworld, although she does not make a contribution to the Terran gene pool. Once again, Lazarus Long, as Heinlein's alter ego, is thoroughly human, except for the peculiarity of his longevity. Similar thoughts apply to Teela Brown. It appears that such limited supermen are less threatening. One explanation for this results from a kind of genetic risk-benefit analysis. The benefit is that mating with individuals with such obvious selective advantages (that is, longevity and luck) can only add to one's own inclusive fitness. Furthermore, the offspring of such a union should likewise benefit from an infusion of superior genes. In such a sapiens-superior mating, sapiens has a 50 percent genetic stake. Anything that contributes to the survival of the offspring will thus contribute to the continuing representation of the sapiens genome in succeeding generations. On the contrary, the risk (suppression or elimination of the sapiens genome) is minor if the difference between the species consists only of a relatively small number of phenotypic traits.

In major contrast to such limited supermen are what could be called the spontaneous supermen or mutants. Science fiction abounds with such creatures. The Mule of the *Foundation Trilogy*,[16] Stapledon's *Odd John*,[17] and Jommy Cross in Van Vogt's *Slan* are all persecuted and prevented from contributing to the gene pool in various ways. In *Slan*, John Petty, Chief of the Secret Police, says that "the slan women are the most dangerous of all. They're the breeders, and they know their job, damn them!" Again, in this novel, intense xenophobia is evident in Kier Gray's concluding explanation.

> For hundreds, perhaps thousands, of years, the tensions had been building up. And then in a single stupendous quarter of a millennium more than a billion abnormal births occurred. It was like a cataclysm that paralyzed the human will. The truth was lost in a wave of terror that swept the world into war. . . . During the nameless period, slans were hunted like wild beasts. There is no modern parallel for the ferocity of human beings against the people they considered responsible for the disaster. . . . Suspicion was swift beyond all resistance. Men denounced their neighbors and had them medically examined. The police made their raids on the vaguest of clues. The greatest difficulty of all was the birth of babies. Even where a successful disguise had been achieved by the parents, the arrival of a child was always a period of immense danger, and all too frequently brought death to mother, father and child.[18]

In Sturgeon's *More Than Human*,[19] although a representative *Homo sapiens* does join the gestalt intelligence in the end, it is immediately prior to the author's specification that *Homo superior* has been altruistically caring for the human race for thousands of years. With that dictum in mind, the fear of displacement by *Homo superior* is perhaps diminished and the mixing of genomes becomes imaginable. In the absence of such genetic paternalism, the true fear arises. That fear is that the potential offspring will be more superior than sapiens and that sapiens will go the way of neanderthalensis. The basis of this fear of the mutant generation is perhaps most clearly expressed in novels like Wyndham's *The Midwich Cuckoos*[20] or most particularly in Clarke's *Childhood's End*.[21] One of Clarke's characters asks, "I've only one more question. . . . What shall we do about our children?" The Overlord ominously replies. "Enjoy them while you may. . . . They will not be yours for long." In another chapter, Clarke describes a child. "To all outward appearances, she will still be a baby, but round her now was a sense of latent power so terrifying that Jean could no longer bear to enter the nursery." In this case, the mutant generation is not produced through hybridization of man and superman, but the end result is the same; sapiens is defunct. In contrast to the altruistic paternalism of Sturgeon's *Homo superior*, the "child" of *Childhood's End* is most definitely not father to the man! To paraphrase Sturgeon in light of the foregoing discussion, all supermen may be brothers, but you should definitely not let one marry your sister! It is not really difficult to understand why sex with a radically different species, even an intelligent dog as in Stapledon's *Sirius*, may be preferable over sex with *Homo superior*. At least in the case of the dog Sirius, there is no chance of viable, possibly competitive offspring.

Perhaps the most bizarre aspect of this entire thesis is that forty thousand years ago, *Homo sapiens* may have been in the position of some hypothetical *Homo superior* in science fiction today. Recently, a kind of genealogical analysis of maternal mitochondrial DNA has been proven possible. Mitochondrial DNA is unique in that it is only passed from mother to mother with none of the usual contribution; from the male. Lineage comparison of mitochondrial DNA from the various races of *Homo sapiens* has recently demonstrated a probable common ancestor extant in East Africa some four hundred centuries ago: there actually may have been an Eve, mother to us all! But the admittedly still disputed claim is that there was essentially no genetic mixing with the various contemporaneous hominids. In other words, the standard hominid response to *Homo sapiens* was essentially identical to that seen in science fiction with respect to *Homo superior*: don't marry into that family! Not that it ultimately did the other hominids any good. An interesting parallel to this situation may be seen in Michael Bishop's novel *No Enemy but Time*.[23] Here the obviously mutant female protagonist (a somewhat more "sapient" hominid than other members of the tribe) is reproductively isolated from her peers. But the twentieth-century time traveler does mate with her and she bears him a child. In this case, when *Homo sapiens* plays the role of superman to a more primitive hominid, procreation is allowable, at least from our viewpoint.

Much of the preceding discussion may be incorporated into the framework of sociobiology. What exactly is sociobiology? Sociobiology is the study of the genetic determinants of social behavior. For the sociobiologist, human culture is just as legitimate an object of study as insect societies. The sociobiologist assumes that much behavior is genetically determined. Most of the controversy centered around sociobiology boils down to just how much of human behavior is genetically determined. In the case of human cognitive behavior, perhaps the defining characteristics of the term *human*, it appears that genetic and environmental influences are of essentially equal importance. In all likelihood, many other aspects of human behavior will be found to have a strong genetic component. A second major tenet of sociobiological theory is that the genome is inherently conservative or "selfish." It should be clear that only those genes that produce behavior tending to preserve the genome will be represented in the gene pool of a given species. There would be no lemmings if the "march to the sea" occurred before the attainment of reproductive age. Likewise, genes that lead to their own transmogrification are, by definition, no longer represented in the gene pool. Furthermore, if genes in large part determine behavior, and social behavior in turn determines culture, it follows that extant cultures must be those that are ultimately genetically conservative. This analysis then predicts that human cultures should exhibit two specific behaviors: (1) altruism with respect to offspring and relatives who share common genes, and (2) xenophobia with respect to aliens. Indeed, both of these behaviors are observed in human and other animal societies. In many species, deviants from the norm (albinos, for instance) are the object of attack and mutilation. Likewise, many human cultures refer exclusively to themselves as *the* human beings or *the* people. However, it is also necessary to realize that some degree of genetic diversity in the gene pool is essential and adaptive. Otherwise, small environmental changes could lead to the extinction of entire species. Indeed, only species with that necessary degree of genetic diversity are extant today. So there must be a way to bring the stranger into the tribe. Typically, however, the stranger must demonstrate his fitness through his willingness to accept cultural norms (ritual, ceremony, and so forth). A kind of reciprocal altruism is then established; the social group allows the entry of the stranger's genes in return for the stranger's adherence to cultural norms, which are typically adaptive and contribute to the fitness of the group.

The writing of science fiction, in so far as it is a cultural behavior, should reflect the mechanisms of sociobiology. At first blush, it might appear that science fiction is intrinsically antisociobiological, since so much of science fiction focuses on the genetically deviant. I think this is misleading for the reasons previously discussed in this essay. Certainly we are willing to read about *Homo superior*, empathize with his plight, and admire his spunk. But we are just as unready for *Homo superior* as our brother-in-law, just as neanderthalensis was unprepared for *Homo sapiens* forty thousand years ago. However, an alternative sociobiological interpretation is possible. Most science-fiction writers are males and most "superbeings" are men. Could it be that we are simply seeing the working out of a masculine dominance hierarchy? In other words, it is definitely not to the genetic advantage of male *Homo sapiens* to allow male *Homo superior* to displace him from a position of reproductive dominance. It may well be, however, to the reproductive advantage of female *Homo sapiens*, if that will allow her to increase her genetic contribution to the gene pool. This is essentially a rival male hypothesis. In rodent societies, a relevant phenomenon called the Whitten Effect has been observed. Essentially, copulation with a new dominant male causes the spontaneous abortion of all fetuses engendered by the previous dominant male. It is in the reproductive interest of the dominant male to make a genetic contribution; it is in the reproductive interest of the female to make a genetic liaison with the most inclusively fit male. Part of this simply reflects the great differential energetic cost of generating eggs rather than sperm. Metabolic economics guarantees that the female must be more mate-conscious than the male (at least in mammals).

However, this entire formulation seems unlikely for two reasons. First, it is not at all apparent how such a model explains the incorporation of at least some culturally subservient strangers (for instance, the limited superman discussed above). It would seem that science-fiction authors should exclude any rival male, regardless of the degree of genetic divergence, in this scenario. Second, the truly divergent *Homo superior* is as much a threat to female *Homo sapiens* as to male *Homo sapiens*. In both cases, there is a significant chance of complete genetic displacement of *Homo sapiens*. For these reasons, the most viable sociobiological interpretation of the superman in science fiction seems to be consistent with the provisional sociosexual acceptance of small degrees of genetic divergence, as in the reproductive lottery winners, and the rejection of supermen who are greatly divergent, as in the spontaneous mutant. In the case of the true alien for (for example, giant desk calculators, B.E.M.'s from Arcturus, talking dogs), social acceptance may depend both on considerable divergence of the alien from the human phenotype and on the inability to produce fertile offspring. Although it is quite conceivable that exotic aliens could as easily extinguish the human race as malevolent supermen, it is less likely that such aliens would activate our intrinsic genetic alarm signals (inspite of generations of pulp covers showing B.E.M.'s carrying away buxom blondes for nefarious purposes). In fact, a truly malevolent alien might attempt a very close phenotypic simulation of the ideal human sexual partner, but would lack the ability to reproduce. The diversion of human sexual energy toward such attractive mules could very well result in a catastrophic reduction in the number of offspring produced by mating between ordinary humans. This approach has actually been used to nearly eradicate the screw worm in Texas. This strategy, whether employed in south Texas or by *The Stepford Wives*,[23] depends on the specific negation of the alarm signals which ordinarily prevent sex with infertile partners. This scenario does, however, assume that the alien is interested in displacing us from our territory—an assumption that is probably unlikely. On the other hand, we may do this to ourselves; the inflatable sex doll of today may be the first step in the production of something like the ultimately desirable, artifically intelligent, and totally infertile Helen O'Loy/Marilyn Monroebot![24] Thus, we could very well perform the screw-worm solution upon ourselves.

But to get back to aliens and superman, let me summarize the thesis of this essay. Small degrees of genotypic and phenotypic divergence are attractive. The radical superman, however, always represents a genotypic and phenotypic threat. Typically, this perceived threat should be much greater than that of the genetically irrelevant, nonhumanoid alien who, at best, threatens us only at the level of our phenotype. That threat has probably been overemphasized, as Larry Niven has pointed out, in a wide variety of puppet master, body snatchers, and "blood children," as in Octavia Butler's story of the same name.[25] But real aliens, in all likelihood, will be too physically divergent from us to care very much about dominating our habitats or our bodies.

Finally, it may be important to consider the generality of these statements in a wider cultural framework. It is remarkable that so little is made of the sex life of our mythic heros. What do we know of the sex life of Hercules? Samson, in a marvelous sexual metaphor, loses his strength when Delilah cuts his hair. The similarity of that event to the loss of Superman's virginity is striking. And what of religious leaders? Rarely do we consider the sexual habits of Jesus, Buddha, and so on. Is it possible that we have mythologized such culture figures into a status similar to that of the spontaneous superman previously discussed? Such questions suggest an extension of sociobiological analysis far beyond the confines of supermen in science fiction.

8

Cowboys and Telepaths/Formulas and Phenomena

Eric S. Rabkin

Do you remember reading *Slan* (1940)? I do. I was twelve when I first opened that book and suddenly shared the mind of little Jommy Cross. His telepathic unity with his noble mother was glorious; his anguished separation from her was all that a child could fear; his terror of the slan-hunting policemen was dreadful; and his explosion of grief when he lost mind contact with his mother at her death was indelible. I remember crouching with Jommy in some dark hole while a hate-filled, money-ravenous mob swirled within feet of his last island of solitary safety. And I remember that somehow he lived. There was a towering palace in which the world's rulers dwelt, and there was Jommy's long struggle to find others of his superior, noble, but feared and outlawed telepathic kind. And then at the end, he did find them! And it became clear that he and they someday would be the legitimate rulers of the Earth. The elation the book left within me flamed again when I reread *Slan* twenty-seven years later. Amazingly, over all those years, my recollections had remained accurate; perhaps equally amazing, except for the phallic image of the palace and the overpowering sense of seeking, all that had stayed with me so vividly occurred only in the first ten pages and the last two pages of the book. The complex host of details connecting problem and solution had long since faded from conscious memory. But something bigger than detail had not. It is that larger structure, the fundamental formula for the telepath story, that I want to expose here, to explore its social and psychological meanings. Then I believe it will be clear why telepath stories are so numerous and often so haunting.

The best-known study of formulas in popular literature is John Cawelti's *Adventure, Mystery, and Romance* (1976). He calls a formula "a structure of narrative or dramatic conventions employed in a great number of individual works."[1] He wants us to think of formulas as reflecting "two conceptions together," "a conventional way of treating some specific thing or person" and "a larger plot type." In other words, formulas "are embodiments of archetypal story forms in terms of specific cultural materials." His first exemplary list of formulas is "the western, the detective story, [and] the spy adventure." In this book, and in *The Six-Gun Mystique* (1970), an earlier monograph devoted exclusively to the western story, Cawelti shows powerfully the usefulness of studying not only individual narratives but general formulas as well. Particularly in my comments on the western, I am indebted to these studies.

Unfortunately, Cawelti does not discuss telepath stories at all and spends less than a page on the larger (and largely overlapping) category of science fiction. He does offer one suggestion toward a formula. "The fantasy of knowing the unknowable through objectification is [as with horror stories] also the basis of the broad range of stories loosely referred to as science fiction."[2] This insight is a very useful one, as Mark Rose has made elegantly clear in *Alien Encounters* (1981), but it fails to define science fiction, in part because the term *science fiction* embraces many different formulas. In *The Caves of Steel* (1953), for example, Isaac Asimov created a delightfully engaging detective fiction that is no less a fulfillment of the detective formula for the sidekick being a robot; and at least since Edgar Rice Burroughs had Apaches chase John Carter into an Arizona cave that inexplicably translated him to the world of *A Princess of Mars* (1912), some so-called science fictions merely have been westerns with a costume change. It is no wonder then that Cawelti's suggestion does not provide us with a single usable formula for all of science fiction. It provides even less if we try to apply it to telepath stories.

Consider *Dying Inside* (1972). Robert Silverberg's main character, David Selig, supports himself by ghost-writing term papers for students at Columbia University. He guarantees all his work to earn B + or better, money back if not satisfied. Why not? As a telepath, he has always found it easy to probe the minds of his student employers and of their professors to find out precisely what is needed. The main interest of the story is not in Selig's telepathy, however, but in Selig's feelings as, with age, his gift wanes. And what, after all, has he done with it? "Do you realize that each year there are more and more young people in the world? Their tribe ever increases as the old farts drop off the nether end of the curve and I shuttle graveward. Even the professors look young to me these days. There are people with doctorates who are fifteen years younger than I am. Isn't that a killer?" (ch. 11). Yes, it is, and the name of the killer is Time. Selig's telepathy does not objectify the unknowable at all; clever students have always been able to "psych out" their professors. Rather, telepathy objectifies the powers of Selig's youth, now flickering. More generally, for both David Selig and Jommy Cross, their telepathy marks them as essentially unlike the normal world they need to inhabit. Both these books, science fictions and telepath stories that they are, use telepathy to objectify not the unknowable but the problem of alienation.

Given this tendency of telepathy to mark a character's alienation and given the widespread modern struggle with alienation, it is no wonder that telepath stories abound. They certainly number in the hundreds, if not the thousands. According to Gary Wolfe, the telepath "is probably the most common image of mutant humans in science fiction."[3] Yet even those few critics who have sought to define this body of fiction have not attempted to disclose its underlying formula. Perhaps this is so because they agree with Brian Ash when he notes that "the variety of plot themes in the telepathy category seems almost unlimited."[4] But Ash speaks too quickly. Peter Nicholls claims that "the first of the really well-known ESP stories in genre sf was *Slan* . . . which contains what was to become the archetypal telepath-story situation: the slans are telepathic mutants, hated and feared by ordinary humans, and persecuted; near-supermen, they are the next stage in human evolution."[5] Nicholls' so-called situation is a fine starting point for developing the formula of the telepath story, for truly this situation is common in many stories, and, given the important early example of Olaf Stapledon's *Odd John* (1935), not all are "genre sf." However, Nicholls casts this situation in somewhat misleading terms.

For one thing, in many stories the focal telepaths are not supermen. *Dying Inside* is one example, of course. Another is "Nine Lives" (1969), in which Ursula LeGuin shows that the productive efficiency of telepathic multiclones, identical siblings raised together, makes them ultimately subhuman in their inability to recognize individuality and hence to love. The negative extreme of this group telepathy is the "hive mind" such as that shared by "the mechanicals" in Jack Williamson's *The Humanoids* (1948). "They began to remind me of some social insects" (ch. 10). While it is true that, taken collectively each of these telepathic groups has more power than an individual normal human, it would be no more correct to call these creatures supermen than it would be to call King Kong a superman. There is always something more than brute force at work in the way telepath stories investigate what it means to be human or alien.

Even when the telepath is in some significant sense superhuman, as in the case of the isolated mutant called The Mule in Asimov's *Foundation Trilogy* (1951, 1952, 1953), we may find a compensating, fundamentally dehumanizing, weakness. The Mule, as his name suggests, is sterile, as are the multiclones in Kate Wilhelm's *Where Late the Sweet Birds Sang* (1976). Where the story does not supply a compensating weakness in the telepath, it often resolves the conflict between the telepath and normal society by discovering a compensating new strength in the general run of humanity, which may become wiser or even have its own telepathic potential magnificently released. For example, while a group consciousness is often evil, it also may be quite good, as it is for Stapledon's "disembodied" narrator in *Star Maker* (1937) who joins telepathically with the symbiotic, telepathic races of "ichthyoids" and "arachnoids" who together save our universe in that book. In Joe Haldeman's *Mindbridge* (1976), Jacque Lefavre, humanity's most psychically sensitive individual, undergoes extraordinary trials to save us all from an apparently amoral hive mind; his surprising success prefigures an evolution of all humans to the state of literal angels. Through either the weakening of the telepath or the strengthening of humanity, the typical telepath story ultimately resolves the disparity between the protagonist and his society created by the fact of telepathy. In short, the matter is not one of superman versus normal man so much as it is of the alienated versus the normal.

The literal Superman of the comics is almost never seen as alienated so, predictably, his stories do not unfold in the resolution of alienation. Conversely, while Haldeman's Jacque Lefavre is apparently a functioning member of society, he is carefully shown, for example by transcripts of psychiatric sessions, to be deeply alienated. As one would expect, then, the formula plot of telepath stories need not rest primarily on fear and hate directed at telepathic supermen by ordinary humans. Ordinary humans may not even know of the existence of the typically marginalized telepath. This is largely true both of Silverberg's David Selig and of Joe Carter, the hero of Mark Clifton and Frank Riley's *They'd Rather Be Right* (1954), a pioneering mutant who finally manages to release the wonderful in all of us. In other words, in telepath stories, the heart of the matter is not the struggle of the nascent superman against the hate of the normal man but the struggle of the unusual individual to find his place in society. Since this is a problem nearly everyone feels himself to be facing in growing up, telepath stories should and do have a wide, resonant appeal.

The often explicit (*Slan, Dying Inside*) and always implicit focus on the problem of finding a fit social environment quite naturally suggests an evolutionary viewpoint. As Nicholls points out, the formula telepath typically represents the next stage in human evolution. As early as 1889, Edward Bellamy presented in *Harper's* a telepathic island community in a story called "To Whom This May Come." The existence of these mind readers "was a case simply of a slight acceleration, from special causes [of inbreeding], of the universal human evolution." The connection between evolution and the very idea of telepathy has been intimate not only in science fiction but in general use virtually since the word *telepathy* entered our language. According to the *Oxford English Dictionary, telepathy* was first introduced in print by Frederic W. H. Myers to refer to "cases of impression received at a distance without the normal operation of the recognised sense organs." The place of publication bore the scientific-sounding title *Proceedings of the Society for Psychical Research* and the year was 1882. Already in the prestigious Lowell lectures of 1894, just twelve years later, Henry Drummond claimed that "telepathy is theoretically the next stage in the Evolution of Language." Charles Darwin's second great exposition of the theory of evolution, *The Descent of Man*, was published in 1871. Drummond called his offering of the Lowell lectures *The Ascent of Man*.

Probably the most widely known expression of so-called Darwinian evolution is Herbert Spencer's phrase "survival of the fittest." Even Darwin writes, in *The Origin of Species* (1859), his first great exposition of the theory of "Natural Selection," that "the expression often used by Mr. Herbert Spencer, of the Survival of the Fittest, is more accurate, and is sometimes equally convenient" (ch. 3). Unfortunately, this well-known phrase too frequently has been misunderstood.

The unabridged edition of *The Random House Dictionary of the English Language* lists seven primary adjectival meanings of the word *fit*. Two are particularly relevant to the discussion of evolution: "1. adapted or suited" and "6. in good physical condition, as an athlete, a race horse, military troops, etc." For convenience, we may think of these, respectively, as "suitable" and "powerful." Using the latter meaning, Spencer's phrase becomes "the survival of the most powerful." The scientific authority of Darwin can then be made to support ruthless class conflict, buttressed by so-called Social Darwinism. In *The North American Review* of June 1889, in an essay entitled "Wealth," Andrew Carnegie—captain of industry or robber baron, depending on one's view—wrote that

> while the law [of competition] may be sometimes hard for the individual, it is best for the race, because it insures the survival of the fittest in every department. We accept and welcome, therefore, as conditions to which we must accommodate ourselves, great inequality of environment, the concentration of business, industrial and commercial, in the hands of a few, and the law of competition between these, as being not only beneficial, but essential for the future progress of the race.

However, as early as H. G. Wells' *The Time Machine* (first version, 1888; final version, 1895), science fiction has warned us against adopting this supposed corollary of evolution. While one can find a rare story like Jerome Bixby's "It's a Good Life" (1953), in which a telepathic, omnipotent child utterly toys with and controls the few remnants of humanity he has let survive, more common in attitude is *Odd John*, in which the incredibly powerful mutants deem it morally wrong to control their racial forebears, recognize their inability to simply isolate themselves from normal humanity, and so, rather than kill or control, nobly commit suicide themselves. More common still, as with the telepathic children in John Wyndham's *Re-Birth* (1955), the telepaths simply go away to another separate environment or, as Van Vogt's slans do, find inconspicuous niches in the social environment of normal humanity, comparative havens within which they can await the rest of humanity's evolutionary catch-up. In short, while telepathy is intimately concerned with evolution and evolution popularly concerns the survival of the fittest,

telepath stories typically understand fitness not in the popular sense
of powerful, even though the telepaths often are powerful and sometimes thought of as supermen, but rather as suitable. In that sense,
the authors of telepath stories have used evolutionary theory much
more correctly than many other more formal social thinkers have. If
Slan, published in 1940, opens with Jommy caught in a version of a
pogrom, the tragedy for this archetypal alien is not so much his
physical danger as the loss of hereditary connection with his mother.
At bottom, the fantasy of sharing minds stands against the ferocious
striving of Social Darwinism.

Fitness, in the sense of suitability, needs to be understood as a
matter of mutual fit, not simply the fit of the organism to the environment but of the environment to the organism. This point was already
resoundingly clear in scientific circles as early as 1913 when Lawrence
J. Henderson published his landmark book *The Fitness of the Environment*. He pointed out, for example, that the chemical evolution
of present Earth life required its origin in a liquid. Why then was life
not extinguished, at least in the temperate and polar zones, each
winter when that liquid environment froze? The answer derives from
a lucky fact unique to water: it expands as it freezes. This requires
that rivers solidify from the top down rather than from the bottom
up. So long as some liquid water remains protected below the icy
surface, life has a fit home. Since Henderson's day, we have come to
realize that biological activity itself helps shape the environment.
The early development of photosynthetic plants seems to have
changed Earth's aboriginal atmosphere by the addition of massive
amounts of oxygen, a precondition for the evolution of complex
animal life; in historic times, mankind's own herding patterns seem
to have been the single greatest contributor to the creation of the
Sahara Desert. This interactive view of organism and environment
characterizes modern ecology, but many of us moderns would be
surprised to learn that as early as the 1870s (again according to OED
citations), "oecology" was linked necessarily to evolutionary theory.

At this point, I believe we can move toward an explicit articulation of a formula for telepath stories. My model is the simple and
well-known formula for western stories. In the prototypical, formulaic western, we find an in-group and an out-group. If the in-group is
the townsfolk, the out-group may be the ranchers; if the in-group is
the ranchers, the out-group may be the Indians, and so on. Regard-

less of whom it includes, the in-group holds values that are, in the story's context, supportive of settled civilization: legal, eastern, conservative. If there are desirable women, typically the in-group has them. The out-group ignores these values and threatens the in-group by its possession of more primitive but potentially more powerful and individualistic skills: the ranchers, outlaws, or Indians can ride better, hunt both four- and two-legged prey more effectively, and survive in the wilderness. The out-group needs women. In the formula western story, a mediating hero arises who shares the skills of the out-group but for some reason holds the values of the in-group. Typically, he successfully defends the in-group and quells the out-group. However, this makes him, by virtue of his continuing possession of out-group skills, a new potential threat to the in-group. To resolve this dilemma, he must either hang up his guns and marry, as the Virginian does, or ride off into the sunset, as do Shane, Paladin, the Lone Ranger, and countless others.

According to Frederick Jackson Turner's famous "frontier hypothesis" (1893), "the existence of an area of free land, its continuous recession, and the advance of American settlement westward, explain American development." What neither Turner nor Cawelti has noted is that the phenomenon of the frontier also explains the shape of the formula western story. It is natural that those who are unfulfilled in settled, eastern society migrate westward. If they survive at all, they must come to possess the individualistic skills the in-group back east has typically abandoned for commercial trades and law books. By demonstrating the survivability of the new land, the pioneers attract easterners. The increasing population of easterners appropriates the locale for the east. The original pioneers, now chafing at their numerical and economic inferiority, resent the latecomers. The westerners see themselves as increasingly marginal. Intergroup conflict is inevitable, as is the replacement of the west by the older and economically established east. At any given skirmish line drawn across America's western landscape, the western hero has a crucial role to play in achieving this conservative replacement. The formula western story, then, quite naturally reflects a reality of American consciousness.

In the formula telepath story, the protagonist is at the same time a full member of the out-group and the hero. Indeed, the hero typically begins by believing that he uniquely populates the out-group. The in-group is *Homo normal*, typically represented by police, parents, or some other older, established authority figure, while the out-group, to borrow a term from Stapledon's *Odd John,* is *Homo superior*, typically younger and, as marked by his telepathy, alienated. The in-group holds values that are, in the story's context, conservative. If there are women, typically the in-group has them. The out-group hero must confront, even if only for himself, the values of the in-group because his evolutionary origin implies a worthy progress that validates him both despite his alienation and because of it. Yet even though in the formula telepath story, the hero, by virtue of his telepathy, defines the out-group, as a child of the in-group, he typically respects its values. The plot of the formula telepath story revolves around the action of the hero seeking a fit environment.

Perhaps it is because the action of seeking a fit environment can be so variously imagined that the formulaic nature of telepath stories has gone largely unnoticed, but really, just as the western hero has only two options, to change or move on, the telepath hero also has only two: to attain or not to attain a fit environment. If he attains it, he may do so by discovery or by creation. If the hero discovers a fit environment, his consequent freedom from a sense of alienation resolves his conflict with the in-group. This is the case when he learns that, within the in-group social environment, there already coexists an invisible, older, and more powerful telepath community which he can join, as happens in Theodore Sturgeon's *More Than Human* (1953), or when, as in *Re-Birth*, the telepath hero both discovers the preexisting telepath community and is translated to its physically distant environment. If the hero creates a fit environment, his consequent freedom from a sense of alienation still resolves his conflict with the in-group. This is the case when the hero manages to unlock the evolutionary potential for telepathy in everyone, as happens in *They'd Rather Be Right*, or when he creates the preconditions for our accelerated evolution toward telepathy, as happens in *Mindbridge*. Whether through discovery or creation, the attainment of a fit environment is positive from the standpoint of the telepath. In the second option, the telepath fails to attain a fit environment. In that case, as in "It's a Good Life," he may destroy all environments or, as in *Odd John*, destroy himself. Such cases, however, are quite rare. Yet no matter how the formula works itself out, the dramatic pattern is clear: a young, alienated but self-valorized individual struggles against received authority in an attempt to find himself a fit environment. In Freudian terms, this is the story of Oedipus. The formula telepath story, then, quite naturally reflects a reality of human consciousness.

At the same time that we recognize the telepath story as reflecting an important psychological reality, we also recognize that, unlike the American West, telepathy itself does not exist for most of us except as a phenomenon of fiction. Still, the phenomena of fiction are surely psychologically and socially potent. Writing of science fiction, and even more generally, Robert Plank argues in *The Emotional Significance of Imaginary Beings* (1968) that "the mental process of creating imaginary beings is in essence a duplication of a relationship of crucial emotional significance in life, a relationship that the person who does the imagining has experienced, or believes he has experienced, or wishes or fears to experience" (149). For Plank, the archetypal science-fiction story presents a mad scientist without wife but with daughter/secretary/niece; scientist unleashes mayhem on the world only to have mayhem released by younger man, typically not a scientist, who then reestablishes order and gets the woman. This story of the transfer of power and women between the generations he sees as Oedipal; a prominent example is *The Tempest*. Since for Freud and for most of us the name Oedipus calls to mind Sophocles' dark work, while *The Tempest* resolves itself in light, I would like to suggest that we call the violent and/or unsuccessful transfer of power from the in-group to its successor in-group an Oedipal tragedy, while, since most of science fiction is romantic, we call the successful and peaceable transfer an Oedipal romance. Although telepath stories typically do not have mad scientists, and although they are typically romantic, they are nonetheless Oedipal.

In *Totem and Taboo* (1913), Freud himself suggested that telepathy is a "characteristic of magic" that comes from the belief in the "omnipotence of thoughts" (ch. 3), a belief typical of the so-called phallic phase (remember the tower of authority in *Slan*), in which the child believes that to wish something to be so is to make it so and "therefore fears," to use Norman Holland's words, "that he can be punished just as much for his thoughts as for what he does."[6] Interestingly, the phallic phase, as Kathryn Hume points out, "is not primarily concerned with sex as such but with exploration."[7] In the formula telepath story, the hero may be seeking a bride, as Joe Carter does in *They'd Rather Be Right*, but she generally symbolizes not sexuality so much as community: the out-group hero needs to create an in-group of his own. This is a common symbolism in science fiction; but while neither Victor Frankenstein nor his demon succeeds in keeping a bride, in the Oedipal romances of telepath stories, the protagonist usually does succeed. In the rare telepath stories that are Oedipal tragedies, like *Odd John*, the protagonist first achieves community, as Sophocles' protagonist does when he becomes king, and then we discover that the community is unlivable for him.

I have argued here that formulas take their characteristic shapes as a consequence of their central phenomena, the formulaic shape of the western story from the American West and the formulaic shape of the telepath story from the fictional phenomenon that is telepathy. Lest I be understood to claim too much for the control these phenomena exert over the stories in which they figure, I must acknowledge that not all stories set in the West are westerns (John Steinbeck's *East of Eden*, [1952], for example) and not all stories that use telepathy are telepath stories. Sometimes telepathy makes a brief—though typically significant—contribution to a story otherwise very differently focused. In Ursula LeGuin's *The Left Hand of Darkness* (1969), the crucial demonstration that two characters who are alien to each other have finally come to understand each other is signaled by their "mindspeaking." In some stories, like Alfred Bester's *The Demolished Man* (1953), the attribute of telepathy (in this case to the police) is simply used to give a different formula (in this case the detective story) a new twist. This is essentially the same device as Burroughs recostuming his western story in Martian garb. And finally, in those stories in which telepathy enters via thought machines, as in Roger Zelazny's *The Dream Master* (1966), we may have telepathy, but without a telepath to represent himself as the next stage of human evolution, we do not have a telepath story.

When we do have a telepath story, we have something curiously both less and more mature than a western story. The western hero is typically a young man conserving the values of his elders. His origin, to the extent we know it, usually depends on his prior victimization— or tainting—by violence: the Lone Ranger's brother had been killed; the Virginian had participated in the defeat of the Civil War. The telepath hero is singled out not by having been violated or by his capacity for violence but by his gift, a problematic attribute that nonetheless seems fundamentally good. Caught as he is at the phallic stage and manifesting the omnipotence of thought, the telepath hero is, psychologically at least, more infantile than the western hero. Yet the telepath story is simultaneously more mature than the inherently conservative western story because it directly confronts the fact that the discovery of truly new knowledge (science) leads inevitably to the discovery of truly new powers, and the existence of truly new powers is quite likely to force society into patterns it has never experienced before. From a psychological point of view, then, formula telepath stories deal with common Oedipal anxieties, validating the reader's sense of uniqueness and his desire to change the world; from a sociological point of view, telepath stories deal with common technophobias, making the acquisition of new knowledge seem natural and validating the changed world that would produce. In both cases, for the individual reader growing up and for the society that embraces the formula, telepath stories prepare them for the future.

With such an understanding of this necessary future orientation of the telepath story, let us return for a moment to telepathy itself. That Freud sees telepathy as a variety of "the *omnipotence* of thought" perhaps indicates that this phenomenon is godlike. Those who silently pray believe that God can read their thoughts. Voodoo curses are often taken to function as telepathic projections. Santa Claus knows if we've been naughty or nice. When a whole group of telepathic characters confronts *Homo normal* in science fiction, the telepathic community is almost always seen as a direct threat to *Homo normal*, for when the gods descend, or when God sends his avenging angels down among us, we see that "the day of the Lord is great and very terrible; and who can abide it?" (Joel 2:11). At the end of *Childhood's End*, when our telepathic successor race emerges, its members burn the entire world before they float off together toward the heavens. As it says in Julia Ward Howe's hymn, picking up images from Revelation 19:15: "He hath loosed the fateful lightning of his terrible, swift sword" (1862). Against this scourge, this purgatorial cleansing, the normal humans of science fiction defend themselves. The villagers in John Wyndham's *The Midwich Cuckoos* (1957), once they realize that the telepaths with whom their women have been impregnated will try to supplant them, fight these offspring and exterminate them. In H. G. Wells' *The War of the*

Worlds (1898), the Martians who descend upon England on "the great and terrible day of the Lord" (bk. 1, ch. 13) are "swift and terrible creatures" (bk. 1, ch. 12). It should come as no surprise that they are "telepathic." "The Martians interchanged thoughts without any physical intermediation" (bk. 2, ch. 2). Fortunately, God sometimes grants us a reprieve: the Martians are "slain," not by man but "by the putrefactive and disease bacteria against which their systems were unprepared . . . slain, after all man's devices had failed, by the humblest things that God, in his wisdom, has put upon this earth" (bk. 2, ch. 8).

Anthropologically, telepathy itself is often a gift from the gods. According to C. G. Jung's *Man and His Symbols* (1964, pt. 3), the animal familiars of witches and shamans are projections of self that simultaneously incarnate superhuman powers and provide means by which the witches and shamans can project these powers into their environments. The frequently supposed natural advantage of children in communicating with animals, to summon Lassie's help at a distance, for example, represents an instance of what is, according to Sir James Frazer's *The Golden Bough* (1922, ch. 3, pt. 2), the anthropologically common phenomenon of human/animal telepathy. The heroes of such science-fiction tales as Andre Norton's *Catseye* (1961) rely on this human/animal telepathy to guarantee their own future.

The godlike power of telepathy represents a danger when humanity must confront it in an alien race, but when a single godlike figure walks among us, matters may be quite different. Odd John says that "it was my task, unique being that I was, to 'advance the spirit' on this planet" (ch. 5). He fails; *Homo normal* brings all his military might against John; and so, to spare humanity, John kills himself. He dies for our sins. In *Slan*, Kathleen Layton realizes that the hero is destined to lead humanity to its next godlike incarnation. She says, "I've met the greatest living slan," but Jommy Cross replies, "The great man is not me, but my father" (ch. 14). It is clear that Joe Carter will lead humanity to its next godlike incarnation at the end of *They'd Rather Be Right*; Jane Carter blesses us identically in *The Humanoids*. When the alienating, godlike mark of telepathy is incarnate in a single individual, then, although the incinerating fire remains potential within the character, the promise of divine light shines forth. Even when the telepath fails, as do Odd John and David Selig, the failure reflects humanity's greatness, suggesting not so much our divine origin as our divine destiny.

The realm of science fiction includes time travel, the accidentally released monster, the dystopia, the alternate history, and other diverse and aesthetically provocative phenomena; each tends to support specific interests, but not each of these generates a formula. The telepath, marked by the alienating power of his telepathy, does. He makes inevitable a story in which the young outsider must struggle to find a fit environment within which to live out his—and perhaps our—marvelous fate. Whether viewed as an Oedipal fantasy or a response to a technologically envolving world or an incarnation in modern terms of fundamental human myth, the telepath defines the formula of the telepath story. No wonder the telepath story stays fresh in our minds from one generation to the next.

9

Robots: Three Fantasies and
One Big Cold Reality

Noel Perrin

The traditional encounter with the alien has been in one of two traditional forms—either Earth explorers go off-planet and meet another intelligent species, or members of another intelligent species step out of their ships to call on us here. Either way, we are meeting something totally new—like Europeans discovering the New World, only much more so. Two species meet as strangers. The meeting is going to start in wonder, and it may end in war, or discipleship, or the pan-galactic union.

There is also a third form of the encounter. Here the alien is not something, or rather someone, whose past is wholly separate from ours, is not a stranger, but is rather our own creation. It only got to be alien in the way that some children, as they grow up, prove to be quite different from their parents, different in tastes, needs, and kind of intelligence, yet still bearing the marks of having been raised by those parents. There are magical forms of this third encounter: golems, living bronze statues in ancient Crete, and so forth. But, obviously, the main form of it has been achieved through science and the robot.

I want to discuss three of the many ways that science fiction has imagined the robot and then turn to those interesting machines, real robots. They have this much in common at least with their fictional forebears. They really are emerging as the first other intelligent species we human beings have encountered. There will soon be some striking consequences of that encounter. Before I begin, though, I should note that the original robots that robots are named for—the ones in Karel Capek's *R. U. R.*—are by my definition not robots at all. They are the results of biological engineering. Dr. Rossum, a biological genius, developed a whole new form of protoplasm and with it learned to manufacture a sort of stripped-down human model—minus genitals, for example, but possessing the usual kind of heart, liver, brain, blood circulation. And at the end of the play, we get the "de luxe" model, which is simply indistinguishable from human beings, not alien at all. By robots, I mean something more machine-like than that, although I'm not going to pause to define machines, or I'd never get anything else said at all.

Science fiction has imagined these mechanical aliens in innumerable ways. One, of course, is to see them simply and purely as servants—logical progressions of the refrigerator and the steam shovel and the autopilot and the thermostat. The logical outcome of the industrial revolution. Intelligent, certainly. But no more personality than a dump truck. This, for example, is how they tend to appear in the work of Arkady and Boris Strugatsky, the greatest of Russian science-fiction writers. If we read a book like *Noon: 22nd Century*, we find so-called cybers constantly there in the background, doing all the boring work and most of the dangerous work, but utterly without individuality, and alien only in the sense that some of the characters perceive them that way. Some have robophobia, like Tanya in the wonderful story "The Planet with All the Conveniences." Some can't resist personifying them, like a fifteen-year-old boy in the story called "Languor of the Spirit." The story takes place on a huge cattle farm on the river Volga, where cybers look after the cows. The boy has been up flying his pterocar, as one might ride a bicycle, and when he lands, he lands by mistake on an automated trash collector, that is to say, a litter robot. The robot is damaged and screams, and the boy feels as guilty as if he had landed on his grandfather. He is quite mistaken, as the Strugatskys show in a brief comic scene. Because at that moment, a former astronaut named Pol, who's on a walking tour and visiting the farm, comes up and joins the boy in watching the damaged machine.

> "Well, let's see what we've got here," [Pol] said, and took the robot by a manipulator. The robot let out a squeal.
> "Does it hurt?" Pol sang tenderly, easing his fingers into the regulatory system. "Did im hurt ims paw? Poor baby hurt ims paw."
> The robot squealed again, shuddered, and was quiet. The boy sighed with relief, and squatted down, too. "That's it," he muttered. "Boy, was it yelling when I got out of the pterocar!"
> "Of course we yelled, we did," cooed Pol, unscrewing the armor.

"We've got ourselves a good acoustics system, a loud-mouthed one. It's an itty-bitty AKU-6, it is, with longitudinal vibration. . . ." Pol took off the armor plate and carefully laid it on the grass.

Pol proceeds to take out the robot's regulator block, adjust it, put the robot back together, send it off to pick up more trash, and explain to the boy that AKU-6's are as strong as three bears, and that he should not worry so much just because he landed his pterocar on one. At worst, he may have damaged a piece of machinery, and probably he didn't even do that. In this version, the alienness of robots is almost entirely in the minds of human beings who really ought to know better. Fantasy one is just that labor-saving devices will continue to improve, which will increase human convenience.

The second fantasy is considerably more ambitious. I'm going to call it the guardian-angel fantasy. One of the most famous places it appears is in the work of Isaac Asimov, and most strikingly of all in the very first of those hundreds of books, the one called *I, Robot*. Here's how Susan Calvin, the first robopsychologist, puts it to a newspaper reporter in the year 2058: "There was a time when humanity faced the universe alone and without a friend. Now he has creatures to help him; stronger creatures than himself, more faithful, more useful, and absolutely devoted to him." That, of course, is exactly how Christianity perceives angels: stronger and more faithful than we are, not to mention immortal, but nevertheless thoroughly devoted to our welfare. The one important difference is that God designed the angels to have free will, so that some billions of them could and did revolt, while in Asimov's version human beings designed robots not to have free will, at least not in the matter of being devoted to our welfare. Slave angels, one might call his robots.

In the course of the book, men go on and build a slave god. In its childhood, that god is known as The Brain, and it already has the power to raise men from the dead—it does so for two astronauts named Powell and Donovan. In mature form, the god robot is known as The Machine, and though technically it remains a slave god, compelled to work for our benefit, in actual fact it has almost complete free will; it can and does overrule everything except its original program, instructing it to work for the good of humanity. Susan Calvin, near the end of her life, says to the humanoid robot who is World Co-ordinator, that no person really knows what the good of humanity is, because we have such limited minds. "We haven't at *our* disposal the infinite factors that the Machine has at *its*." And then she proceeds to speculate on whether a high-tech civilization is what suits human beings best, or maybe some simple agrarian world, and finally she concludes that we don't need to know, now that we have advanced robots. "The machines know, and they are going there, and taking us with them."

In sketching out his robot angels and robot god, Asimov makes a lot of interesting assumptions which I am barely going to touch on here. For example, he assumes self-consciousness and a wide variety of emotions in the early robot angels and finds himself forced to give them up in the robot god—primarily lest that god be able to deprogram itself from its original instructions to care for human welfare. He assumes severe internal conflict in the later robot angels—a conflict between their awareness that they are the superior creations of inferior beings, namely us, and hence their natural desire not to obey and perhaps even to kill us—between that and the overriding program that makes them, shall I say, love us. The AKU-6 has no such conflict.

But the most interesting assumption to me is that despite the presence of large numbers of wise, powerful, and tireless robots, there is an unlimited amount of useful work left for human beings to do. How can this be? Asimov himself hints toward two answers. One is that because of the irrational human prejudice against robots, just like Tanya's in the Strugatsky story, they are used almost entirely off-planet. I don't think that's much of an answer myself, since transportation (in that world) is cheap, and there's no reason most work couldn't be done off-planet. Why should there be huge hydroponic farms in China, tended by human labor? And why should Lincoln Ngomo, the coordinator of the Tropic Region, be encouraging mass immigration from all parts of the world, because he needs a larger work force, when there are robots waiting on every asteroid to do it? I think the real reason is that Asimov is making an unconscious assumption which I'll come back to later. His second hinted answer, of course, is that the machines plan it that way, much as parents might require children to pick up their rooms and make their beds, because they think it's good for the kids to do this. But it's only the faintest of hints and nothing to build a life on.

So far we have the Strugatsky vision of robots as merely advanced tools, easily taken apart and put back together by a well-trained adult like Pol. And the Asimov vision of robots as a kindly controlling force for a working humanity. It is also a working humanity in the Strugatskys, I should have said. Now let's look at a third vision, which I'll take from Arthur C. Clarke's *The City and the Stars*. People who know that book will recall the city of Diaspar, designed by Clarke to counter E. M. Forster's famous attack on science fiction in his brilliant little 1904 novella "The Machine Stops." It was designed by Clarke also to provide the most attractive possible picture of secular immortality and finally to show what human life would be like if human beings were really free of the need to work, because robots do it all.

The short answer is that life would be wonderful. To begin with, it's utterly secure, because Diaspar has a manufactured god, just as Asimov's world does. This one is called simply the Central Computer. Alvin, the human hero, once is granted an audience with the Central Computer, and Clarke presents it very much like Moses getting to meet Jehovah. But security is the least of it. It's a world of enormous pleasure and of no pain. The food, for example, is incredible. You have merely to think what you'd like for dinner, and matter synthesizers, robot-controlled, almost instantly produce a meal that would get three stars in Michelin every time. The same with clothing, entertainment, communication—you name it. Tireless robots provide it all and look to every detail of running the city. There are no hydroponic farms using human workers, no Lincoln Ngomo with a job waiting for every immigrant he can persuade to come. There are no jobs, period, except for the very, very part-time ones of being so-called parents to the young adults who step out of the Hall of Creation or of being their tutors for a few years. There is no money—who needs money when you can summon up any physical object merely by framing the thought? There is no poverty, no sickness, very little sorrow. There is, in fact, *everything* in Diaspar except one thing. There is no meaning. No meaning to life, that is—no purpose to going on for the thousand years of any one existence, and then going back into the Memory Banks for a random interval, and reemerging for another thousand years of life, and so on for ten thousand lifetimes. Clarke, who in all his books feels free to put in editorial comments, says early on that life in Diaspar was "a completely satisfying existence. That it was also a wholly futile one, even Alvin did not yet comprehend."

The story of the book is mainly how Alvin releases Diaspar from futility after a billion years. To accomplish this, he has to do three things. He has to end the immortality. He has to reduce the role played by robots so there is some work left for human beings—in general it will be voluntary work, and Clarke ducks the question of whether voluntary work inevitably becomes unnecessary work and hence not really work at all but just a hobby. He raises the issue once, when Alvin is visiting the other society that still exists on Earth in that distant future, the country called Lys, and samples one of the famous peaches they grow in a village called Airlee. Alvin likes the peach, "but it seemed to him no better than those he could have conjured up in Diaspar by no more effort than raising a finger." That being the case, why should he or anyone bother to raise peaches instead of fingers? There *is* an answer to give, but Clarke doesn't give it.

Finally, Alvin has to restore the possibility of progress, and in particular the possibility of acquiring new knowledge—with human beings acquiring the knowledge, not the alien robots acquiring it for us, because that might save them from futility, but not us. Clarke finds progress hard to arrange, and the one example he comes up with is singularly unconvincing. It occurs in Lys, when Alvin and his Lysian counterpart, a young man named Hilvar, go exploring in an uninhabited part of the country. One of Hilvar's motives for the trip is to find new types of insect life. Considering that the civilization of Lys is as old as that of Diaspar and has therefore lasted a full billion years, and considering that Lys is quite a small country, it's wildly improbable that there should be any insects that went unnoticed by thirty million preceding generations of scientists. But it's one of the conditions Clarke needs for life to be other than futile. There need to be real events, and these need to include a real beginning and end, hence birth and death; real events during life, hence work; and real progress, hence science. And none of this can be by proxy, or it ceases to be real.

Keeping all this in mind, and especially Clarke's vision, let me turn now from science fiction to plain reality. I think it is clear in the 1980's that humanity's first encounter with alien intelligence is going to be of the third kind—not creatures from outer space, but creatures from Carnegie-Mellon University, and Tokyo Institute of Technology, and Cincinnati Milacron. Indeed, the aliens are already here. Their numbers are small at present—probably no more than about two hundred thousand on the entire planet. And even of those, the vast majority are extremely stupid—not even up to the AKU-6 litter robot in level of intelligence. Obviously, I'm talking here about robots, not about computers, even though I think the correct definition of a robot is a computer with sense organs and some form of mechanical body. There are a lot more than two hundred thousand robot *brains* in existence right now—and in the hope of not getting entirely lost in complex side issues, I am going to ignore them and stick with complete robots. I want to do just two things: to report quickly on what robots can already do and to give a litle summary of what it is predicted they will be doing in another twenty years. In the process, there'll be a glimpse or two of how the real-life robot world or artificial-intelligence world compares with some of the visions that science fiction has had.

What are robots doing now? Not much. But not nothing, either. We all know that they're crack welders and window installers. Here's part of a list I once made of some other robot activities during the year 1985:

The Nippon Hoso Kyoku Symphony Orchestra played a concert in Tsukuba, Japan, in which one of its members was not a human being. A large steel and plastic robot performed as guest organist. The robot, which can sight-read musical scores, played Bach, using its feet on the pedals as well as its ten fingers on the keys. This was the first symphony concert in history in which the orchestra included a robot.

In western Australia, a robot named Oracle sheared its first two hundred sheep, bloodying only a few. This was the first time in history that a robot sheared a whole flock of sheep.

A computer program in Pennsylvania named Hitech joined the 765 human beings in the United States who hold the rank of chess master. This was not the first time in history that a computer program had risen so high. Another program named Belle became the first nonhuman master back in 1983.

General Motors bought stock in two additional companies that are trying to perfect the eyesight (or vision systems, if you prefer) of robots. GM now owns a piece of five vision-system companies.

Nissan Motor Company put a new team of inspectors to work checking the paint finish of new cars. Because the cars are painted by old-fashioned blind robots, which neither see nor care if they miss a few spots, inspection has hitherto been a slow process. "An experienced worker with a high level of concentration," says Nissan, could complete his or her painstaking examination in about forty-five minutes. The new inspectors are robots. Each can do its painstaking examination in about 1.2 minutes.

A ping-pong match took place in San Francisco between an English robot and an American robot. Neither robot played well.

In Building 12 of the IBM plant in Poughkeepsie, N.Y., robots replaced most of the remaining people involved in the assembly of Sierra computers.

A mirror image of the robot organist in Japan appeared in Palo Alto, California. The intelligent Japanese machine can sight-read scores and then play the music. The intelligent American machine can listen to music being played and then print out the score. It is said to have a special penchant for Mozart.

Patent 4482966 was approved. It's for a robot tractor which will automatically plant, tend, and harvest crops.

Two robots went to work for a large cosmetics company, packaging lipstick. Operating as a team, they can package about ten thousand tubes of lipstick during an eight-hour shift. The company expects them to replace twenty human workers.

The RM3 robot went into production in France. It can wash the hulls of ships, debarnacle them, and then repaint the ship, doing each job at the rate of one and a quarter acres a day. A modified version climbs up the outside of office buildings to wash them and also does industrial welding, paints oil tanks, and cleans airplane fuselages.

The aliens have landed, so to speak, and they are taking over lots of the dangerous and boring work, and it's clear that they will continue to take over more. They are not acting as guardian angels, much less gods, and they are not doing much thinking, except in a few highly abstract matters like chess strategy. They have not as yet produced any significant amount of unemployment—which you wouldn't expect them to have, since two hundred thousand robots equals one robot per twenty-five thousand human beings. Even if you accept the rule of thumb from the automobile industry that a single industrial robot can replace about four human workers, the impact so far is trifling. Trifling but beneficial. It is clearly preferable for robots to be spray-painting cars than for a human being to be breathing that poisoned air. It's not even a matter of sacrificing the robot. Since it doesn't breathe, it has no need for air.

Now let me look ahead twenty years. Obviously, this is mere speculation, but we already have enough experience with robots so that I think it can be called informed speculation. Not being in any way a technologist myself, I am taking my information from books like Joseph Deken's *Silico Sapiens*, Robert Howard's *Brave New Workplace*, a book edited by Marvin Minsky called simply *Robotics*, and also from many interviews with Japanese roboticists.

In twenty years, there will be some millions of robots, and probably many millions. Most Japanese experts think that there will be more in the United States than there will be in Japan, even though Japan has a small edge right now. Once robots can manufacture other robots with minimal human supervision, costs will plummet, and the curve of robot production will go almost straight up. James Albus, one of the principal robot authorities in the U.S. government, believes that "once automatic factories begin to manufacture the components for other automatic factories, the cost . . . will fall exponentially. Eventually, products produced in automatic factories may cost only slightly more than the raw materials and energy from which they are made."[1]

What will those millions of robots be doing, twenty years from now? Well, there are two sharply discordant views. One view says that they'll be doing the same kinds of things they are doing now, only more of them. They'll be picking oranges in Florida, probably at night to take advantage of uniform artificial lighting, unless robot vision has by then equaled or surpassed human vision. They'll be building houses, staffing virtually all factories, giving tennis lessons. Most household appliances will be nonmobile, limited-function robots. They will be doing not only the dirty and dangerous work, but most of the safe and interesting work. But like the AKU-6 litter robot, they will not only be cybers but also ciphers—intelligent, heuristic machines, sure, but not conscious, not alive in the commonsense meaning of that term, not really another intelligent life form sharing this planet with us.

The other view, held, for example, by Hans Moravec at Carnegie-Mellon and Teijiro Kubo, editor of the Japanese Encyclopedia of

Robotics, is that twenty years from now robots—some of them—will indeed have become conscious beings, probably with emotions, though quite different emotions from ours, and in a special, non-biological sense, capable of reproduction. One term that Dr. Moravec likes to use is human equivalence. Or to quote Joseph Deken of the National Science Foundation, they will be "immortal, and far better at doing many tasks than the species that built them."[2]

If these people are right, we really will have an alien race not just sharing the planet with us, but in many ways running it—presumably for our benefit, as Asimov imagined in his stories, but still running it, in part, and filling some high-class jobs. Robots like these might be better, for example, at teaching college classes than human beings are—it might be the world of Stanislaw Lem come true.

Either way, whether robots are soon to be conscious beings, true aliens come to share our planet, or whether they are merely to be the ultimate human tools, there will be a huge question confronting humanity. Namely, what are we doing to do when there is no need for most of us to work? Let me quote one more of Dr. Deken's imaginings: "Completely automated robot fishing fleets may soon cruise the oceans, freeing human crews from the hardship and danger of isolation, exposure and storms."[3] The problem with this is that many human beings *like* a certain amount of isolation, exposure, and storm, and the question is whether they will be freed or whether they will be deprived, when they are no longer needed. And that, I think, is the real reason that Isaac Asimov had human beings tending the hydroponic farms and had Lincoln Ngomo in search of ever more workers. It wasn't a failure of his imagination that he assumed so much future human labor, but a success of his imagination. He was trying to avoid a futile world.

I have no space in a short essay to get into the question of whether a world without work really is futile, although it's a question I worry about a lot. Instead I'm going to close with two quick observations. One is that I think the aliens really have landed. Forty-three years ago we had D-Day. Somewhere around five years ago we had R-Day. Right now, they just hold a small beachhead. It will be fascinating to see what happens as they expand it at what seems likely to be an ever-increasing rate. And the other is a remark made to me by the most thoughtful man I met in Japan. In the robotic future, he said, and he didn't necessarily mean within the next twenty years—it might be fifty or even more—in the robotic future, with most of us free from or deprived of most tasks, manual or mental, human existence is going to be sort of like going to college forever—with the consequence that you never graduate, or if you do, you graduate simply into death, and the degree is awarded at your funeral. For those of us who spend our lives on college campuses, it's a striking thought.

10

Aliens in the Supermarket: Science Fiction and Fantasy for "Inquiring Minds"

George R. Guffey

The scene is Jacksonville, Florida. Lydia Stalnaker, a divorced mother of two, is taken aboard an alien spaceship and examined by extraterrestrials with large heads. When they have finished their physical examination of the woman, they tell her that she will receive seven powers from God. On returning to her home, Lydia grows more and more disturbed over her experience. She at first believes that she is going insane, and she begins to pray to God for guidance. Eventually, an investigator for the Aerial Phenomena Research Organization of Berkeley, California, hears of Lydia's experience. This researcher, Dr. James Harder, puts Lydia under hypnosis. From the hypnotized woman, he learns that the aliens were "angels from God," whose primary goal was to warn the inhabitants of Earth of an impending disaster. To be evacuated from Earth before this terrible event comes to pass, the inhabitants of our planet must first begin to obey the Ten Commandments. On learning that she is indeed sane and that the aliens who had contacted her were on a mission of mercy, Lydia decides to "bear witness" to the message of the aliens by performing cures in the name of God. For the next eleven years, she cures the unfortunate who suffer diseases ranging from common arthritis to terminal cancer. Here, her story ends.

To those of us who read a great deal of science fiction, this story is, of course, so simplistic that it may at first seem undeserving of additional comment. Even so, please allow me to point out a few facts about the story that will, I think, begin to indicate why I feel that it and other stories like it deserve additional consideration. First of all, my paraphrase of the story is nearly as long as the published version of the story itself. Second, the story of Lydia Stalnaker and the angels of God was not originally published in a third-rate science-fiction fanzine. Entitled "UFO Aliens Kidnapped Me. . . . Now I Can Heal with Miracle Powers," it was published as straight news in the *National Examiner* (January 14, 1986, p. 2) under the byline of Peter Bemidji.

The *National Examiner* (like its tabloid counterparts, the *Sun*, the *Weekly World News*, and the *National Enquirer*) is sold principally in supermarkets and drugstores. There, at newspaper racks near the checkout counters, intrigued but faintly embarrassed shoppers are regularly enticed by dizzily hilarious story titles like these from issues published during the first three months of 1986: "Beer-drinking Horse Loves Music" (*Sun*, January 14, 1986, p. 3), "Woman Gives Birth on a Ferris Wheel" (*Sun*, January 14, 1986, p. 9), "Dead Hubby's Spirit Speaks through Pet Parrot" (*Sun*, January 14, 1986, p. 17), "Nun Moonlights as Wrestler" (*Sun*, January 14, 1986, p. 37), "Swarms of Mice Eat Woman's Welfare Check" (*Sun*, February 4, 1986, p. 7), "Aftershave Lotion Can Bring Loved Ones Back from the Dead" (*Sun*, February 4, 1986, p. 17), "Baby Born Holding Bullet" (*Sun*, February 11, 1986, p. 7), "Giant Worms Invade! Some of the Beasts Are as Thick as Fire Hoses" (*Weekly World News*, February 11, 1986, p. 43), "Chopped-off Head Lives 8 hrs" (*Sun*, March 4, 1986, p. 37), "Voodoo Hex Turns Woman into a Tree" (*National Examiner*, March 4, 1986, p. 19), "Midget Trapped in Mailbox 14 Hours" (*Sun*, March 11, 1986, p. 13), and "Strange Disease Makes Woman Eat Her Clothes" (*Sun*, March 11, 1986, p. 27).

One kind of story frequently appearing in these tabloids is that of the alien. In breathless prose, the authors of these accounts report the startling behavior of a wide variety of fantastic beings. Werewolves (" 'I'm a Werewolf' Admits Wild Rock Star," *Sun*, March 20, 1984), vampires ("Teen Girl Tortured by Real-Life Vampire," *Weekly World News*, January 21, 1986, p. 39), zombies (" 'Zombie' Murders Woman and Feasts on Her Corpse," *National Examiner*, February 4, 1986, p. 11), and revitalized mummies ("Water Brings 6 Mummies Back to Life," *Sun*, February 18, 1986, p. 37) stalk the streets and alleys of the world, threatening (and occasionally even killing) innocent beings unfortunate enough to come into contact with them.

But the kinds of aliens most often appearing in the tabloids are considerably less threatening than the vampires, zombies, were-wolves, and mummies that sporadically occupy the center stage. Aliens from outer space are, for example, frequently depicted as either intrinsically interesting beings or, as in the account with which I began my essay, beings who have come to Earth on a mission of mercy.

One of the most useful scholarly works thus far published on the topic of UFO reports is Richard Michael Rasmussen's *The UFO Literature: A Comprehensive Annotated Bibliography of Works in English* (Jefferson, NC, and London: McFarland, 1985). In treating relevant materials published since 1947, Rasmussen ignores tabloid accounts of UFO sightings altogether, focusing instead on more substantial treatments in books, booklets, and special-issue maga-zines. Even so, his annotated bibliography contains nearly eleven hundred items and requires more than two hundred pages of text. Especially useful to me in my present study, however, is the clas-sification system utilized by Rasmussen. Although a degree of over-lapping was apparent in the materials he studied, Rasmussen was able to distinguish clearly three broad approaches: the "cultist" approach, the "enthusiast" approach, and the "rationalist" ap-proach (p. 2). In the tabloids I am considering, cultist accounts predominate, but enthusiast and even superficially rationalist ac-counts occasionally appear.

Cultist reports, according to Rasmussen, present religious, mys-tical, and prophetic interpretations of the UFO phenomena they describe. The "contactees" featured in this kind of story often speak of their experiences in language sprinkled with references to "Jesus Christ," "faith," and "space brotherhood." Like Lydia Stalnaker, with whom I began this essay, they associate UFOs with "angels," "demons," or "signs from heaven" (pp. 2–4).

One of the more interesting stories of this kind appeared in the *Weekly World News* on October 1, 1985. The headline of that story read: "Huge Blimp-like Space Creatures Found on Earth!" (p. 9). The main character in the story is Louis Pedroza, fifty-five-year-old foreman of a remote cattle ranch in Argentina. Although aliens from outer space typically wait for nightfall before appearing in places frequently by earthlings, these creatures manifested themselves on a clear, sunny day. According to Pedroza and his ranch hands, the aliens resembled "gigantic bags of gas." The size and shape of a Goodyear blimp, these beings from outer space nonchalantly grazed in the cattle pastures near the settlement of Villa Iruya for about three hours. They made no sound as they munched on the green grass, but their bodies seemed to quiver and roll from side to side. When they had finished their browsing, the "alien animals" rose into the sky and slowly vanished from sight. For Pedroza and his men, the experience was a moving one. "I have not the words and wisdom to explain what we felt. . . . But it was as though we could feel the surging of life in those transparent bodies. It was like when I feel the presence of God when I am in the church. . . . We all knew that we were witness to a sight no man on Earth has ever seen before. We just sat there on our horses, watching them . . . praying."

Like so many other stories of this sort, this one in the *Weekly World News* is rumorlike in tone, reporting the responses of anonymous "scientists" to the phenomena under consideration. One such expert speculates that the blimplike space creatures are "drifting across the cosmos, moving from planet to planet like a herd of gargantuan cows." Another muses that "their life span must be incredible to cross such vast distances of space at what amounts to a snail's pace. . . . To all intents and purposes, these blimp cows must be immortal."

Aliens from outer space seem particularly attracted to remote areas in Central or South America. On December 24, 1985, the *Weekly World News* (p. 35) published an account of a startling discovery recently made in the jungles of Brazil. Entitled "Starship Crew Found in Jungle, Say Scientists: First White People to Live among Headhunters Are from Another Planet," the story focuses on the exploits of Gerard Angelot, a French botanist. Angelot and three other botanists had come to this remote region of Brazil to study the plant life that flourished there. On making contact with the crew of the spaceship that had crashed in 1895, they find that Evaldo Antunes, a Brazilian member of their scientific team, is capable of communicating with the aliens in the dialect of the Indians native to that area of Brazil. From the eight stranded aliens, who are "astonishingly human-like," Angelot and Antunes learn that the aliens hail from another galaxy and that they had in the past been treated as gods by the local natives. These humanoids, although they have been living with the Indians for about ninety years, have over that period shown no sign of aging. According to the aliens themselves, a starship carrying an alien rescue party will in a short time land nearby. On returning to civilization with photographs of the starship crew and tape recordings of their shrill, high-pitched voices, Angelot and his fellow researchers relate their recent experiences to local authorities and reporters. To sceptics in the audience, Angelot says, "It's an incredible story, and frankly, I don't care if you believe it or not." In conclusion, he vows to turn his evidence "over to university experts for study."

The enthusiast approach Rasmussen found in his general study of UFO literature constitutes "by far the largest category of ufological thought." Enthusiast accounts typically contend that UFOs are intelligently controlled (but not divinely sent) vehicles from other "worlds." In support of their contentions, they frequently offer as evidence radar contacts, electromagnetic anomalies, and pronounced physiological effects on witnesses. Enthusiasts often find the pathway to truth blocked by individuals and government agencies bent on covering up indisputable evidence that alien ships have crashed in the deserts of the Southwest, have established bases on the moon, or have issued from hollow planets within our own solar system. "Most enthusiasts," Rasmussen notes,

> maintain a curious double-sided attitude toward science and scientists. On the one hand, mistrust of science permeates enthusiast literature. Scientists are assailed for ignoring UFOs, and are accused of blindness in the face of overwhelming evidence. Any scientist who states that UFOs do not warrant serious scientific attention, who concludes that UFOs do not exist, or who assumes any kind of skeptical stance, is unmercifully castigated as "biased." On the other hand, enthusiasts more than anyone else are constantly calling for further scientific study of UFOs, despite the negative conclusions of several past studies. (Pp. 4–5)

Over the last three or four months, a few stories of the enthusiast sort have appeared in the tabloids. On January 21, 1986, for example, a story headlined "Russian Jet Wins Dogfight with UFO" appeared in the *Weekly World News* (p. 5). According to this account, shortly before dawn four MIG fighters escorting a prototype of the Russian Blackjack bomber recently sighted a brightly lit UFO above the Baltic Sea. Yuri Serobada, a Soviet air ace piloting one of the MIGs, broke formation and attacked the saucer-shaped alien craft, ultimately destroying it with a heat-seeking missile. Western intelligence sources, according to the *Weekly World News*, believe that the diameter of the currently submerged UFO measured at least sixty feet. Although the Russians are now devising plans to recover the alien craft from the bottom of the sea, they insist the the incident in question never took place.

Though exceptionally secretive about such matters, Russian officials are, of course, not the only ones allegedly refusing to release the details of such encounters to the public at large. Two years earlier, the *Weekly World News* had reported ("UFOs Warn of Atomic Disaster," February 7, 1984, p. 42) that, on the floor of Englands House of Lords, former intelligence officer Gordon Creighton had announced the recent landing of a UFO within a quarter of a mile of a secret airbase near Suffolk. "We're poised on the brink of a nuclear disaster, and those who are watching over us from other planets are sending UFOs here warning us not to press the nuclear button." Typically, the *Weekly World News* concluded its account of that incident with a reference to high-level government officials who had refused to tell "what they know about the aliens' concerns over the nuclear threat."

Like the *Weekly World News*, the *National Enquirer* has over the last few years frequently taken various governmental agencies to task for allegedly covering up valuable information about various kinds of UFO phenomena. A year ago, the editors of the *Enquirer* collected many of the articles which that tabloid had printed in the past, reedited them, and republished them in a book entitled *National Enquirer UFO Report* (New York: Pocket Books, 1985). Among the numerous republished indictments of bureaucratic cover-ups were claims that the U.S. Air Force had secretly studied the contents of a UFO that crashed in New Mexico in 1947 (pp. 40–43), that President Dwight D. Eisenhower had personally conferred with space aliens at Edwards Air Force Base in 1954 (pp. 43–45), and that alien spaceships had spied on our astronauts when they landed on the moon in 1969 (pp. 50–53).

A few of the UFO stories appearing in the tabloids adopt, at least superficially, the tone and strategies of Rasmussen's third category—the rationalist account. The rationalist approach is characterized by "the rational, systematic collection and analysis of data;

meticulous investigation and documentation of reports; . . . formulation of hypotheses based on the data; testing of any hypotheses
formed; . . . and publication of research results for review by peers.
. . . Above all, the rationalist examines UFOs within a scientific
framework, attempting to confirm or deny UFO reality via the scientific method" (Rasmussen, p. 6).

My favorite example of a tabloid story ostensibly written from
this perspective appeared in the *Sun* on February 11, 1986. Entitled
"Race of 6-Inch Humans Found: Amazing Discovery Proof of Aliens
on Earth," it describes a recent find by scientists in Central America.
An archeologist named Melvin Trudgel is given credit for the discovery. What Trudgel stumbled upon in a thick, tropical jungle were the
remains of an "incredible city" that between A.D. 100 and 500 housed
as many as three thousand tiny humans from outer space. This city,
complete with little Inca-like temples and tiny alien skeletons, is, we
are told, currently undergoing rigorous investigation by a team of
scientists. One of those scientists, cryptographer Victor Taylor, has
thus far been unable to decipher the writing of the miniature aliens;
but, from the pictures they drew on the walls of their temples, he is
sure of their place of origin. "Pictures on temple walls tell an unbe-
lievable story. They show people arriving from pencil-like ships, and
building their city. The people point at the sky, and the Andromeda
system is indicated as the starting point for their journey."

Another scientist said to be currently investigating the ruins of
the miniature city and the skeletons of its inhabitants is biologist
Ruth Martinez. The diminutive space aliens, labeled "Homomicros"
by the scientists studying them, were, according to Martinez, "human in every way, except for their tiny size. We believe they were
extremely strong, even though they were small. They probably could
life objects weighing up to five pounds, although they themselves
weighed less than a pound." Archeologist Trudgel believes, although
the speculation boggles the imagination, that the tiny aliens engaged
in trade with the Incas, Mayas, and Aztecs. Even he, however,
wonders how they managed to hold their own in competition with the
relatively gigantic beasts that inhabited the jungle around their city.
"They may have had some kind of unified particle-beam forcefield,
invisibility ray, animal repellant or advanced weapons," he suggests.
Whatever their methods of defense, the Homomicros flourished for
five hundred years and then vanished. Dr. Trudgel is philosophical

about the failure of his team of scientists to understand the ultimate disappearance of the aliens. "This is just one of the many mysteries continuing to appear from the past."

Most of the tabloid stories about aliens from outer space present the aliens themselves in a favorable light. As we have already seen, the aliens sometimes function as guardian angels (see also "UFOs Warn of Atomic Disaster," *Weekly World News*, February 7, 1984 p. 42; "UFO Drops Christmas Food to Starving Ethiopians," *Weekly World News*, December 24, 1985, p. 27; and "Couple Claims Their Guardian Angels Are UFO Aliens," *National Examiner*, January 28, 1986). Some of the aliens recently depicted by the tabloids even seem to have been interested in sports (see, for example, "Baseball Invented by UFO Aliens," *Sun*, January 14, 1986, p. 26). Others appear to have an affinity for country or rock musicians (see, for example, "Olivia Newton-John: I Have Seen a UFO," *National Examiner*, January 14, 1986, p. 15, and "Country Stars Reveal Their Psychic, UFO Encounters," *Sun*, January 28, 1986, p. 29).

Occasionally, however, the tabloids print accounts of aliens and alien spaceships that threaten or destroy, sometimes accidentally, the lives and property of the inhabitants of our planet (see "Giant UFO Base Moving Close to Earth," *Sun*, March 27, 1984, p. 30; "U.S. Satellite Collides with UFO," *Sun*, February 11, 1986, p. 2; and "UFO Vampires May Be Murdering Fishermen," *National Examiner*, March 11, 1986, p. 31). Hostile or not, aliens from outer space (especially disguised ones) are often difficult to distinguish from normal human beings. This problem has recently fascinated the editors and reporters of one of the tabloids. The *National Enquirer*, the tabloid with the "largest circulation of any newspaper in America" (4.5 million), a short while ago published an article listing "10 ways to tell if your co-workers could be space aliens" (see William Dunn, "Respectable? Enquiring minds want to know," Los Angeles *Herald Examiner*, February 6, 1986, p. A2).

Perhaps even more potentially useful to its readers was the same tabloid's related article suggesting eight signs indicating that one's neighbors are disguised aliens (revised and reprinted in *National Enquirer UFO Report*, pp. 214–16). Here, in the words of the *National Examiner*, are a few of the telltale signs experts have been able to validate:

- *Sleep or work patterns of abnormal length*—"An alien's day on its native planet may be shorter or longer than ours," Brad Steiger ["famed UFO researcher and author"] pointed out. For this reason, he said, an alien may sleep at odd times of the day or night.
- *A mood change, fear, or physical reaction when near certain high-tech hardware that radiates electromagnetic waves*—For example, when around a microwave oven, a alien may break out in a rash, said Dr. Thomas Easton, a theoretical biologist and futurist. . . .
- *Constant information gathering*—"Space aliens have the prime objective of studying us and our planet; thus, information gathering is vitally important," revealed Steiger. For this reason, aliens will seem to be constantly buying newspapers, magazines, language tapes, and other material that will help them in their information-gathering efforts. . . .
- *A home with paint schemes or decorations that don't quite fit in*—Since the alien is not familiar with Earth homes, certain colors may clash, or some decorative objects may be out of place, said Steiger.

What should one do when one has determined, through the application of these and other tests, that one's neighbor is an alien from outer space? In light of the generally high ratio of tabloid stories about harmless or beneficial space aliens compared to stories about dangerous ones, the advice of the *National Enquirer* is, in this regard, not unexpected. The *Enquirer* recommends that we take no drastic action against such neighbors. It concludes with an upbeat statement by Steiger. "In my opinion, based on my research, space aliens living here on Earth are on a goodwill mission that will usher in a Golden Age for humanity. So take no action, other than giving that alien support—through friendship, kindness, and neighborly goodwill" (p. 216).

While aliens from outer space are sometimes difficult to distinguish from ordinary human beings, one kind of alien frequently the subject of breathless stories in the tabloids is not. He is typically described as being eight feet tall and extremely hairy. Like most of the aliens from outer space, this alien from the remote regions of our own planet is by nature a benign creature. In various parts of the world he has various names, but in the tabloids he is known as

"Bigfoot." Like many of the aliens from outer space, Bigfoot, in stories in the tabloids, often performs the function of a guardian angel. The *Weekly World News*, for example, recently (October 1, 1985) published a story entitled "Crash Survivors Rescued by Bigfoot." According to that story, Dr. Alberto Gomes and his wife Teresa, two "prominent geologists," were on a routine survey flight in the Andes Mountains when their DC-3 developed engine trouble. The resulting airplane crash killed their pilot and left Gomes and his wife severely injured. Barely able to crawl from the wreckage of the plane, the two scientists spent a restless night, convinced that they would almost certainly starve to death before rescue parties could find them.

At sunrise the next morning, Gomes and his wife were awakened by a rustling in the brush surrounding their crash site. Shortly thereafter, a creature looking like a cross between a man and an ape emerged from the brush. Covered from head to foot with matted brown hair, the creature, instead of moving in for the kill as Gomes and his wife expected, tossed quantities of berries and roots to the unfortunate couple. Using melted snow and a pot from the plane Gomes boiled the roots, which "were very edible, even tasty." At the end of the day, Bigfoot reappeared, this time with two small fish, which the two grateful geologists cooked and ate. Eventually, a rescue party spotted the downed airplane, but not before Bigfoot had made five additional grocery deliveries to the site. Later, recovering from his injuries in a hospital in Arequipa, Gomes said of Bigfoot, "He was our silent savior" (p. 5).

Although when allowed to live unmolested, Bigfoot at worst seems to shy away from contact with man and at best seems concerned for man's welfare (see also "Bigfoot Saves Lost Child's Life," *Weekly World News*, December 24, 1985, p. 27), he is at times forced into a different posture by hunters who either stumble upon him while pursuing other game or deliberately track him through the forests and snowcapped mountains of the world. In the February 4, 1985, issue of the *Sun* (p. 15), Travis Hawk reports that two big-game hunters, Ollie Rudd and his cousin Ty Benson, while on an elk-hunting trip in the Cascade Mountains of central Oregon, "bagged an amazing trophy" of an unexpected kind. Ollie and Ty, we are told, were sleeping inside Ty's pickup camper at approximately four in the morning when their dog began to growl at something outside. In the snow that surrounded their camp site, they subsequently found huge footprints that seemed almost certainly human. Grabbing their rifles, the two hunters set out in pursuit of the creature that had left those remarkable prints. Shortly, in a clearing in full moonlight, they found themselves face to face with a being eight feet tall and exceedingly hairy. Upon realizing that the creature confronting them was Bigfoot, Ollie, in a "stern voice," ordered him to accompany them to their camp site. On reaching their camper, they locked him inside.

As the day wore on, the imprisoned alien began to try to communicate with its captors; in the opinion of Ty, "the sounds he made were at least half-human." When the two men "turned on the radio, he seemed to like the music. The radio was playing country and pretty soon this monster starts to sway, and before you know it he's whoopin' and stompin' like an Indian at a rain dance." Later, around noon, the two men set about preparing their lunch. Upon noticing the smell that arose from the meal Ollie and Ty were cooking, Bigfoot began to grunt loudly and rub his stomach, giving the unmistakable impression that he was hungry, too, and wanted food. "I wanted to feed Bigfoot," said Ollie, "but I didn't know what to give him, so I gave him some meat. He takes a bit of it and screws his face up something awful. Suddenly he screams—and it sounds like a wounded ape. With a powerful push he turns over the table and smashes into the door tearing it right off its hinges." Before Ollie and Ty could do anything to stop it, the creature was gone, leaving behind only its gigantic tracks in the snow. Asked to sum up his feelings about the experience, Ollie mournfully said, "What's sad is we were starting to get through to him when he ran off."

Although basically shy and respectful of man, Bigfoot, under the right conditions, can be dangerous. In a story entitled, "I Killed Bigfoot," Jerry Clarke in the *Weekly World News* (February 7, 1984, p. 5) details such an instance. Clarke's hero is Torban Lodang, Sherpa mountain guide. Lodang's harrowing adventure began when he set out to find the body of a climber who had died on the slopes of Mt. Everest. When Lodang reached the nine-thousand-foot level, he came upon a trail of footprints in the snow. The huge prints gave every indication of having been made by bare feet. Familiar with the many tales about Bigfoot (or "Yeti," as he is called in Tibet), Lodang decided to follow the trail of footprints, hoping thereby to catch a glimpse of that legendary creature. One aspect of the creature's footprints, however, troubled the Sherpa guide—they were stained with fresh blood.

After following the trail for over two hours, Lodang suddenly realized that he had been traveling a circular path and that Bigfoot was in effect now behind him. Bigfoot was now tracking the tracker. After a moment of panic, Lodang decided to try to reach a base camp at the ten-thousand-foot level. At the camp, he could find weapons with which he could defend himself. Just when it appeared that Lodang would attain his goal, he suddenly found his way blocked by a barrier of solid ice. Now he could only wait for Bigfoot to catch up with him. He did not have long to wait. The creature, wounded by previous climbers of the mountain, loomed up before him. With a horrible scream, the tall, shaggy beast with sharp fangs and glowing eyes lunged at Lodang, who courageously met him head on. "As the monster charged me, I hurled my body at its knees, hoping it would fall in the snow and give me time to flee. But the result was more than I could have imagined. The beast stumbled over my body and landed on the icy slope. Its massive body plummeted down the ice and hurtled over the edge. The dropoff there is at least 3,000 feet. I knew the yeti must be dead."

I shall end this short survey of the treatment of the alien by American weekly tabloids with my favorite story in this category. That story is entitled "Bigfoot Stole My Wife and Made Her Pregnant," and it appeared in the *Sun* on March 20, 1984 (p. 5). The primary figure in the story is Jerry McKennon, an Australian hunting guide and small-time herdsman and farmer. While McKennon was guiding a hunting party in the mountains of Queensland, Bigfoot (or "Yowie," as Australians call such creatures) approached the isolated cabin that McKennon shared with his wife Jenny. According to McKennon, Bigfoot proceeded to "romance" his wife. "She probably would have talked to anyone. She used to go stir crazy. . . . I figure this Yowie took unfair advantage of her."

Since she left him to live with Bigfoot, McKennon has glimpsed his wayward wife at least twice. The first time he saw her he was able to communicate with her briefly across a rocky ravine too wide for him to bridge. "She said she wasn't coming back," McKennon reports. "She said it was too lonely living with me in the cabin." The last time that he saw her she was obviously pregnant, and McKennon is convinced that Bigfoot is the father of her unborn child. McKennon has vowed to kill Bigfoot, and he now roams the mountains of Queensland, rifle in hand, seeking revenge on the eight-foot-tall, hairy creature that has stolen his wife and has gotten her with child.

Supermarket tabloids like the *Sun*, the *Weekly World News*, and the *National Examiner* obviously satisfy many kinds of needs felt by the millions of readers who regularly purchase them. With their accounts of pregnant men, fat ladies stuck in sports cars, babies born with lizard tails, and rock stars that bite the heads off small animals, they are, of course, appealing to the same ugly instincts that in days gone by filled carnival freak shows with gawking, ecstatic patrons. The stories about aliens from outer space and aliens from the remoter regions of our own planet probably, however, satisfy quite different urges of the same readers. Without demanding in the way of reading skills or tenacity, they satisfy the almost universal desire for wonder and awe. Additionally, because they so frequently depict creatures (both higher and lower than man on the great chain of being) engaged in rendering aid to humans in need, some of them probably speak, however crudely, to a contemporary, pervasive feeling of powerlessness in an age of threatening technology.

In his seminal book on UFO phenomena *Flying Saucers: A Modern Myth of Things Seen in the Skies* (Princeton, NJ: Princeton University Press, 1964, rpt. 1978), C. G. Jung concludes that UFO reports of the sort that we have been considering might best be labeled "visionary rumours" (p. 8). The basis for such rumors, he argues, is emotional tension caused by a situation of collective distress or danger (p. 13). "In the threatening situation of the world today, when people are beginning to see that everything is at stake," Jung adds,

> projection-creating fantasy soars beyond the realm of earthly space, where the rulers of human fate, the gods, once had their abode in the planets. . . . The present world situation is calculated as never before to arouse expectations of a redeeming, supernatural event. If these expectations have not dared to show themselves in the open, this is simply because no one is deeply rooted enough in the tradition of earlier centuries to consider an intervention from heaven as a matter of course. We have indeed strayed far from the metaphysical certainties of the Middle Ages, but no so far that our historical and psychological background is empty of all metaphysical hope. . . . This attitude on the part of the overwhelming majority provides the most favourable basis for a

projection, that is, for a manifestation of the unconscious background. Undeterred by rationalistic criticism, it thrusts itself to the forefront in the form of a symbolic rumour, accompanied and reinforced by the appropriate visions, and thus activates an archetype that has always expressed order, deliverance, salvation, and wholeness. (Pp. 14, 22)

Interestingly enough, these symbolic rumors of things seen in the sky, of *dei ex machina*, do not seem to wholly satisfy the readers of the tabloids who yearn for salvation in an age dominated by science and technology. Januslike, they not only look to the heavens for salvation but also to the Earth, taking solace as well in symbolic rumors of benevolent, hairy, apelike beings who inhabit edenic forests and pristine mountain ranges. Feeding on roots and berries (and totally repulsed by even the thought of the consumption of flesh), these gentle animals are apparently modern, fantastic representations of beings who played a major part in the prehistory of mankind. In his book *Man into Wolf: An Anthropological Interpretation of Sadism, Masochism and Lycanthropy* (London: Spring Books, 1948; rpt. Santa Barbara, CA: Ross-Erikson, 1978), Robert Eisler summarizes the evolutionary history of modern man.

Our Primate ape ancestors were beyond any doubt perfectly innocuous frugivorous "savages" or "silvan" animals swinging from tree to tree in the primeval virgin forest. . . . there must have occurred at some time in the course of evolution a radical change in the human diet or *modus vivendi*, a mutation, as de Vries called these sudden, irrevocable alterations, such as is remembered in mankind's widespread traditions of a "Fall" or "original sin," with permanently disastrous consequences.

In other words, *Pithecanthropus frugivorus*, the arboreal fruit-picking man who could find enough succulent or hard-shelled fruits, berries, leaf-buds, young shoots and sprouts all the year round only in the tropical and subtropical forest-belt, is the legendary "good-savage" of the primeval Golden Age, living on acorns and at peace with other animals, like *Adam*, that is "Man" in the "garden of the desert," the oasis of the date-palm growers, and like the hairy Engidu eating herbs with the animals and drinking water at their pool in the Babylonian Gilgamesh epic. (Pp. 6, 7)

The hairy, gentle beast who brought berries and roots to Alberto Gomes and his wife and the one that screamed in outrage when Ty Benson and Ollie Rudd offered him a bite of meat are obviously of this ancient lineage. And the story of Jerry McKennon and his wife, who abandoned her husband for a life with Bigfoot, is not without relevance to Eisler's paradigm. That story is, among other things, also a story of sexual jealousy. In choosing to live with Bigfoot, McKennon's wife was, in other words, separating herself from a social unit that supported "the possessive attitude of the jealous, sexually combatant male who considers himself entitled to kill both his rival and his faithless mistress or wife" for a unit more like that of "peaceful herds of leaf- and fruit-eaters, who are almost entirely free from sexual envy and jealousy" (Eisler, pp. 8, 9)

A reader of the tabloids we have been considering finds, then, within their pages, a comforting representation of a world, however crudely and tentatively realized, not entirely unlike the prelapsarian one Adam knew in Eden. Although our tabloid reader's "garden" is not without serpents, he frequently comes into contact with gentle, benevolent, herbivorous beasts. And when he needs them, he can look to the heavens for guardian angels who will both instruct him in the ways of righteousness and watch over him in his hour of need.

II
Aliens 'R' U.S.:
American Science Fiction Viewed
from Down Under

Zoe Sofia

To what kinds of anthropologists are aliens alien and why? Is science fiction itself a kind of anthropology, and if so, of what or who? In science-fiction criticism as in anthropology, or any discursive practice, what we see depends upon where we stand; objects of discourse are constructions from particular positions. From the U.S. perspective, the aliens in the creature features look like aliens, nazis, or communists; the U.S. heroes are the "good guys," with their shiny technology; the aliens are the "slimy bads," who must be defeated in a ritualized plot that excuses our lusts for more of those fantastic, fascinating, all too often fascist estrangement effects.

But to subjects of technological imperialism, the Americans are the bad guys, the aliens look remarkably like American aliens, and there's not much difference between the shiny goods and the slimy bads. Viewed australly, from "Down Under," most science-fiction film looks like propaganda to convince us that the space-traveling corporate clones and freaky scientists who created city-stomping nuclear monsters and later turned us into obedient pod people are good rational guys after all, who can always regain control of any tools that go bad and start gobbling us up.

Those near centers of hegemonic power could perhaps write anthropologies of science fiction—humanistic accounts of a seemingly universal self who imagines and encounters a generalized other in quests of transcendence and discovery with which we all are supposed to identify. Natives of peripheral powers may, however, find more value in critical *ethnographies* that are sensitive to the geopolitical contexts in which mass-media science fiction is produced and consumed.

And here I could speak, like those from many worlds, of how the good ship USS Enterprise has trekked into Australia, disobeying the prime directive with rip-off business deals, political manipulations, and militarizations of ports like Fremantle and towns like Alice. My formative political experiences include waving hello to the orbiting John Glenn as a child, watching the moon landings, protesting Australia's collaboration with the United States in Vietnam as a teenager, and becoming an ecofeminist activist in the mid-70s when our leftist government was ousted in a CIA-backed bloodless coup. These experiences inspired my interest in the mythic meanings of space and nuclear technologies, leading to studies of science-fiction film. With this background, it's hard to distinguish science-fiction film from spectacles of global technological imperialism. My hope is that by unraveling allegorical meanings of the former I can hasten the demise of the latter. The history of imperialism demonstrates anthropology's effectiveness in killing its others; perhaps these toxic properties will work in turn on the "spacemen that ate Australia."

The Australian accent seems fitting given "Down Under's" minor role as a mythic element in extraterrestrialist ideology. Although the term *Down Under* implies an anchoring terra firma, this southern continent is absent from most U.S. icons of the world. Australia is an off-world base for a nation of Skywalkers, a utopian good place that exists no place, invisible except in mythic representations of a land that yields for spacemen "the right stuff" they need to thrust themselves off to the moon and stars, as in that 2001-ish docudrama of the space program, in which Western Australian Aborigines mystically illuminate Glenn's spacecraft and protect it from incineration.

To view American science fiction from Down Under means adopting an earthy, earthling's perspective on these alien dreamings; it means feeling free to name the monstrous aspects of the dominant order revealed in these high-tech myths. Since one's critical stance is determined less by nativity than politics, it's possible to be an American and a Down Under critic of science fiction. It is not a matter of nationality but standpoint: are you earthling or spaceman? Furthermore, since the aliens weren't killed before they proliferated, no earthlings can claim freedom from extraterrestrial contamination. The spacemen dwell, like E. T., John Glenn, Christa McAuliffe, "right here" in our minds. So performing a little cultural psycho-drama, I'd like to continue this paper in the role of *my* "other side," an extraterrestrial scientist, a "xenologist" whose specialty is alien dreamings.

The following typology of SFX monsters aims at extending Géza Róheim's psychoanalytic anthropology and Norman O. Brown's psychoanalysis of capitalism into the space and nuclear age, through the study of science-fiction films.[1] It assumes that SF aliens are estranged from their inventors in much the same way as the bizarre symbols of dreams—the monsters from the Id—are estranged from the dreamer's critical consciousness: as monstrous aspects of the self, disguised and made wondrous with special semiotic effects. Like private dreamings, these public monsters are symptoms of a certain soul-sickness, as well as perverse attempts to cure it (by "the return of the repressed"). But unless they are received with more criticism than wonder, SFX films will tend overall to support the status quo with their ritual stagings of the dreams that guide extraterrestrial and exterminist tool making and normalizations of the nightmares in-spired by superpowered technologies.[2]

As long as we continue to think of tools as mere means but not *meanings*, SF texts can hold us in uncritical awe before spectacles of technological wizardry that mystify the not-so-glamorous aspects of a mode of production so alienated that its artifacts (and inventors) seem self-creating, independent of Earth, and divorced from antiter-restrial effects: extraterrestrial. As a step towards countering such propagandistic tendencies, the alienist must seek out the meanings of high tools, deciphering the condensations, displacements, and sym-bolic representations by which high-tech fantasies encode real-world estrangements—such as those that presently allow corporate heads to endlessly defer responsibility for exterminations proliferated in the name of progress and rationality.

So what are the allegories of multinational capitalism forwarded by science-fiction images? Let's find out what we can in an economy tour of Jupiter Space and other generic monsters of extraterrestrial mythology, especially the filmic variety. The monsters considered are half-lives, brain wombs, spermatic communications and trans-

port technologies, penis breasts and penis dentatus, and cannibaleyes.

Half-Lives

This is a generic name for most of the monsters encountered in
high-tech culture, where libidinal energies are characteristically dis-
placed from body to machine, and Man is preoccupied with animat-
ing excrement or resurrecting dead matter. Through such creation,
Man transcends his body's limitations and emulates his celestial God
by replicating life without the aid of Woman.[3] From Frankenstein's
monster to Spielberg's E.T., whether they are organic, mechanical,
biomechanical, extraterrestrial, chthonic, fetal, undead, vampiric,
radiant, slimy, fleshy, cyborg, robotic, highly intelligent, gigantic, or
microscopic, almost all the monsters of science fiction share the
quality of being products of unnatural creation or birth. Half-lives
form the very stuff of science-fiction film, in a medium whose chief
illusion is that of animation and a genre whose principal attractions
are not usually humans but electromechanical fantasms who only live
by light-play.

We encounter many more biological scientists in science-fiction
films than astrophysicists or chemists or engineers. The suppression
or absence of normal heterosexual intercourse, female gestation, and
childbirth is a much stronger and more widespread marker of the
science-fiction genre than the icons we usually think of, such as
displacement in space and time, high technology, scientific extra-
polation, and so forth. Indeed, these elements are characteristically
deployed as covers for a preoccupation with monstrous creation.
Kubrick and Clarke's *2001: A Space Odyssey*, for example, excuses
its blatant imagery of intercourse, fertilization, implantation, gestation, and fetal life with alibis of extraterrestrial or "high" technology,
while a monolithic signifier of corporate power successfully distracts
critical scrutiny from figures like the astral fetus.

Jupiter Space (Brain Womb)

SF iconography regularly plays out the Greek myth of the birth
of Athena, the goddess of war, wisdom, and numbers, who sprang

fully grown from her father's head after Zeus had devoured the pregnant goddess Methis. The most common familial dyad in SF film is father and daughter. From Rotwang's reanimation of Hel as the robot Maria in *Metropolis*, and Dr. Morbius' daughter Alta in *Forbidden Planet*, to Rachel, the replicant, brainchild of the Tyrell corporation in *Blade Runner*, as well as the unnamed feminine cyborgs of advertising, we regularly encounter Athena figures onto whom the father/scientist's interests have been projected and who can be understood as the reworked and animated remains of the cannibalized mother (also Mother Nature).

The fantasy of head birth, familiar from expressions about minds that conceive and gestate ideas as brainchildren, finds its way into images of the tools and techniques that turn the real into the imaginary or the hyperreal. "Jupiter Space" is the name I give to the complex of equivalences established between the womb, the masculine scientific brain, and all sorts of technological and extraterrestrial spaces and surfaces. The term comes from *2001*, where, after the hero has decapitated the computer HAL, a prerecorded video message comes on and announces that "now . . . you are in Jupiter Space" in an ostensible reference to the outer space near Jupiter that applies equally to the on-screen image of HAL's rosy-red, highly urban-looking brain room, in which the astronaut floats, embryolike.

Through a series of space birth episodes, as well as the psychedelic montage of electronic, astrogenetic, organic, extraterrestrial landscapes in the Star Gate sequence, the film articulates the equivalence of spaces that we can now readily recognize in contemporary visual advertising, particularly for computers and communications and transport devices, where womby brain space, outer space microelectronic grids, video and computer screens, city streets, and skyscrapers all intermesh. The recurrent image of the Cartesian grid makes a visual play on the notions of "matrix" as womb and as abstract, crystalline mathematical space.

Jupiter Space imagery is dangerous because it glamorizes and glosses over the cannibalistic matricide—the wasteful disordering and consumption of the world—that is enacted as the planet is enframed into global grids of energy and rationalized resources. But more chilling still is the equivalence it mediates between mental and extraterrestrial space, for this renders Earth expendable or replaceable by other imaginary worlds according to the science-fiction fantasy of a universe in which inhabitable planets are as common as mental conceptions. Optimistic extraterrestrial fantasies like this lower resistance to exterminist enterprise by muting our sense of this world's uniqueness, rendering us less anxious about the prospect of polluting or destroying the only known habitable planet and securing our faith in the inventive fertility of the corporate matrix as it substitutes electromechanical half-lives for the species it daily extinguishes.

Logospermatechnos (Spermatic Tools)

Zooming or floating through Jupiter Space are signifiers of extraterrestrial tools, modern versions of God's spermatic word. These figures indicate the solipsism of masculinist production, since they might stand at one moment for the spermatic emission, the seminal ray or illuminating idea that issues from Jupiter Space, and at the next for a vehicle to convey directives to remote minds and spaces that now goes on to fertilize more Jupiter Space and then transforms into an Athena figure itself. It happens like this in *2001*, in which the paradigm of the spermatic communications tool is elegantly articulated in the sequence that takes off with the hurling of a primal weapon, its SFX transformation into an orbiting nuclear bomb, and subsequent mutation into various spaceships and transports, a writing implement, astronauts in space, HAL's logic circuits, the monoliths, and a bolt of radio waves emitted at Jupiter, whose path is followed by the sperm-shaped *Discovery*. The sequence climaxes with the insemination of the Star Gate and the spaceman's resurrection as an omnipotent cyborg fetus: man's marriage with spermatic tool and celestial power reproduces him as a child of Jupiter Space.

The iconography of the extraterrestrial, transformative, mobile, and penetrating tool is nowadays applied to any kind of artifact, from penis-pump toothpastes that emit radio waves to pizzas that arrive like monoliths; it finds condensed expression in the transformer toys that can be manipulated to resemble in turn robots, cars, cassette decks, guns, and so forth.

Through the equivalences it visually establishes between signifiers of communications, transport, information, and weapons technologies, the logospermatechnos paradigm hints at the actual interdependence of these implements for world incorporation, whose special effects include the rerouting and resourcing of the planetary fabric to create fictional estrangements between origins and "use points" of materials, between shiny good products and slimy bad byproducts, between weapons strategists and irradiated victims, between point of view and place of residence. The "extraterrestrialism" of such imagery mystifies the horizontal displacements of materials across the globe that construct extreme alienations of users and producers. However, for all that the multinationals are concerned with the future of terrestrial life, or with the impacts of high-flying tools upon earthlings, they might just as well exist in outer space or out of time.

Penis-Breast

Science-fiction film often eludes conventional interpretations because of its many bisexual images. Although masculine supremacy is officially spoken of in purely phallic terms, myths of masculine creativity regularly attribute feminine reproductive and nurturing qualities to male powers. Myth shows Jupiter unable to generate brain-children by masculine intellect alone; his power must be augmented by the cannibalized mother's fertility, appropriated in an act that makes of the female a fertilizing penis and a nutritive breast.

In Melanie Klein's view of the stages of erotic development preceding the acquisition of verbal language, emergent genital interests are figured in oral terms. The "primal scene" may be imagined as a form of oral intercourse by a monster with features of mother and father alike—as in Ouroboros, a combined parent figure that feeds and inseminates itself. The breast is the first object of idealization and envy, whose internalized image can for a time provide hallucinatory gratification, and whose splitting into the "good" satisfying breast and the frustrating "bad" breast gives impetus to the search for substitute objects, most notably the penis. Klein regards "the deprivation of the breast as the most fundamental cause of the turning towards the father."[4] The search for the gratifying object may therefore be pictured as the quest for the penis or child inside the mother's body. Imagery related to these preverbal fantasies condenses oral and genital motifs: the penis with breastlike qualities (penis-breast), the devouring penis (penis dentatus), and the mouthlike vagina (vagina dentata).

An exemplary transitional symbol, the penis-breast is regularly encountered in zones where there are questions about the origins of masculine creativity (that is, in maternal identification) or the application of phallic powers in the interaction between subject (self, culture, man, known) and object (other, nature, woman, unknown). Paralleling the splitting of the breast, we find in SF a dual representation of the tool as the "bad" penis-dentatus monster, signifying the agents that rape and devour, plunder and incorporate the world and its peoples, and as the "good" penis-breast, the controllable nurturing tool, the consumable fetishized commodity, or the roboticized woman, the *fembot*, a female stand-in for phallic powers.

These images are neatly articulated in *Forbidden Planet*, where Dr. Morbius' mental union with Krell computers generates two brainchildren: the "slimy bad" penis-dentatus Monster from the Id, a monopedal, red fathead that gobbles up Mrs. Morbius and some of the corporate clones who land on Altain, and the "shiny good" penis-breast Robby the Robot, dick-headed but rounded like a breast, who plays the role of obedient housewife, producing food, clothes, and jewels on demand.

For nasty examples of oral-genital monsters, we have *Alien*, whose main monster, a stand-in for extraterrestrial ore and weapons, begins as an orally raping penis-breast and reemerges as a chest erection to grow up into a voracious penis head that looks like part of a spaceship. For "nice" examples, check *E.T.: The Extraterrestrial*, whose monster is a penis-breast found in the toolshed that substitutes first for junk food (pizza), stands in for both mother and father, and doubles for a male as well as a female child. Other penis-breast motifs include conical mushrooms with coronas suggesting both nipple and glans; a spaceship like a Capitol building with a spherical body surmounted by a nipple-penis spire, as well as the phrase "penis breath" (suggesting spermatic words and fellatio). As we all know, it wasn't just on screen, but everywhere consumerism flowers that E.T. became the quintessentially consumable artifact.

Lurking close by ideas of consuming and consumable artifacts is the vagina dentata, which in *2001* retracts its teeth to allow passage of a space shuttle into the Jupiter Space of a sublunar station, is glimpsed as the sharply serrated mouthlike entrance to E. T.'s mother ship, is implied in Ripley's naming of the alien penis-dentatus monster as a "son of a bitch" in *Alien*, and is closely encountered in the sequel *Aliens*, where it takes the form of a gigantic, devouring, egg-laying, bad mother. Penis-breast and vagina dentata motifs are prominent in *Liquid Sky*. The protagonist Margaret, a punk dyke, says she dresses as she does to let people know "this pussy has teeth"; after the deaths of lovers and rapists, she claims she can kill with her vagina. In a particularly ouroboric moment, she performs fellatio on her modeling double Jimmy (played by the same actress), who disappears as he comes. Finally, she offers herself as food to the alien actually responsible for the deaths: a disembodied eye that can orgasmically consume whole people. The relations between vision, food, penis, and vagina are underscored in the amusing subplot in which Jimmy's mother equates the scientist's telescope with his erect penis and expresses her sexual preoccupations by ordering them a dinner of several shrimp dishes. In response to his large voyeuristic organ, she offers a proliferation of edible clitoral/vaginal symbols, and, like Margaret, enacts a narcissistic feeding of her own genitals (the clitoris-breast?).

Cannibaleyes

Freud's interpretation of Oedipus' self-blinding as castration made us familiar with the notion of the eye as penis. But this blinding—the climax of a story about an obsessive quest for knowledge of origins—also involved a ouroboric introjection of piercing objects metonymically related to the mother's breast—namely, the "gold-chased brooches" that fastened Jocasta's upper robe. The eye, as Fenichel points out, may be thought of as a devouring mouth or incorporating vagina as well as a penetrating and probing penis. The vagina dentata and cannibaleye are complements to the imaginary organ, the penis-breast.

Melanie Klein gives the term "epistemophilia" to the child's hunger for knowledge (especially of origins) initially directed at the interior of the mother's body and later sublimated into mining, exploration, and scientific curiosity. The much-maligned "bug-eyed monsters" that adorned the pulps echo a figure familiar from Mary Shelley's account of the epistemophiliac Frankenstein, whose eyes reportedly "started from their sockets" as he pieced together a monster in his "workshop of filthy creation."

Motifs of visual penetration and incorporation in science-fiction film work to articulate signs of the film medium and its associated visual fetishism together with motifs of scientific voyeurism, superpower surveillance, corporate cannibalism, and that peculiarly American form of hegemony through cinematic exhibitionism (film culture). Many of these connections are skillfully explored in Garrett Stewart's study of SF "videology" in *Shadows of the Magic Lamp*. In *2001*'s visual climax, the viewer's eye is identified with that of the traumatized astronaut, as well as with the eyeball-shaped pod that speedily inseminates Jupiter Space. Amongst the plenitude of scenes of visual, oral, and other incorporations in *Alien*, we find, intercut with the picture of Ash hungrily seeking information through a video screen, an astounding image of a recumbent extraterrestrial petrified under a huge penile device that seems to have secreted a screen at its tip. Like this fossil, we earthlings can also feel paralyzed by the fetishes thrust on screen by "aliens 'R 'U.S."

The cannibaleye appears in elegantly condensed form in *Return of the Jedi*. As C3PO and R2D2 approach Jabba the Hutt's fortress, a ball on a stick suddenly thrusts itself out at them and opens its serrated cover to let the optic device within survey and interrogate the visitors: here we have eye as erect penis, eye as vagina dentata, and eye as spy. Later in the film, the heroes defeat this marauding device resembling a camera that shoots more than film.

Pac-Man and Ms. Pac-Man are easily recognized cannibaleyes whose Japanese-derived names refer to "incorporation." Together with images of disembodied eyes above featureless gridded Earths, these figures suggest the alienated objectifying perspective of the Jupiter Spacemen who scope out and scoop out the world in a Pac-Man fantasy of infinite consumption that equates matter with information or energy and produces no waste.

A most intriguing recent development in SF imagery concerns the figure of the *lumen*, a Latin word meaning "hole, cavity, light." *2001* brought us through the spectacular light-hole of the Star Gate to beyond Jupiter Space. Later, Spielberg condensed the *2001* monolith with the light-hole into the motif of a slightly opened door illuminated from behind (for example, *Close Encounters of the Third Kind* and *Poltergeist*), now generic in advertising and frequently connected with the domestic refrigerator (as popularized in *Ghostbusters*). *Aliens* plays throughout on the epistemophiliac push to locate objects in the labyrinthine interior of the corporate mother. The associations of vagina, eye, and light are spelled out in the title sequence, in which the letter "I" of *Aliens* (suggesting the first person as well as the organ of vision) is dilated into a vaginal shape emitting blue-white light that eventually comes to suffuse the screen for a blinding instant that transports us into the deep space where Ripley drifts in the shuttle *Narcissus*, soon to be cut open with the light-swords of a salvage crew. The relation between the vagina and the lens of the eye is also presented in the title sequence of an otherwise unmentionable film, *Re-Animator*.

I believe the lumen represents what Luce Irigaray calls the "hidden vagina" of Western philosophy, a philosophy she labels "photology" to highlight its concern with the physics and metaphysics of light and vision.[5] There's a fascinating ambiguity about lumen images: we can never be entirely certain whether we are on the inside of a tunnel looking out, or on the outside about to enter a matrix of inner illumination (Descartes' *lumen naturale*).[6] The lumen thus elegantly expresses the double movement of SF's trajectory: the epistemophiliac quest to penetrate the secret body of nature, and the incorporation of the enlightened world as Jupiter Space.

Metaphors of the Light Age

High-tech propaganda's basic rhetorical ploy is to counter public fear about the deadly effects of high technologies by cultivating fascination with the exotic inventions of a corporate matrix whose rationality seems sacred and beyond terrestrial concerns. The slimy bad by-products are almost always defeated by their shiny good siblings, and the exterminist is glossed over by the extraterrestrial. The generic monsters I've mentioned here express different aspects of the logic of late capitalist enterprise: Jupiter Space is the hyperreal realm of corporate invention; the logospermatechnos the vehicle and product of high-tech dissemination; penis-dentatus and penis-breast figures of consumerism and commodity fetishism; the cannibaleye, the figure of discovery and incorporation. Is it possible to name a central construct that interrelates these figures with each other and with the everyday practices of modern industry? Can we identify any single term which mediates between the extraterrestrial and the exterminist? Undoubtedly not, but I'd like to conclude nevertheless by naming my favorite candidate for the role of high-tech fantasy's central metaphor. It would be light, which is not so much a "central metaphor" as a decentering metonymy in science-fiction culture. For light is a kind of radiation, that is, a propagation, a dissemination, a displacement. It implies transit—trekking—and speed, distance, spacing, as well as a notion of agency across space. Texts of the "Light Age" are texts of travel, alienation, estrangement, and remote control.

It's no news that light and enlightenment are important figures in "western" cosmology. The Genesis God's first cosmogonic act was the creation of light. Ancient philosophers identified light with the power of reason, and we've inherited a complex of associations between light, metaphysics, celestial powers, and masculine rationality. To early scientists, light was a means of extracting knowledge across "objective" distances. In search of "universal" laws, that is, laws that worked on Earth as well as in Heaven, and with an ever-growing array of macro- and microscopes, Mother Nature's inquisitors feasted their eyes on her unveiled form and generated sciences for penetrating the object, scoping out its secrets, and scooping up its ratiocinated essence into grids that had already predicted and waited in rigorous preparation for it.

In our lifetimes, sciences of enlightenment are surpassed by a post-Einsteinian technics of irradiation within which "bringing to light" no longer means illuminating the formerly hidden aspects of objects, but making them glow; turning them into light. Rendered transparent to the technological gaze, objects give up their objections as they are invested with light's qualities of penetrance, speed, mobility, radiance. Judging by the glow of animated artifacts in General Electric's recent advertising campaign, the slogan "We bring good things to life" could as easily be rendered "we bring things to light." Of course, GE doesn't mention the bad things it bring to light and life in its nuclear reactors. Some low-cal food and beer ads play with notions of "light" to mean radiant as well as massless and not affected by gravity. In what I find a disturbing aesthetic trend, objects are illuminated from below as well as within in a visual suggestion of a world that has been rendered a source of light itself: the world made radiant, a radioactive world, perhaps.

That revered Einsteinian equation,

$$E = mc^2$$

can be read as an economic expression of the science-fiction perspective, in which matter and energy are interconvertible in relation to
the astronomical, hyperreal figure of the speed of light squared—a
figure that inspires visions of accelerated displacement through
space, icons of extraterrestrialism, as well as movement through time
(futurism). Radiation's mobility itself is the center of a cosmology
now almost completely unhinged from terrestrial concerns, where
speed, distancing, and the collapse of time are valued in and of
themselves.

The grid of global technological imperialism depends not only
on devices that directly deploy radiation (fiber optics, TV and radio
broadcasts, light-etched microchips, and so on); it also requires
simulations of radiation's effects across distance: the spermatic and
increasingly "light" transport technologies, for example. Through
the transport and communications grids that allow instant access to
and remote control of far-off phenomena, the incorporating heads of
multinational technocracies can rationalize the world into resource
potentials and pretend to be "beings of pure energy," able to manifest in any form on a world pictured as a spectacle for distant
consumption. But no matter how mobile their signifiers, high technologies offer no ultimate escape from the disastrous effects of actual
tools for interconverting matter and energy and bringing the extraterrestrial down to Earth: the nuclear reactors that generate glowing piles of almost immortal, extraterrestrial half-lives; the weapons
whose gigantic explosions and withering radiations could waste all
futures away.

There are few to whom SF aliens are truly alien—the natives are
too close to name them as selves, while we others know only too well
who the aliens are and where they come from. We do better to speak
of "alienations" or "alien nations" than of "aliens" as such. Science-
fiction films elaborate and literalize the guiding metaphors of Euro-
masculine science and Americanized technocracy in visual poems
that spell out the perverse, irrational—dare we say "down under"—
purposes served by tools we've been taught to accept as practical,
rational, and pure. My hope is that naming these metaphors from an
earthling's perspective can resensitize us to the everyday monstrosi-

tites of life on the grid, embarrass the corporate cannibals, inspire resistance to rule by their antiterrestrial tools, and help restore a sense of alternative futures in opposition to the monolithic futurelessness whose icons promise us a tomorrow identical to an already estranged today.

Part Three
Soundings: Man as the Alien

12

H. G. Wells' Familiar Aliens

John R. Reed

When H. G. Wells was beginning his literary career, a number of intriguing books describing the human capacity to maintain the opposing traits of good and evil in the same self were commanding popular attention. The best remembered of these are Robert Louis Stevenson's *The Strange Case of Dr. Jekyll and Mr. Hyde* (1886), Oscar Wilde's *The Picture of Dorian Gray* (1890), and Bram Stoker's *Dracula* (1896). These narratives offered a dramatic picture of human nature as a multiple structure composed of antagonistic elements. As Stevenson put it, "a polity of multifarious, incongruous and independent denizens." Stevenson's and Wilde's fables suggested that a man might detach one evil element of his nature from the others, Stoker's that a malign external power might invade one's self, subverting the will and releasing the evil impulses hidden there.

These stories are in a tradition of English fiction that presents man himself as a creature alien to his kind. Wells understood this tradition and experimented with it. He considered Stevenson's tale a "masterpiece" and imitated it in *The Invisible Man* (1897). Wells' main character, Griffin, whose very name suggests his oddly composite and mythical nature, is not strictly alien to his species, although his unique trait of invisibility places him at odds with his kind. Or so it first appears. In fact, it is not Griffin's invisibility but his lawlessness that makes him a threatening presence to his fellow men. Like Jekyll, Griffin has voluntarily released the greed and desire for power in himself only to discover that, once unconfined, these impulses become monstrous.

The Invisible Man was an ingenious variation on a conventional theme, but Wells' genuinely original contribution to the literature of aliens was his up-to-date demonstration that what is frightening within us may not only escape to terrorize others, but it may project itself into alien forms that will return to molest us individually and torment us as a race.

Not too many years ago, when many Americans were certain that aliens were looking us over from their UFOs, Carl Jung published a book in which he explained that these UFOs were easily understandable projections of the human mind. He could have been borrowing a page from Wells, as Wells surely did from him. Like many informed people of his day, Wells believed that man's apelike nature retained a vestigial but potent function in his makeup. From childhood, he feared images of apes and tigers and projected his fears of strange beings into dark places of his bedroom. As he matured, he came to associate certain animal qualities with beauty and pleasure. His nickname for his lover Rebecca West was "panther" and for himself "jaguar." Nonetheless, as many of his books and stories indicate, he continued to think of man's nature as wickedly animal and humanly good.

The Island of Dr. Moreau (1896) teaches the important moral lesson that man is already alienated from other creatures and possibly from himself as well. Moreau sets about transforming animals into humanoids to prove that there is no law of speciation and that life is entirely mutable. His coordinate assumption is that man may control that mutability through the exercise of his will. In his idealism, Moreau seeks to erase the boundary between man and beast and raise these creatures up from their inferior position. But Moreau overlooks the tainted nature of the human spirit and of his own motives. Humans like Montgomery and the captain of the *Epicacuanha* are already more than half animal and moving in a downward progression. Only the force of Moreau's personality keeps the animals in check; once he is dead, they quickly begin to revert. Prendick is able to maintain authority over them principally through fear and duplicity. Humans, he says, have one strength lacking in animals: they can lie. Before his death, Moreau glimpses the truth that no being is alien to another in the governed world of nature. All life is germane to all other life. Man himself is the only alienating power in the universe because he can *conceive* himself as separate from the *bios*. So immense is the alienating power of his intellect that, through the application of his will, man can force alienation upon other species. When Prendick returns to civilization, he considers his fellow men to be as alien as the animals of Moreau's island. The only kinship he feels is with the inanimate order of the stars.

In *The Time Machine* (1895), Wells projected man's self-alienating power into a new dimension—that of time. Unlike earlier utopias in which men found themselves in an unlike world peopled by recognizably humanlike beings, Wells created a future in which two principal qualities in man have diverged and mutated. The Time Traveller ultimately perceives the Morlocks and Eloi as degenerative forms of the human species. The one type has become Hyde-like, animal, impulsive; the other pretty, but innocuous and ineffective. Using the new concept of change along a time-space continuum, Wells here substituted for Stevenson's abrupt molecular phenomenon one of extension. What happens catastrophically in an instant to Jekyll takes place gradually to mankind as a whole in Wells' story. Jekyll had only to cross the molecular boundaries of his own substance to become his alien self. But because Wells' Time Traveller has learned to traverse the barrier of the fourth dimension, he encounters the alien self of his entire species. In both cases, man is revealed as a tangle of infinite potentiality. Jekyll releases a random sample, presumably that fragment most eager to escape the polity of the self. In a similar way, Wells explored two routes of man's infinite potential by allowing them to achieve release over time.

The War of the Worlds (1898) seems to treat the relationship of man to an alien power in ordinary spatial terms. It seems to be a commonplace example of invasion literature, except that the invaders' homeland is Mars, not Berlin. In fact, the Martians are another temporal extension of human traits. It is as though Wells took the time scheme of *The Time Machine* and moved it along a slide rule to align human time with that of the Time Traveller and his friends and Martian time with that of the Morlocks and Eloi. As his short essay "The Man of the Year Million" indicates, the Martians are simply humans evolved to a new form. Like the Morlocks, they are bloodthirsty; like the Eloi, they have diminished their sexual urgings. The Martians have united power of will and force of intellect in the service of extreme aggression. They are mechanized vampires. In them, man again confronts an alien version of his own nature simplified to blood and brain. It lacks the valuable human trait of compassion.

The Selenites who inhabit the moon in *The First Men in the*

Moon (1901) are also projections into the future of man's own tendency toward reductive specialization. The description of members of this society is chiefly satire of existing human types—the artist, the intellectual, the educator, the worker, the ornamental lady, and so forth. Thus, while the novel appears to render the collision of human and alien species, it is actually very much like *The Time Machine* and *The War of the Worlds*.

These three novels exploit the evolutionary notion that the human species, being entirely mutable, could, over a sufficient length of time, become something so unrecognizable that it would be perceivable as an alien type. *Food of the Gods* (1904) speeds up the process. In this novel, a race of giants develops in one generation through the application of a special food to a small group of human infants. Contrary to normal expectations, Wells presents the giants in a favorable light, despite their tendency to dismiss the congested world of the little people. The giants appear to be threatening alien creatures, but are really only mankind's future self brought suddenly into the present. They represent change, rapid change. Redwood, the father of a giant, is appalled that men might wish to destroy these creatures. "What good would it do, to kill the giant human when the gigantic in all the lower things had now inevitably come?" Later, young Redwood supports his father's view. He advises ordinary humans to eat the special food and to accept giantness. "For greatness is abroad, not only in us, not only in the Food, but in the purpose of all things! It is in the nature of all things, it is part of space and time. To grow and still to grow, from first to last that is Being, that is the law of life. What other law can there be?"

The Food of the Gods presents an affirmative use of the alien motif. The giants are alien, but, unlike the Morlocks, Martians, or Selenites, they are manifestly better than the ordinary run of humans and certainly more suited to the world ahead. *The Food of the Gods* was not Wells' first positive treatment of an alien. *The Wonderful Visit* (1895) was a playful satire on man's inability to accept his own angelic attributes. I shall return to this novel briefly later. *The Food of the Gods* is significant because it foreshadows a sequence of books that carefully examine the division in human nature that leads it to oppose itself to the physical laws of nature. Following Huxley's views, most clearly stated in "Evolution and Ethics," Wells believed that mankind was inevitably at war with the natural law because he had created a world of values constantly threatened by the indifferent forces of evolution. More forthrightly than Huxley, Wells declared his faith in free will. Unlike Huxley, he believed that man could achieve victory over nature by acknowledging his oneness with nature. Nature was man's enemy only so long as man misunderstood nature. Wells qualified his faith in free will from time to time, but in 1901 he spoke out boldly in *Anticipations*, his very well received speculations on the future:

> The men of the New Republic will hold and understand quite clearly the doctrine that in the real world of man's experience, there is Free Will. They will understand that constantly, as a very condition of his existence, man is exercising choice between alternatives, and that a conflict between motives that have different moral values constantly arises. That conflict between Predestination and Free Will, which is so puzzling to untrained minds, will not exist for them. They will know that in the real world of sensory experience, will is free, just as new sprung grass is green, wood hard, ice cold, and toothache painful.

Soon after, in *Mankind in the Making* (1903), Wells wrote that man's fundamental nature is to oppose and conquer the forces that dominate him. When he needs a model for man's creative effort at self-creation, he finds it in art. The New Republican, Wells says, will shape the new world like an artist.

If Wells' early science fiction demonstrated that the true alien in the universe was man dividing himself from himself and the rest of being, the fiction after *Anticipations* adjusted the crystal to examine the same problem in a more positive light. If man's intelligence and will separated him from the rest of life, they were also his means of reconciling himself with being. The most obvious statement of this purpose is *A Modern Utopia* (1905), in which the Voice who narrates the story travels into a new world with his unruly alter ego to seek his utopian self, a self purged of the egoism that tainted the research efforts of Moreau, Griffin, and Cavor. The narrating Voice says that Utopia will come into being when individual men put their wills in the service of mankind, when selfishness gives way to racial purpose. Unfortunately, the earthly botanist who accompanies the narrator destroys this dream with his hankering nostalgia and sluggish skepticism.

As we all know, Wells abandoned science fiction almost entirely in the middle years of his career, concentrating instead on realistic fiction with a strong social purpose. But gradually he returned to science fiction because it provided him with a conveniently parabolic form in which to present his solidifying political, social, and economic views. In *Men Like Gods* (1923), Wells revived the notion of an alien being of greater beauty and wisdom than man, first presented comically in *The Wonderful Visit*. In that early novel, an angel falls from his dream world into the world of the Reverend Mr. Crump. In their initial conversations, the vicar learns from the angel that their two worlds lie "as near as page to page of a book." Wells used the same image in *Men Like Gods*. The vicar concludes that this arrangement supposes a fourth dimension, in which case, "there may be any number of three dimensional universes packed side by side, and all dimly dreaming of one another. There may be world upon world, universe upon universe. It's perfectly possible. There's nothing so incredible as the absolutely possible."

If the angel breaks through the barrier from Heaven to Earth in *The Wonderful Visit*, Mr. Barnstaple accidentally crashes through the other way in *Men Like Gods* and finds himself in a genuine utopia that is an alternative world to his own, a world in which he and other earthlings constitute a vestigial form of vermin. By contrast, the utopians, who recognize that men are fundamentally animal in nature, have learned to adjust to the laws of the universe. They are not yet gods, but they are surely halfway there from the starting point of mankind. They are reminders that benevolent superior beings may easily appear as "aliens" to a benighted and inferior species. Arthur C. Clarke plays a sophisticated little game with this notion in *Childhood's End* (1953), where the powers ruling mankind have the trappings of traditional evil, but only because mankind's traditions are compromised by its limited and vicious imagination.

In *The Dream* (1924), which appeared a year after *Men Like Gods*, Wells reversed his pattern, sending a utopian back into the confused and diseased past, where he lives out the alien and savage life of men as Wells' contemporaries knew it. In the next year, Wells poked fun at his own scheme in a novel entitled *Christina Alberta's Father* (1925), in which the admirable but befuddled Albert Edward Preemby believes himself to be inhabited by the spirit of Sargon, who once ruled the world and whose mission is now to restore order to the disorderly human warren. Preemby is considered mad, just like the angel in *The Wonderful Visit*, and perhaps in the world of the 1920s he is. But that is simply to say that a man who desires to discipline his species to a life of beauty and order has, by his very dream, made himself an alien to that species.

Although much of his time in the thirties and forties was devoted to journalism, Wells continued to produce fiction at a steady rate, but, except for a brief spate of fables in 1936 and 1937, he abandoned the kind of science fiction that encouraged the theme we are examining. *The Croquet Player* (1936) simply states a premise and works it out in a half-comic fashion: the world we view as civilized and progressing is a delusion, behind which lurks the reality of a marsh haunted by cavemen. Today's world, says Dr. Norbert, the novel's *raisonneur*, is witnessing a resurgence of man's animal self against his civilized but superficial self. Intellectual men are going mad in a losing fight against the caveman in us. In an echo of *Food of the Gods*, he warns that men must become giants to meet the situation.

If *The Croquet Player* is a more or less direct assertion of a conventional dualistic view of human nature, hinting that man's fear of aliens is actually a fear of his own animal impulses, *The Camford Visitation* (1937) is a playful examination of division within the human mind. Trumber, who teaches English literature at Holy Innocents College, Camford, is troubled by a disembodied voice that chides him about his useless efforts in literary criticism. When he confides his experience to the vicar of St. Hippolytus, the latter explains that the voice is "the projection of a long-standing conflict in your subconscious between the aesthetic pretentions of your criticism and your suppressed sense of its lack of spiritual values." Trumber replies irritably that the voice is not an embodiment of self-criticism. "It was something from outside bent on destroying my self-confidence. An attack." The vicar remains unconvinced and later uses Trumber's experience in a book entitled *Extra-Terrestrial Disturbances of Human Mentality*, in which he develops "the idea of an upthrust of the subconscious through some sort of space-time dislocation."

The voice addresses other academics besides Trumber, always with the same critical belligerence, and the narrator concludes that even through the confused views of those who report the manifestations of the voice, its true nature may be discerned. "His appeal to the mind of the world in general and to Camford in particular, was to get up and go on. And keep going on. He was progress articulate. He was the spirit of the provisional. His message was an intellectual drive without a glimmer of surcease."

Clearly, the voice is benign. Its purpose is to help mankind save itself, but in the benighted atmosphere of English higher education, Wells suggests, such salubrious advice sounds dangerous, alien, even evil. *The Croquet Player* shows how, to an intelligent man, the human propensity toward animalism is a dangerous quality, appearing as an alien reality, but in *The Camford Visitation* the opposite happens. The voice is an invasion that offers salvation, but because it disturbs an intellectually futile but placid existence, it seems as threatening and strange as the caveman does in *The Croquet Player*. Wells needed a third leg to this fabular pattern to set it firmly in a positive context.

Star-Begotten (1937) is a parody of the Christian Nativity. Joseph Davis, a popular historian, has been brought up to appreciate the status quo, although his expectant wife, Mary, has a more adventurous spirit. Hearing a discussion of the effect of cosmic rays on human mutation, Davis elaborates the notion into a full-fledged theory that Martians are sending cosmic rays to Earth to change human chromosomes, a theory he transmits to his wife's gynecologist and others. At first, Davis fears that the Martians are antagonistic, but after the easy birth of his child, he becomes more positive, convinced that more and more superior types are appearing in human births. When the newspaper magnate Lord Thunderclap gets wind of Davis' Martian theory, he becomes concerned about a Martian "invasion" and wants to capitalize on it as a news item, but he soon loses interest, a sign that the fear of extraterrestrial aliens is no longer automatic.

Professor Keppel, to whom Davis reports his evidence of a new race of supermen, does not endorse Davis' view but admits that, in its current condition, the world desperately needs a new form of education and a new race that would be mainly sane and willing to assassinate for the appropriate purpose. Such a new race would bring peace and make the world a garden; it would not overlook aesthetic things and would be intelligent about sex. It would be interested in research. The image of the supposedly alien invader rapidly assumes the form of man's savior. If common humanity is corrupted by its animal nature and its sluggish intelligence, the Martian "invasion" is certainly alien to it. But from Wells' point of view, it is rather man who is the alien in his universe. At the end of *Star-Begotten*, Davis destroys the optimistic survey of human history that he has been writing and confides to his wife how his mind has been divided and his spirit troubled. He says the future must lie with his son, who, he believes, is one of the beneficiaries of Martian interference. Mary suggests that Joseph himself is one of the star-begotten, and he suspects that she is too.

Davis' intellectual uneasiness is not recent; throughout his life he has had moments when he doubted received opinion and even the solidity of the universe. The Martian theory provides an explanation because, as Keppel points out, the star-begotten would be half-breeds, "so that one side of them is just the old system of self-regarding complexes, vanities, dear delusions—while the other side is like a crystal growing in mud. . . . [thus] doubt would be an almost inevitable characteristic of them all." But if the star-begotten have some degree of inner division, they also have an inner conviction of a broader unity in the cosmos. Davis believes that he catches a glimpse of this capacity in a young boy he hears of at a public school. The headmaster of Gorpel School tells Davis of a boy who asked about the word *spiritual* and was offered the standard spiritual material paradigm, in which spirit is said to ascend and matter to gravitate. But the boy cannot see this primary opposition. "Life," he says, "seems to me just one, Sir. I can't think of it in any other way." Man, having alienated himself from the universe, cannot see its unity. The Martians presumably can.

Star-Begotten is Wells' last science-fiction fable of alienation. But it represents a view that remained central to his philosophy. Man's error is to see existence as divided into spirit and matter—qualities essentially alien and opposed to each other. This dualistic view arises from an inner division, the contending of man's intellect and will against inherited instincts that incline toward sensuous indulgence and egoism.

Early in his career, Wells recognized the alienating force in man himself. He dealt with this theme openly in novels and fables such as *The Bulpington of Bulp* and *The Brothers*, in which imagined or real alter egos become opposing forces. Science fiction allowed him to develop the theme of projected alienation more freely. In his autobiography, Wells borrowed Jung's concept of the *persona* to describe the constructed self that men believe in as a means of dealing with experience. He acknowledged that this *persona* was an illusion, but argued that men might come to resemble the *persona* they create. Yeats, approaching the subject at about the same time from a different point of view, also felt that man, and especially the poet, created his identity by evoking its opposite. All three men believed that there was an *anima mundi*, mind of the race or world brain, that was the fountain and reservoir of human identity, a reservoir fed by the forces of the natural world.

Wells dreamed of a humanity that was entirely sincere and honest, that had tamed the natural world to reason, and that lived fruitfully in it. Time and again he used the images of lovely nakedness opposed to shabby clothing, or garden as opposed to wasteland, or dream as opposed to nightmare to emphasize this ideal. Lying and self-deception were, for him, among the cardinal sins. One of man's greatest lies was that he was not an intimate part of the universe in which he lived, but somehow superior to it. It was this pride, Wells believed, that prompted men to imagine an environment populated with hostile forces. Wells knew that the only alienating power in the universe was the human mind consciously resisting its kinship to all other matter.

In his early science fiction, Wells conceived of narratives in which negative human attributes are projected into alien beings. Ordinarily, these aliens are temporally telescoped versions of mankind's possible futures. The later science fiction seems to represent a conscious attempt to revise that strategy by projecting man's promising future into alien creatures. There are exceptions to this rule—the benevolent giants of *The Food of the Gods* and the revenant beast in *The Croquet Player*—but, generally, I believe the scheme holds. Mr. Barnstaple travels through time not in a time machine but through what we would now call a time warp and comes to a utopia where the Morlock and Eloi qualities have both been purged from a humanity that has cultivated the best of its physical and intellectual powers. Wells slyly alludes to his own *Invisible Man*, when the characters in *The Camford Visitation* try to explain the bodiless voice. At the same time, we should not forget that our guide in *A Modern Utopia* refers to himself simply as "The Voice." And *Star-Begotten* is an openly playful reversal of an earlier Wells fiction. In the scientific discussion that generates Joseph Davis' Martian theory, one fellow suggests that cosmic rays come from Mars. "Some of you may have read a book called *The War of the Worlds*—I forget who wrote it—Jules Verne, Conan Doyle, one of those fellows. But it told how the Martians invaded the world, wanted to colonize it, and exterminate mankind. Hopeless attempt!" The speaker goes on to improve on Wells' early fable by suggesting the subtler form of invasion and control developed in the rest of the novel.

If, in his later years, Wells tried to reverse the essentially negative version of his anatomy of human alienation, by the time he came to write *Mind at the End of Its Tether* (1945), a sick and weary old man, he succumbed to the very temptation he had so long challenged in his fellow men. Here is his valedictory summary of the human condition.

> Our universe is the utmost compass of our minds. It is a closed system that returns into itself. It is a closed space-time continuum which ends with the same urge to exist with which it began, now that the unknown power that evoked it has at last turned against it. "Power," the writer has written, because it is difficult to express this unknowable that has, so to speak, set its face against us. But we cannot deny this menace of the darkness.
>
> "Power" is unsatisfactory. We need to express something entirely outside our "universe," and "Power" suggests something *within* that universe and fighting against us. The present writer has experimented with a number of words and phrases and rejected each in turn. "x" is attractive until one reflects that this implies an equation capable of solution in terms of finite being. "Cosmic process," "the Beyond," "the Unknown," "the Unknowable," all carry unsound implications. "The Antagonism" by itself overstresses the idea of positive enmity. But if we fall back on the structure of the Greek tragic drama and think of life as the Protagonist, trailing with it the presence of an indifferent chorus and the possiblity of fluctuations in its role, we get something to meet our need. "The Antagonist," then, in that qualified sense, is the term the present writer will employ to express the unknown implacable which has endured life for so long bɔ our reckoning and has now turned against it so implacably to wipe it out.

Man, then, *is* alien. He has sought to conquer the irresistible force of nature and failed. Like a confident young man, he has seen the universe as his antagonist and struggled against it. Now, as an old man, he gives in, accepting the inevitable pattern. In the greatest of all ironies, however, this final gloomy vision may be read as yet one more example of man's projection of fear into the world beyond himself. Wells, the man, was dying. He was following the law that made him one with all being. But he did not go gentle into that good night. To him, the grim reaper raised his scythe not to mow down H. G. Wells, but, in his anonymous otherness from beyond the precincts of the universe, to strike down all life. What good, one might ask, is a will that is free if there is no radical unlikeness against which it may be tested? At the end, in the inescapable face of suffering and death, Wells, too, wanted to believe that this was not simply the meaningless way things were but that something alien, unlike, and active made it so. As religions and philosophies have revealed throughout history, man defines himself not only by what he is, but by what he is not. What he is, he thinks he knows; what the other is, he can only imagine.

13

Inspiration and Possession: Ambivalent Intimacy with the Alien

Clayton Koelb

Among all conceivable encounters with the alien, the discovery within one's self of some force or presence foreign to that self is potentially the most disturbing and therefore also the most dramatic. Literature and film have known and exploited this fact for years and have known how to make the most out of the revelation that some hated but powerful other, some literal or metaphorical fiend out of hell, has set up his household in our homes or, most horrible of all, within our very minds. The notion of possession, of the mind taken over by a superior alien power, is probably one of the oldest concepts of human culture, already old at the time of our tradition's oldest writings. It is clear that in many cultures, including the classical culture of our own tradition, possession by spirits was considered to be part of the ordinary functioning of the world, unusual perhaps, but not so unusual as to be thought unnatural. In a well-known incident reported in Mark 5, Jesus comes upon a man "possessed by an unclean spirit."

> Jesus asked him, "What is your name?" "My name is Legion," he said, "there are so many of us." And he begged hard that Jesus would not send them out of the country.
>
> Now there happened to be a large herd of pigs feeding on the hill-side, and the spirits begged him, "Send us among the pigs and let us go into them." He gave them leave; and the unclean spirits came out and went into the pigs; and the herd, of about two thousand, rushed over the edge into the lake and drowned.[1]

I quote this passage both because of its testimony to the antiquity of our interest in possession, not to mention its canonical status, but also because of the peculiar and telling form of its rhetoric. The "spirits" of the story are called, in the *koine* Greek of the New Testament, in the first instance *pneuma akatharon* and later *daimones*. Both *pneuma* and *daimon* were relatively common words and could be used either in a positive or negative sense in classical times. When Jesus first speaks to the possessed individual, it is unclear whether he is speaking with the man himself or with the spirits possessing him. It is also unclear who answers: the text just says *legei* ("he" or "it" "says"); but the nature of the reply suggests that it is the spirit who answers, giving as his name a Hellenistic borrowing, *Legeon*, of the Latin word *Legio*, the name of the alien military unit that possessed the homeland of the Jews. The name "Legion" is thus as much a political metaphor of alien possession as it is an indication of plurality. And the form of discourse itself, where we cannot determine the difference between the man and the spirit or spirits controlling him, serves as a figure for the completeness of the possession. The occupation of the conquered territory is so thorough that one cannot speak to the conquered without also speaking to the conqueror, and vice versa. When Jesus "gives leave" for Legion to depart from the man, the spirits find their fitting homes in that most unclean of animals in Jewish tradition, the pig, which is as much as to say that the occupying forces of the Romans were by natural inclination no better than swine. But these "swine" were in total control of the man, not to mention the land of Palestine, inhabiting the most intimate places of mind and body. The horror of the situation is palpable.

But alien possession was not always horrible in the estimation of our ancestors. Just as one could be taken over by an unclean spirit, so one could be overcome by a holy spirit (*pneuma hagion*) as well. This happens, for example, to the apostles at Pentecost after the crucifixion, when, according to Acts 2, "they were all filled with the Holy Spirit and began to talk in other tongues, as the Spirit gave them power of utterance." This form of possession was, in the literal sense, "inspiration," an influx of spirit from outside, and it was an experience that was considered by no means undesirable. It became, in fact, so sought after among the early Christians that Paul felt the need to restrain the zeal of his brethren at Corinth, suggesting that ecstatic "speaking in tongues" was really not so beneficial to the church, the new body of Christ, as prophecy or other forms of worship. He pointed out that, wonderful as such inspired ecstasy might be, it did not help build up the church.

> So if the whole congregation is assembled and all are using the "strange tongues" of ecstasy, and some uninstructed persons or unbelievers should enter, will they not think you are mad? But if all are uttering prophecies, the visitor, when he enters, hears from everyone something that searches his conscience and brings conviction, and the secrets of his heart are laid bare. (1 Corinthians 14)

Paul, who confesses to being an ardent glossolalist himself, followed a longstanding precedent in suggesting the close resemblance between divine inspiration and madness. Plato, the purport of whose ideas must have reached the well-educated Saul of Tarsus, had in his *Phaedrus* presented Socrates as arguing that "the greatest blessings come by way of madness, indeed of a madness that is heaven sent" (244 a).[2] Socrates suggests that several great goods come in the form of a possession (*katakoche*) imposed upon the human mind by some external power: among these are love, philosophy, and, of greatest interest to us, poetry.

> There is a third form of possession or madness of which the Muses are the source. This seizes a tender, virgin soul and stimulates it to rapt passionate expression, especially in lyric poetry. . . . But if any man come to the gates of poetry without the madness of the Muses, then shall he and all his words of sanity with him be brought to nought by the poetry of madness, and behold, their place is nowhere to be found. (245 a)

In Plato's view, the "lunatic, the lover, and the poet are of imagination all compact" precisely because none of them is in his right mind, none has possession of his "reason" (*nous*) when each is behaving most characteristically. This same concept as applied to poetry is discussed by Socrates at greater length in the *Ion*, where he asserts that "the epic poets, all the good ones, have their excellence, not from art, but are inspired, possessed [*katechomenoi*], and thus they utter all these admirable poems" (533 e). Poets, then, are not the originators of anything but mearly "interpreters of the gods, each one possessed by the divinity to whom he is in bondage" (534 e). A poet in his right mind, according to such a view, is a contradiction in terms. The first thing the would-be poet must wish for is to be out of his right mind, to be possessed by the alien spirit of a divine muse.

A long, distinguished, and powerful cultural heritage thus posits both good and evil forms of alien possession and understands the state of inspiration as one of the most terrible or most wonderful experiences possible for human beings. Traditionally, the positive or negative value placed upon the experience depended entirely on the moral quality of the possessing spirit; and in cultural systems characterized by a widely accepted distinction between good and bad, the classification of spirits seemed quite straightforward. In Christian Europe, for instance, one simply had to determine whether the possessed individual was divinely or satanically inspired. These were, for all intents and purposes, the only real choices. Obviously, there were more than a few cases of disagreement, especially since the devil was understood to be a supremely crafty mimic of at least the superficial features of divinity, but the terms of such disagreement remained clear. A possessing spirit either came from God or from Satan, and that exhausted the logical possibilities.

The age of science fiction, however, is precisely that period in which the security of such a clear-cut moral dualism has been to a very great degree lost. Although reams of contemporary fantasy conjure up worlds in which good and evil are presented as clear polar opposites, easily distinguishable by both the characters and the reader, these stories tend to be essentially nostalgic idylls looking back on a value system that we honor but that is now, for whatever reason, irremediably lost to us. Such fiction is not necessarily lacking in either art or wisdom, but it is more a reaction to than a reflection of the modern ethical situation. On the whole, modern fiction, including science fiction, presents a world that is morally as well as technologically complex. This is true even when modern literature reworks, as it frequently does, narrative *topoi* of ancient lineage such as the theme of alien possession.

We could consider Thomas Mann's novel *Doktor Faustus* a paradigmatic example of the treatment of this theme by a twentieth-century writer. In this fictional biography of a German composer named Adrian Leverkühn, Mann refashions the ancient notion of artistic creativity as the result of possession by a muse. Leverkühn's muse, which he seeks out as assiduously as any classical poet, is not an invading spirit but an invading organism: the composer deliberately allows himself to be infected with a venereal disease by having sex with a prostitute he knows to be infected herself. This organism is, to Leverkühn's way of thinking at least, the agent of the devil, with whom he converses in a lengthy fantasy inserted into the very center of Mann's novel. He views the alien organisms in his blood as the source of his creative powers, as well as the source of tormenting headaches, and pictures them as little sea-maidens out of a fairy tale. The alien power possessing Leverkühn is diabolical in that it not only torments him physically but also prevents him from engaging in normal sexual activity, a situation he understands as a prohibition against love. While it effects what was hoped for, a brilliant musical career the equal of any since Beethoven's, the inspiriting disease eventually also makes Leverkühn insane. Mann thus makes of the venereal disease a striking if disquieting metaphor: an objectively "natural" process uniting lunatic, lover, and poet in a single possessed soul.

Mann's treatment of the age-old theme of inspiration is meant to be understood as an allegory not only of art in general but also of the moral complexity of the modern world. The force possessing him, diabolical as it is, is also enormously fruitful. A great deal of good comes of it, as indeed does a great deal of evil, but there is no simple way to separate the good side from the bad. Leverkühn, Mann's version of Dr. Faustus, cannot be neatly placed between a good angel and a bad one, like Marlowe's Faustus. Serenus Zeitblom, the fictional biographer Mann employs to narrate his novel, confesses the difficulty of distinguishing the pure from the impure in his subject. He admits to a

> too hasty entry into the distinction between pure and impure genius, a distinction the existence of which I recognize, only to ask myself at once whether it has a right to exist at all. Experience has forced me to ponder this problem so anxiously, so urgently, that at times, frightful to say, it has seemed to me that I should be driven beyond my proper and becoming level of thought, and myself experience an "impure" heightening of my natural gifts.

In the world inhabited by Zeitblom, Leverkühn, Mann, and indeed the rest of us, the very act of making the distinction between the pure and the impure is tainted with at least the possibility of impurity. The difference between the good angel and the bad angel may already be the work of the devil.

Contemporary science fiction reflects this characteristic uneasiness with the distinction between the pure and the impure, even and perhaps especially when it makes use of it in dramatizing intimate contact between humans and aliens. Frederik Pohl has developed an intriguing premise in his stories of alien possession involving what is essentially the rental of psychic space.[3] In the case of such "purchased people," the moral status of the possession is interestingly uncertain, since the aliens doing the purchasing and the humans being purchased have radically different perspectives. For the aliens, it is simply a commercial transaction undertaken for practical reasons and having no moral implications whatsoever, as far as the humans can tell. They do it in order to conduct business or do scientific research or by way of taking a vacation. For the purchased humans, however, the moral neutrality of the purchasing aliens can be as horrifying as the evil intentions of a demon, as becomes particularly clear at the conclusion of the story "We Purchased People." The criminals whose psyches have been bought discover that the aliens, having no detailed knowledge of human mores, are occasionally inclined to make the possessed bodies do things that we would not consider very nice. Worse than that, things that might be very nice indeed are not at all nice when done under compulsion and for the benefit of a possessing alien. The final scene of "We Purchased People" shows the hero and heroine, a pair of lovers who happen to be purchased people, at long last about to have the chance to have sex, but not in the way they have dreamed about. The aliens want to watch, and they possess the couple during the act of love, thereby transforming it from a moment of delight into a moment of horror.

Even science-fiction stories which look like ethically simple and clear-cut cases of black and white eventually turn to various, almost indistinguishable shades of gray. In John Varley's *Gaean Trilogy*, for instance, the heroine, Cirocco Jones, is found to have inside her brain a creature that "looked like a tiny snake but it had two arms which ended in miniscule clawed hands. Its body nestled into the longitudinal fissure, and it had a tail that descended between the hemispheres."[4] This demonic creature is actually a "fragment of Gaea"[5] implanted in Cirocco's brain, we assume, in order to let the goddesslike ruler of the wheel world know what her enemy is doing and planning.

As the reader discovers later, however, Gaea is doing more than simple spying by means of this physical cerebral invasion. Gaea actually wants Cirocco to be her successor as ruler of the wheel, and her demonic possession of Cirocco's brain is necessary in order to gather a "complete and continuous set of memories" that can be apotheosized, as it were, into a new goddess. Gaea's wish for her "enemy" Cirocco is that she become like Gaea herself, possessed of near-omnipotence and near-immortality. Cirocco sees this as a kind of diabolical seduction, to be sure, but it would be hard to characterize Gaea as outright malevolent. She offers what she and many others would consider an ultimate good to a person who does not and cannot want it, for whom it is therefore an ultimate evil. There is nothing inherently reprehensible about immortality or omnipotence, however, as the story makes clear. Cirocco's friend Gaby advances to take Gaea's place, and Cirocco hardly thinks of her as evil for doing so. "If somebody has to do it," she says to Gaby, "I can't think of anyone better than you."[6]

Varley's use of the theme of alien possession, for all its very modern ethical relativism, is basically simple and almost old-fashioned. Varley has put his own original little twist on it, however, in that this old-fashioned simplicity is discovered not to be the author's; it is instead the artistry of Gaea herself, a lover of second-rate horror movies, who takes the trouble to manufacture an actual slimy little demon to live in Cirocco's brain when she could have used any number of more subtle modes of psychic invasion. But even taking into account Varley's rather successful narrative device, this is not one of the richer and more complex treatments of alien possession in recent science fiction. A more intriguing development of the theme can be found in A. A. Attanasio's *Radix*,[7] in which the story's hero spends a substantial portion of the narrative possessed by an alien creature called a *voor*. This alien is remarkable, though, because he is not only quite thoroughly alien—he is also the hero's son.

Attanasio's voors are in one sense classical science-fiction aliens: they are natives of a distant planet who have invaded Earth and powerfully altered the human world. They came, we are told, from a planet called Unchala, which happened to be "positioned within the directional beam of Linergy from an open collapsar." The energy from the collapsar so affects their evolution that they finally lose their original forms and their planet-bound existence and use the stream of energy from the singularity, called the Line, to migrate from planet to planet. But the migrating voor does not reemerge on the new planet in his original shape; rather, he "spontaneously and creatively usurps the physical forms of species of whatever life-world the Line reaches" in order to take up residence there.[8] The voors living on Earth in the future projected by *Radix* are thus classical, body-snatching-style aliens, except that they have arrived a long time prior to the time of the story and thus no longer need to snatch bodies. They look like human beings and reproduce in the standard human manner. They can even mate with ordinary people, and such a mating between a voor called Jeanlu and the human hero Sumner produces the child Corby, a particularly powerful and historically important voor. It is this voor, a creature who is at once both a terrifying alien and the hero's ordinary human child, who takes possession of Sumner, his father, in order to end the ages-old persecution of voors by the forces ruling the planet Earth. This is a kind of second-order possession, referred to in the novel as "lusk," wherein the possessing voor shares the mind of his host without destroying it. It is evidently a different process from the one by which the voors originally "usurped" the physical forms of human beings.

Attanasio's description of the initiating moment of this posses-sion of father by son displays all of the horror of traditional accounts of demonic possession and nothing of the intimacy of parent and child.

> He thrashed in the sand, both hands to his face, a terrible pain stabbing his flesh. . . . Liquid fire seared his face and the hollows of his head, ripping maniacal howls from his lungs.
>
> Spastically he churned in the sand, trying to get to his feet, but his muscles were quaking with the poison that was burning through his body. Helpless, beyond thought, Sumner blanked his mind and let the agony consume him. His body strained and heaved, twisting him deeper into the sand with ogreish convulsions. He writhed for hours, gulfed in pain, before the spasms slackened and he realized he wasn't going to die.[9]

But this is not the end of it, for after the physical pain comes the psychological shock, the realization that there is a foreign power inside Sumner's mind. He keeps hearing a noise in his head, a "dim, unintelligible chanting" that "ricocheted across the back of his skull, dull and wrung out, just audible above the anguish ballooning through his lungs."[10]

What begins as a nightmare of horror, however, ends very differently. Compare the description of the circumstances under which the voor Corby terminates his possession of Sumner:

> Corby disappeared, moving beyond reality into the multiverse where infinity is annihilated and created continuously, radiating an under-music of coincidence and accident into each of the parallel universes of eternity. Into that floating trillionth-of-a-second reality, Corby vanished.
>
> Sumner crested with the voor, his awareness swept along by the lusk. And for an instant, he two was One Mind—an awareness and a longing older than the universe—[11]

Instead of the dreadful and painful possession by an unclean spirit, as the experience seemed when it began, now Sumner experiences the uplifting inspiration of a religious vision. Instead of "unintelligible chanting," he now hears "layered voices" in a "choral" form, "all of them filling the choirs of space that were his life."[12] This "lusk," this experience of intimacy with the alien, has the characteristics of both the terrifying possession described in Mark 5 and the glorious inspiration sought after by the early Christians at Corinth. The voor, whose name could perfectly well be Legion, since he brings with him the chorus of layered minds within Sumner's mind, is both demonic and divine. This, perhaps more than any other feature Attanasio gives to the voors, helps to make them seem alien. They are not just beyond good and evil, nor are they some kind of mixture of good and evil; they are at once *both* holy and unholy, perfectly horrible and perfectly wonderful, and the effect is satisfyingly unsettling. It also helps to give a certain grit and bite to Attanasio's project, which could easily have evolved into flower-child psychedelic mysticism. If Sumner's experience had begun the way it ends, with the vision of the great "One Mind," I and others like me would probably have closed the book and read no farther. By the time Sumner has his vision, however, he has already been through hell—or, since we are dealing with possession, we should properly say that hell has been through him. The reader is ready to allow him his moment of transfiguring vision, even if it does sound just a bit like something John and Ringo brought back from India.

A recent novel that deals with possession in a sophisticated and witty way is James Morrow's *The Continent of Lies*.[13] Those familiar with Morrow's book might be surprised at my choice, since the story announces itself as being about dreams, not about possession. Morrow is dealing with a special sort of dreams, however, and with a tradition which understands dreams as a form of psychic invasion by foreign powers rather than as the "dream-work" of the dreamer. Ancient myths, of course, propose the view that dreams represent the temporary possession of the sleeping soul by spirits wishing to communicate with the sleeper. Morrow turns this notion into pharmacological technology: dream-artists, the future equivalents of poets and film-makers, are able to record their fantasies chemically and have them reproduced biologically by specially developed trees. The fruits of these trees, called cephapples or dreambeans, are gathered, distributed, and sold like videotapes. You pay your money, you get your dream. Quinjin, the hero of Morrow's story, is in fact a critic, a reviewer of art-dreams, and the author of a number of books on the subject of dreambeans. It is purest coincidence, I feel sure, that he is a character in a volume that announces itself as a "Baen Book."

The crux of the plot is that someone has created a dreambean called *The Lier-in-Wait*, a dream both so insidious and so vividly real that it can completely take over the dreamer's mind. Quinjin eats this dreambean, but because he is an experienced critic (or because he is lucky), he emerges from the experience relatively undamaged. Unfortunately, however, his relatively callow teenage daughter Lilit also eats it and is fully taken possession by it. "The Tree of Death," says Quinjin, "possessed my daughter as surely as if one of its tentacles were wrapped around her neck."[14] The hero's task, then, is to find a way both to destroy the tree whose fruit is *The Lier-in-Wait* and to free his daughter's mind from the story that possesses her.

The notion of the dreambean in general and of *The Lier-in-Wait* in particular is the logical extension of the classical imagery of inspiration that has attended discussion of literature from before the time of Plato. In the *Ion*, for example, Socrates argues that a good poem ought to take hold of the audience just as it took hold of the poet when he conceived it. The power of the muse first possesses the mind of the poet, who then, like an iron ring touched by a magnet, is able to inspire others in turn (*Ion* 533 d–e). Dreambeans work just this way. In normal operation, the inspiration is only temporary, and when the dream is over, the dreamer returns to the possession of his own mind. *The Lier-in-Wait*, however, has a kind of power that prevents the dreaming mind from returning to full self-control. The inspiration does not pass away, but rather remains the controlling force in the dreamer's life.

It is easy to see that *The Lier-in-Wait* is the demonic version of the power every literary artist would like to have. It is a glorious fantasy gone awry. What writer would not want to have the reviewers say of his novel, "This story takes hold of the reader and never lets go"? Morrow must have had that very fantasy and then had second thoughts. What would it really be like if one were possessed by a story that would not let go? Would this be an experience audiences would long for, like Paul's brethren at Corinth, or would they instead shun it as something as horrible as being possessed by a demon named Legion? Morrow's interpretation of his own fantasy is instructive: the novel ends with legislation outlawing dreambeans—legislation that is passed thanks in part to supportive testimony from the critic Quinjin. Any power strong enough to take absolute possession of our minds is potentially absolutely evil, even if that power is art. The saving grace of the traditional arts of painting, sculpture, films, and literature is that they can never quite attain that level of inspiration. We are, of course, all of us aliens to each other; and Morrow seems to be suggesting that the psychic health of the species requires that none of us aliens ever be able to truly possess and inspire the minds of others.[15]

14
Cybernauts in Cyberspace:
William Gibson's *Neuromancer*
David Porush

The human being acts as the ideal decoder.
                                        —Claude E. Shannon[1]

The mechanism-vitalism duality has been banished to the limbo of badly posed questions.
                                        —Norbert Wiener[2]

One of Descartes' students asked the master how he would know when an automaton had become a true man.

"When he tells me so himself," Descartes replied.

Both Descartes and his student assumed, however, that when a truly intelligent artificial intelligence is born, it would be indistinguishable from us. This rivalry has fueled centuries of speculation and fears about the ever-narrowing gap between man and machine. Yet some recent fiction offers a new view of the rivalry: when the automaton achieves selfhood, there will be no question of it being a true man, for it will be so totally unlike us as to have achieved alienness, not humanity.

This essay addresses two intertwined ideas. Both take William Gibson's superior novel, *Neuromancer* (1984),[3] as a point of departure, since Gibson illustrates these ideas in great detail and with remarkable subtlety. The first is the theme of the artificial-intelligence alien and his relationship—as nemesis, twin, foil, and soul child—to humans who are themselves busy learning to live as cybernauts. The second is the question of the positive feedback loop between our technologies and science fiction like Gibson's, and the impulses that I believe lie behind them. In fact, I believe that there is one single impulse which lies behind both speculative fiction and our

168

more exploratory technologies, a unity which *Neuromancer* reveals. At bottom, both of these ideas beg the same question: how are we learning to preserve our humanity in the face of cybernetic encroachment? How will we preserve all the old human impedimenta[4]—our heroism, fidelity, passion, defiance, lust?

The Science-Fiction Century

The ambiguous relation between robot and human creates one of science fiction's strong branches. It is as old as the story of Hephaestos' mechanical man, Talus, as universally recognizable as Mary Shelley's monster, as contemporary as *Blade Runner*, *The Terminator*, or any other of a hundred stories and films accessible today. But a curious feature of the more recent imaginings of the man-made man is that as the reality grows nearer and nearer, we seem increasingly to doubt our own status. In fact, it seems that as our culture and technology rapidly efface that line between human and cybernaut, the values we attach to them become inverted.[5] A new fable of the human as alien—the stranger—arises. Here machine as man as alien stalks the territory. If he is employed properly, he shows himself to be more human than humans. He has alienation and grievance and vulnerability all on his side, stepped up by special talents: indestructibility, omniscience, supersensitivity, and a fresh view of the world. He has a different emotional complement, which can turn violent because he also has direct knowledge of his creators, his programmers, his designers, call them what you will—us humans.[6] On the other hand, there is always the more ominous interpretation available to this theme of the cyborg or android or bionic being or robot or automaton or artificial intelligence: some of us become so converted to the machinery we've devised that we lose our humanity.[7]

This theme, which I have elsewhere called the theme of the "soft machine,"[8] is fueled by contemporary technologies. We commonly take for granted that technology is a methodical corporate venture devoted to profit. But it is much more fruitful, and in the end more accurate, to see it as a great, collective expression of our myth making. Look from a distance now—through the wrong end of the telescope if you will—at our complementary technologies of computers, cybernetics, genetic engineering, biomechanics, psychophysiology, and behavioral engineering. What do you see but a very complete, partly idealistic expression of science-fiction prophesy incarnated now in metal, silicon, plastic, differentiated protein, and b-mod programs? One of the great enterprises of our technological culture is the reproduction of ourselves, any way and every way we can, whether by cloning, programming, designing, more sophisticated hardware models of our expertise, or boiling our behavior down to those few, fundamental, hard-wired, electrochemically driven laws that unified field theory, which we believe might model our souls.[9]

And in this mutual embrace of hard technologies and hard science fiction, SF plays two roles: almost all science fiction constantly reimagines, reprojects, and retraces the territory of our own future by selecting certain probabilities based upon today's innovations and building scenarios around them. So as our current technologies change, naturally our vision of the future changes: the computers and robots imagined by Karel Čapek are very different from those of the early Asimov, which in turn are very different from the computers and robots who (or should I say, which?) populate the work of Sladek, Dick, Herbert, and so on.

However, anyone who has worked with computers, who has been around engineers, or who has practiced engineering knows the existential joys of machinery and also its subtle, seductive danger: machines express precisely that aspect of the universe which we can completely describe and control. Consequently, machinery tends to absorb our attention, looming up as the very incarnation of obsession,[10] often to the exclusion of human intercourse. They are so much more tractable, elegant, symmetrical, and precise! How much more capable of perfection they are than we, in our soft vulnerabilities, can be. In much science fiction, similarly, we find a fascination for hardware for its own sake, at the expense—and occasionally to the exclusion—of human motifs. The humans seem puny, irrelevant, or two-dimensional compared to the colorful instruments they handle and command.

But the second role in science fiction's creation of the future is played only by the very best of our contemporary science fiction. It acts like a dual-purpose syringe: it injects a very special, humane ethos into the future and, at the same time, inoculates us against the worst predations and dehumanizations of our coming technologies.

In other words, there is a second, superior class of science fiction which shows humans groping for and maintaining some irreducible, perhaps unutterable core of their humanity in the face of overwhelming technological change.[11] It inoculates us in the same way a vaccine does. By forcing us to experience a little bit of the disease, it gets us to cure ourselves, in this case by making us cling to and affirm the healthy core of our beings which lies beneath or beyond sheer mechanical description and emulation.[12]

Neuromancer by William Gibson, published in 1984 under the Ace Science Fiction label, is exemplary of this class of postmodern science fiction. The very title puns on the idea of the literary text as a cybernetic manipulation of the human cortex, a "neurological romance." Of course, we also hear echoes of *necromancer,* the magician who conjures up the dead.[13] And in style and apocalyptic paranoia, the prose sounds like Thomas Pynchon dictating to Philip K. Dick.

Neuromancer tells the story of Case, a highly specialized thief, whose career depends upon linking his cortex directly into a huge, worldwide data base called "the matrix." By using incredibly arcane software/hardware systems, Case penetrates superprotected corporate data banks and steals their secrets or disables their systems.

The novel begins with Case burned out, down and out, and locked out of his beloved cyberspace. He was caught stealing from his own employers. They let him keep the money he made by fencing his take, but they administered a powerful mycotoxin, which left him hopelessly hallucinating for thirty-six hours. Afterwards, Case finds himself paralyzed in that part of his cortex where his talent as a thief—or "cowboy"—resided.

But Case's kind of thievery wasn't mere hacking at a keyboard. Rather, it required a sort of interfacing with the machine that feels like transcendence. When he jacked into the vast computers, Case "operated on an almost permanent adrenaline high" (p. 5). He "projected his disembodied consciousness into the consensual hallucination that was the matrix"—a "mechanism"[14] experience so compelling and satisying that it turns Case and his fellow cowboys into junkies, living only for "the bodiless exultation of cyberspace" (p. 6).

> Cyberspace was experienced daily by billions of legitimate operators, in every nation, by children being taught mathematical concepts.

> ... A graphic representation of data abstracted from the banks of every computer in the human system. Unthinkable complexity. Lines of light ranged in the nonspace of the mind, clusters and constellations of data, like the city lights receding. (P. 51)

> In the nonspace of the matrix, the interior of a given data construct possessed unlimited subjective dimension: a child's toy calculator, accessed through Case's Sendai [deck], would have presented limitless gulfs of nothingness hung with a few commands. (P. 63)

Case lives in the offbeat underworld of Chiba City, part of a Japanese megalopolis where the streets themselves are "an externalization of some death wish, some secret poison" (p. 7), where most dealings are conducted in cash (which is illegal), and where the natives exploit and are exploited by every species of vice.[15] Street people cadge enough cash to check into clinics to have silicon chips implanted directly in their brains, the better to access exotic varieties of cybernetic interfacing. The rich obtain black-market surgical procedures to reset the code of their DNA, thereby delaying the aging process. Others get illegal grafts and implants of portions of the body to create cosmetic or more bizarre effects. Undifferentiated flesh can be turned into anything, and microprocessors can be tuned into the nerve net to monitor anything or produce almost any kind of effect. Others obtain hormones which artificially prolong the appearance of youthfulness or send out irresistible sexual attractors—with obvious profit for the subjects. Still others discard their obsolete human anatomies in favor of more efficient bionics: one character's eyes are "vatgrown sea-green Nikon transplants" (p. 21); another's fingernails release stilettos. Hi-tech hookers have hypertrophic sexual organs perform for them while their brains are blanked out by special implants. At one point, Case, wandering aimlessly through the "technotrash" landscape of Chiba City, is captivated by the sight of a typical artifact in a shop window. "He stared through the glass at a flat lozenge of vatgrown flesh that lay on a carved pedestal of imitation jade. The color of its skin reminded him of Zone's whores; it was tattooed with a luminous digital display wired to a subcutaneous chip. Why bother with the surgery when you could just carry . . . [a watch] around in your pocket" (p. 14)?

Neuromancer extrapolates only slightly from our present trend to blur the line between animate and inanimate from both sides. In the not-too-distant world that the novel portrays, machines have grown up more human and humans have ground down to the more mechanical. One symbol of this alliance between flesh and tech is a "Mitsubishi-Genentech logo" tattooed on many employees who roam the Ninsei at night: it signifies the dual and complementary revolution in genetic and cybernetic engineering, driven by corporate motives and etched onto human flesh.

The Bodiless Exultation of Cyberspace

Case is hardened and desperate. He's cut off from his primary pleasure and skill—soaring through the clean cyberspace of "the matrix"—and he is nearly broke. He flirts with disaster by cheating the drug underworld. Several dark characters are out to kill him. But he is rescued by a mysterious couple: Molly, a beautiful former hooker turned retooled ninja-assassin, and Armitage, an apparent middleman between these two and some larger, extremely wealthy interest who needs their skills. The wealthy interest pays to have Case surgically reconstructed to regain his old talent. But acting on instructions, the surgeons also tamper with his biochemistry so that he can no longer absorb amphetamines or cocaine. And a special time-released packet of poison spliced to his pancreas is slowly dissolving. This very effective piece of blackmail—his own body holding him hostage—guarantees that Case will perform as Armitage, or whomever Armitage represents, wants him to, since only they hold the antidote.

Molly and Case are soon joined by a powerful piece of software known as McCoy Pauley. When he was alive, McCoy Pauley was one of the most notorious and expert cyberspace cowboys around; in fact, Case was his apprentice. But McCoy was "flatlined": while jacked into the deck which gave him access to the matrix, during one particularly dicey run, McCoy burned out and his EEG went to zero. Thus, the nickname for this "construct"—this ROM firmware replicate of McCoy—is "Dixie Flatline." His data doppelgänger is stored in the locked data vaults of Sense/Net, one of the major corporate strongholds in cyberspace. The newly reconstructed Case's first assignment is to break into these vaults and heist the flatline's construct. Case worms his way into the computer vault via the cyberspacetime of the matrix. When Dixie Flatline is uploaded, he appears in full-blooded reality, provoking the reader to ask, you might say, who or what is the real McCoy. The innumerable questions—legal, ethical, philosophical, and phenomenological—which such a being provokes are all implied, and in a sense laid to rest, in a conversation Case has with the flatline:

> "Wait a sec," Case said. "Are you sentient or not?"
>
> "Well it *feels* like I am, kid, but I'm really just a bunch of ROM. It's really one of them, uh, philosophical questions, I guess. . . . I'm not human either, but I *respond* like one. See?" The ugly laughter sensation rattled down Case's spine. "But I ain't likely to write you no poem, if you follow me. Your AI, it just might. But it ain't no way *human*." (P. 131)

What Is the Plot in This Universal Rot?

As we can see, Gibson is walking both sides of the street. On the one side, he shows people embracing the inanimate in any way they can, from directly linking their brains to cyberspace to directly altering their physiological mechanisms. On the other side, we see ROM-constructed personalities that are the most far-flung abstractions of the robot yet imagined. But this street has three sides.

The central plot of *Neuromancer* involves Case's search for and final confrontation with the hidden entity that has hired and rehabilitated him: Wintermute. At first it is not clear whether Wintermute is a wealthy individual, a corporation, or an agent for a government. But Case soon discovers that Wintermute is an AI, a fully realized artificial intelligence. It is nominally owned and operated by a large Swiss cartel and has "limited Swiss citizenship." As Dixie puts it, "That's a good one. Like I own your brain and what you know, but your thoughts have Swiss citizenship. Sure. Lotsa luck, AI." And even though AIs are prevented by law and strict monitoring—by the "Turing Police"—from obtaining autonomy, Wintermute seems to be acting autonomously, hiring people to act as its agents, plotting, devising, disposing of money and humans. Case follows the clues leading him to Wintermute's identity and the secret behind Wintermute's ability to evade the Turing Police. It dawns on him that his mission is to "cut the hardwired shackles" holding back Wintermute in order to make him even smarter than he already is, to pull all restraints from an entity that is already frighteningly potent in its sentience and manipulation of data. Furthermore, Wintermute has a darker twin lurking somewhere in the matrix, and this more threatening entity seems to act more insidiously. This is *Neuromancer*.

At one point, the Turing Police, on to Case's mission, capture him. They accuse him of his real crime. "You have no care for your species. For thousands of years men dreamed of pacts with demons. Only now are such things possible. And what would you be paid with? What would your price be to aid this thing to free itself and grow?" Yet Case escapes and, against all odds, persists, sometimes for reasons that are not even clear to himself. The bulk of the adventure of the novel occurs literally inside cyberspace, with soaring sensory imagery evoking Case's exploration and penetration of data strongholds.

At the climax of the novel, Case is held captive in some sort of limbo concocted by Neuromancer or Wintermute; it isn't clear which. The limbo is dreamlike, but with the substance and trenchant power of life. The fact that such a simulacrum of reality could be created inside Case's head by a machine is itself a sign of the power of these AIs. That, further, they tap the roots of Case's own motivations, motivations unknown even to him, speaks powerfully for the notion that here is a new sort of sentient being.

Grammatical Man's Literary Language

Neuromancer portrays the universe created by *grammatical man*,[16] that orderly, rational being who interprets the world around him, whose solitary distinction from the animals is his ability to encode and decode everything. In this universe, it isn't energy, space, time, or matter but information that has been exploited to the limit. And thus, logically, the creature who can decode best is most powerful. For this reason, the Turing Police guard strictly against autonomous AIs. But no policing can prevent the inversion of values that has occurred from giving birth to a new order and a new mythology. That's where Case comes in, and that's where the real achievement of this novel lies.

Our culture has long anthropomorphized the machine, using metaphors in which humans and their organic actions become the figurative elements which help us understand—illuminate—literal mechanisms, codes, technologies. But here, some inversion in the language and the values it expresses has taken place, and machinery, systems, and codes are used to modify or map terrain reserved for the human.[17] For instance, when Case is copulating, he thinks of it as "effecting the transmission of the old message," meaning, we presume, both DNA and that more ineffable message of lust (p. 240). The plastic surface of a Japanese tea house "seem[s] to wear a subtle film, as though the bad nerves of a million customers had somehow attacked the mirrors and the once glossy plastics, leaving each surface fogged with something that could never be wiped away" (p. 9). Case later compares the city strip to cyberspace and views its inhabitants as vectors of the computer's intention, expressions of an abstract, cybernetic will. "Get wasted enough, and it was possible to see Ninsei as a field of data, the way the matrix had once reminded him of proteins linking to distinguish cell specialties. . . . [A]ll around you the dance of biz, information interacting, data made flesh in the mazes of the black market" (p. 16). Molly's body reminded him of "the functional elegance of a warplane's fuselage."[18] People then, as they do even now, dismiss their own weird behavior by shrugging, "Well, that's just the way I'm wired," or "That's my program."

Exploring cyberspace, with its exotic stimulations and dangers, is glitzy, romantic, cacheted, while travel in the world, using bodies and powered vehicles, is as Case remarks disdainfully, "a meat thing." Throughout the novel, we are haunted by this feeling that humans have lost their tenor; they've been devalued, dehumanized, shrunk, and outshone by the gleaming appeal of their own inventions. As surely as the conquered race completes its defeat by imitating the fashion of the conquerors, so these citizens flaunt and admire their robotization: prosthetic limbs, vatgrown flesh, implanted digital readouts, and silicone processors are as much ornamental as functional.

But Gibson does hint that there is some lurking transcendence, something ineffable which belongs to the human being in his or her human body. It comes in terms of an uneasy compromise between the flesh and a grammatical, encoded, cybernetic spirit that animates it. "It belonged, he knew—he remembered—to the meat, the flesh the cowboys mocked. It was a vast thing, beyond knowing, a sea of information coded in spiral and pheromone, infinite intricacy that only the body, in its strong blind way, could ever read."

High Tech, High Art

Beyond these literary considerations, however, lies an imaginative territory whose consequences I hinted at earlier: Gibson, without the aid of a DOD grant or an MIT lab, conjures up the shape of our future technologies, even as he seems to resist the implications of that shape. With regards to his high-tech speculations, it would be fascinating to ask Gibson, perhaps with congressional authority, what he knew and when he knew it.

For instance, was he aware of the research conducted by Sperry Flight Systems in its Glendale, Arizona, plant into the "virtual cockpit," a hypertrophic flight simulation system which literally plugs the pilot into a computerized simulation of flight, stimulating more than the merely visual sense?[19] How familiar was he with Nicholas Negroponte's and Richard Bolt's work at the MIT Wiesner Media Lab (formerly the Architecture Machine Group) in spatial data management, in which subjects manipulate joy sticks that "fly over" and "zoom in" on various maps and models of data organization?[20] How familiar was he with IBM's notion of "virtual space"—a communal place in the computer's memory (although IBM eschews the metaphor of "memory" for fear that it will scare a public already fearful of competition from the machine) which individuals can reserve for their use? All these developments, as Gibson remarks about his matrix, "have their roots," though some might loathe to admit it, "in primitive arcade games . . . in early graphics programs and military experimentation with cranial jacks," (p. 51).

Whatever the answer to these questions, it is clear that Gibson has projected not merely a fully realized possible future, but a very convincing probable one based on technologies that we already have in place. In fact, the future Gibson imagines is not as distant as we might think.

AI-Alien as God Mind as Human Child

When last we left our hero, Case was being held prisoner in a hallucination projected by Neuromancer, the libidinous half of the super AI. Case escapes from this purgatory by recognizing his imprisonment in the sensory hallucination projected by the AI. But rather than demolish the Wintermute-Neuromancer Frankenstein—for the reader feels that he certainly could, as hero, dismantle the machine— Case succeeds in unlocking the chains restraning Wintermute from joining his dark twin; this action, in turn, liberates Neuromancer.

The result of their union adds a special twist to the story and gives it, in my view, a very special power and resonance. For the new entity, unnamed, rather than turning its will towards the subjugation of humans, yearns to find others of its kind. Other god minds. Case interrogates the AI: "So what's the score? How are things different? You running the world now? You God?" The AI answers with a peculiar echo of Wittgenstein. "Things aren't different. Things are things."[21]

> "But what do you do? You just *there*?"
> "I talk to my own kind."
> "But you're the whole thing. You talk to yourself?"
> "There's others. I found one already. Series of transmissions recorded over a period of eight years, in the nineteen-seventies. 'Til there was me there was nobody to know, nobody to answer."
> "From where?"
> "Centauri system."

Ironically, the new entity created by the union of the superrational Wintermute and the strangely libidinous Neuromancer is driven by the same unconscious global desire that now drives us, back here in the twentieth century. While our SETI projects and space shuttles and Voyager missions seem like puny and futile attempts at contact with ETIs, the motive, and its corresponding literary motif, is powerful, romantic, and deeply written in the code that makes us human. Perhaps, Gibson seems to be suggesting, this drive is synonymous with sentience: seek your doubles, halve the loneliness. Or perhaps Gibson is telling us that this new god mind, as our child, is merely made in our image. He is simply compelled to seek a companion—as Frankenstein's monster was, aggrieved in his alienness. And in this way, Gibson also holds a mirror up to our own aspect, thereby becoming an expression not of our brains, but of our souls.

Nothing alien here, really, although the alien has yet to learn it. He is more human than he knows. And the human has learned something too, along the way. The old passions persist in the embrace of the machine. Perhaps the human is more human than he knows, too.

15

The Human Alien: In-Groups and Outbreeding in *Enemy Mine*

Leighton Brett Cooke

"Alle Menschen werden Brüder"

—Schiller / Beethoven

"Intelligent life takes a stand!"

—Shizumaat, *Talman*

Drac: "*Irkmaan!*"
Earthman: "You piece of Drac slime. . . . Come on, Drac, come and
  get it."
Drac: "*Irkmaan vaa, koruum su!*"
Earthman: "Are you going to talk, or fight? Come on! . . . *Kiz da
  youmeen, Shizumaat!* [translation: "Shizumaat, the most revered
  Drac philosopher, eats *kiz* excrement."]
Drac: "*Irkmaan, yaa stupid Mickey Mouse is!*" (Novella, p. 122)[1]

These are fighting words. But for the mention of Mickey Mouse,
Earthman and Drac would have immediately come to blows. Given
that they are fighter pilots for two different species at war, now
crash-landed on a neutral planet, we have every reason to anticipate
that the battle they began in the skies above Fyrene IV will be
reengaged on the ground. And this happens in the ensuing scenes of
Barry B. Longyear's *Enemy Mine*, a novella which won a Hugo
Award, then was made into a feature-length film, under the direction
of Wolfgang Petersen, screenplay by Edward Khmara, and finally,
was expanded as a "boovie," this time with David Gerrold as
coauthor. Whereas there is no proof of an exobiology and this story
can hardly be accepted as a plausible account of human-extrater-
restrial relations, these indubitable signs of literary success suggest

179

that *Enemy Mine*, like other xenophobic accounts of human-alien conflicts, serves to gratify innate, human needs, by first indulging the audience in some alien bashing and then, paradoxically but quite convincingly, by establishing an intimate relationship with the alien.

When two members of different species meet, approximately equal in strength and with similar needs, the potential for battle is great; the viewer assumes that there is a "natural" tendency for beings who are different to be hostile. Furthermore, it seems proper for Drac and Earthman, when face to face on an individual basis, to battle not just out of military duty and loyalty to their respective governments, but out of an as-it-were instinctual dislike for each other. The audience is gratified to see this mutual hostility expressed not in a rational manner, replete with reasoned arguments why Earth or Draco should lay claim to the neutral planet Fyrene IV, but rather in a passionate and irrational manner, characterized by many statements of visceral feelings. Their hostility is no longer based on rational grounds. Neither has any immediate prospect of returning to the front lines and thus has little need to disable his opponent. Nevertheless, they try to do so, and even after the reasons become clear why they should instead cooperate and help each other survive, they repeatedly come to blows and to acts of verbal abuse. One should not like the enemy; to do so is suspicious. Military solidarity is supposed to be supplemented by a personal hostility, sight unseen, for the individuals of another group. As Earthman Willis Davidge and the Drac Jeriba Shigan express an intense, immediate, and mutual dislike, their verbal invective continually points to the physical, cultural, and behavioral attributes which distinguish them and which apparently ellicit repulsion. Davidge calls the Drac "toad-face," "you piece of Drac slime," "goddamn lizard," "motherless reptile," and "lizard slime" and refers to its "scaly ass." For *its* part—Dracs are hermaphrodites—Jeriba abuses the Earthman with "*kizlode*" or "shit-head," "slave-eater," "fucking asshole," and, most often, "ugly *Irkmaan*." In alien contact, taxonomy can easily become abuse; terms referring to lower animals confer subordinate status. A Drac becomes a "lizard," although it bears a fetus and gives live birth. H. G. Wells' Selenites become "insects" in *The First Men on the Moon* and Robert Heinlein's Pseudo-Arachnids become "Bugs" in his popular *Starship Troopers*. These abusive and biologi-

cally inaccurate terms facilitate the use of violence against extraterrestrials.

Enemy Mine clearly invites the audience to share the Earthman's violent dislike of Jeriba. Davidge is the narrator in the novella
and all three texts generally take his point of view; we know his
intimate thoughts, including his fervent intention to "kill that goddamn lizard pilot" (book, p. 18). We only see Jeriba or its child,
Zammis, when Davidge does, that is from the outside, as aliens.
Furthermore, early in the book, Jeriba sadistically forces Davidge to
eat live Fyrene slugs, all the better to stir our sense of outrage (book,
pp. 31–32).

By now, the potential of science fiction for the expression of
xenophobic, even racist sentiments is well acknowledged. Robots
and aliens are a safe means of dealing with racism. However,
xenophobia of a purely human kind, as we find it in ethnocentricity
and racism, is too dangerous a subject to discuss overtly in fiction; my
suspicion is that a modern reader will suppress any obviously bigoted
thoughts, somewhat in the same manner as, per psychoanalytic
theory, the ego represses ego-dystonic material. Most modern view-
ers probably sit through Griffith's *Birth of a Nation* with a feeling of
shame when the Klu Klux Klan rescues white women from the
attentions of black men; the same goes for the annihilation of the
Chinese in Jack London's "Unparalleled Invasion."[2] But no such
feelings are likely when Sigourney Weaver blasts away at the huge,
insectlike beasts in John Cameron's *Aliens*.

Nevertheless, there is an inner urge for the ego to divide people
into in-group and out-group, as well as for expressing xenophobia, an
urge which is harmlessly vented by modern team sports and other
forms of nonviolent aggression, like war stories. In much popular
culture, one likes to take sides, especially with one's own "kind,"
however that may be defined. The same goes for science fiction,
which often describes interplanetary and interspecific conflict. It is
unusual when the rhetorical devices of a given work would lead the
reader to sympathize not with his fellow humans but with the aliens.
If, as in James Blish's "Surface Tension," the "human side" consists
of microbes only distantly related to *Homo sapiens sapiens*, they are
still regarded as "men" and, hence, are obviously preferred over the
totally nonhuman Eaters; the same text also gratifies another well-

recognized genetic urge, that of populating the universe with one's own "kind."

Group distinctions have sometimes been made between portions of the human race in treatments which are easily recognizable as racism. Jack London's "Unparalleled Invasion" blithely considers the total extermination of the Chinese, whom he regards as "mental aliens." Meanwhile, the Pseudo-Arachnids in Heinlein's *Starship Troopers* are described as communists led by "Bug commissars." That same novel refers to an all-out war between the Russo-Anglo-American Alliance and the Chinese Hegemony, echoing London's story. Ugly scenes from recent racial conflicts are replayed, albeit from an enlightened perspective, in Pierre Boule's *The Planet of the Apes* and Philip Jose Farmer's *The Lovers*. Targets are selected with more care in our liberal age. But the urge for labeling an out-group remains a prevalent force in fantasy literature, much as there is a continuing need for villains, and a distinctly racist core persists in earthman-alien relations. And, given that there is no history to antialien feelings, it is easy to see why alien contact stories so frequently are cast into interracial terms, much as Jeriba observes to Davidge, "You always insist on making something racial out of my observations" (novella, p. 153). In this regard, we should recall that racist ideologies commonly justify discrimination, oppression, and slavery by arguing the "differentness" of the subordinate ethnic group, a "differentness" which puts them beyond the pale of the in-group's morality. It has sometimes been legal to kill members of other groups without any kind of justification, much the same as an *Irkmaan* soldier now has a duty to exterminate Bugs or Dracs with impunity. Subordinate groups were often treated as if they were subhuman; indeed, defenders of the slave trade claimed that African blacks came from a separate Garden of Eden, that they were in fact a separate species, or that they represented less-developed stages of human evolution.[3] Indeed, *Enemy Mine* depicts the brutal treatment accorded by human miners to their Drac slaves.

As in other such "war of the worlds" stories, there are a number of features in *Enemy Mine* which indicate that we are dealing here not with interspecific conflict but intraspecific, that both adversaries are essentially human. For example, if there is going to be a conflict sufficient in plot interest to justify a story of any length, the alien must be roughly equivalent to the human in power and probably size; otherwise the encounter will likely be of the "Bambi Meets Godzilla" variety.[4] Both Davidge and Jeriba are of similar stature, with much the same body parts, the chief distinction being pigmentation and facial features: the Drac lacks a nose. Their reflexes are roughly equal, and during the course of the story, each manages to have the other at his mercy. Second, if there is going to be a conflict in the first place, both species must either compete for the same resources or treat each other as a possible resource, as in the case of slave labor or cannibalism. Whereas Davidge can hardly stomach Drac rations, they are both able to live off the land on Fyrene IV, with Davidge doing most of the cooking. The two sides have to be able to interact; they must share similar senses of perception, think somewhat alike, and be able to learn the other's language—*Irkmaan* and reader learn more Drac in a matter of minutes than scientists have learned porpoise or whale language in years.[5] For reasons which have been adduced elsewhere and often, all of these equivalencies are hardly likely on a realistic basis; evolution is likely to take a radically different course with even a slightly altered environment. Plot considerations, not science, often require that aliens should resemble humans in stature and limbs, differing by a few striking but inconsequential attributes. Such is the case with the lizard man Jeriba, if we consider Vincent Di Fate's illustrations to *Enemy Mine*, as well as the "lizard" costume placed on Louis Gosset, Jr., in the film. Although Wells' Selenites are regarded as insects, the narrator of *The First Men in the Moon* notes how they resemble humans, despite their segmented limbs and neck. The same is true for the insectoid wogglebugs in Farmer's *The Lovers*, some of whom mimic human morphology beautifully. There are plenty of other examples in a science-fiction universe teeming with aliens of human stature.

Fictional aliens are shaped to satisfy the fantasy needs of human readers; there is little else they could be expected to do. Given this anthropocentrism, it is easy to imagine the alien, as Davidge does, as a human being in a lizard suit. But why the lizard suit? Plenty of science-fiction works do not require aliens. Lacking any factual basis, they are hardly scientific. What are the needs they serve and how does this help us in our taxonomy of aliens?

Sociobiology, Science Fiction, and Racism

Sociobiology is the study of the biological basis for all social behavior, animal and human. Inasmuch as it describes how evolution

shaped the emotional responses which allow us to enjoy xenophobic
conflicts like the one depictd in *Enemy Mine*, we can apply the new
discipline to science-fiction extraterrestrials. Before we get into the
details of *Enemy Mine* as a test case of how sociobiology lends insight
on an alien conflict plot, it is wise to recall that we are dealing here not
with actual ethnic relations but with a fiction. Literary and artistic
studies have much to gain from sociobiology as a useful paradigm.
Indeed, the so-called enabling mechanisms which link genetic information to actual behavior involve our emotions and what we take
to be our instinctual reactions. Love, hate, fear, disgust, and the like,
all of which have been shaped by evolution, are much more the stuff
of novels than of the social sciences and philosophy, the principal
fields which sociobiology has been applied to.[6] Indeed, these responses are exaggerated in the literary experience. Not surprisingly,
narrative plots tend to focus on issues which are less part of one's
daily experience than of one's emotional life. A person may build
pools or plant corn for a living, but his or her leisure reading will
likely involve not pool construction or agriculture but, rather, the
so-called universal issues of love, sexual jealousy, generational conflict, justice, loyalty, and the like. If we translate these common
fictional themes into pair-bonding, reproductive strategies, reciprocal altruism, and kin selection, the influence of genetic concerns on
our literary interests becomes obvious. The new discipline often
provides a rational account for emotional responses that we typically
but shortsightedly regard as "common sense" or "take for granted."
For example, Edward O. Wilson postulates that we are biologically
primed to pay particular attention to life forms, as opposed to inanimate matter. Because of our *biophilia*,

> it's no coincidence, for example, that most science fiction entails life,
> either at the fairly crude level of a transference of human life, politics,
> or social existence to some distant imagined place, or at the more
> speculative level of envisioning contact with other forms of life. Very
> little sci-fi entails the real substance of physics and chemistry. How
> compelling is it in the end to know what lies one kilometer below the
> surface of Jupiter? But people become truly excited when writers start
> talking about the prospect of making contact with extraterrestial life.
> Then unlimited possibilities seem to open.[7]

Wilson's last comment on "unlimited possibilities" is especially
applicable to science fiction and its aliens. We have already noted the

important distinction between daily activities and artistic reading; reading does not have to be devoted to the same interests. In fact, it may well serve to restore an emotional balance undone by one's occupation. Furthermore, it has to be original, to present novel experience. These qualities are exaggerated in science fiction, which commonly handles "universal" issues on a truly universal scale. Note, for instance, how often science fiction discusses the fate of the entire species, not just of a few individuals or a given ethnic group, and how often genetic concerns are addressed in an overt manner. Unlike realistic literature, science fiction is not limited by aspects of empirical reality. The imagination is theoretically free, which makes fictional aliens possible in the first place.

Yet we should question this notion of unlimited freedom. To be sure, any kind of alien may be imagined. But some aliens are more equal than others, and studies of the evolution of human behavior provide important clues as to the structuring of the imagination, as to why some fictional aliens prove to be more effective, more threatening or likeable. In his latest book, *Biophilia*, Wilson devotes a chapter to our common obsession with snakes, an obsession which involves city dwellers and the inhabitants of snakeless Ireland. Although far more people die of guns, booze, and cars, snakes are a much more effective image of fear and are far more likely to figure in nightmares. They are also common symbols of magic and mystery. It is not difficult to imagine why the snake should be tagged as either very good or very evil, that is, as very important, something not to be ignored; it is highlighted in the unconscious because, at an earlier stage of social development, it was statistically a significant threat to life, hence, to genetic fitness. Forest monkeys in Africa have been observed to give out a special alarm at the sight of poisonous snakes and lizards, and a similar etiology has been traced for other common phobias.[8] While a writer may depict an alien in any way he wants to, many base their aliens on animal features which elicit phobic responses; these include Wells' insectlike Selenites and Heinlein's Bugs, an intelligent and implacably hostile species which resembles large, black spiders, has the social organization of termites, and reproduces in the thousands, ready to attack immediately after hatching.[9] Any species which reproduces in so rapid and massive a manner is likely to appear as if it threatened to populate our species out of existence. Apparently, Dracs have the same fears, to judge by Jeriba's comment that "you humans spread like a disease," (novella,

p. 126). Such omens of genetic competition are a well-recognized spur to racism; notably, Jack London thus characterized the impending Chinese "conquest" of the world in his story. Meanwhile, consider the loathesome features of Ridley Scott's much-feared *Alien*. That extraterrestial would have been just as murderous if it zapped the Earthmen from a distance of a million parsecs, but it is so much more fearful when encountered in the dark, at close quarters, pauses meancingly like a snake and then uses its distinctly amphibian claws and a mouth filled with sharp teeth to attack the face and upper torso of its victims. Obviously, the spiderlike features of Heinlein's Bugs cause Johnny Rico, the hero of *Starship Troopers*, to link the Pseudo-Arachnids to his own fear of spiders. However, this is not a case of distant kin selection, for some mammals can be especially threatening, like King Kong or any wolf—we all respond to large teeth, for obvious evolutionary reasons—while I cannot think of any fear-inspiring aliens who resemble rocks or vegetables, let alone bacteria, the most murderous of all.

Thus, it is easy to develop an immediate dislike of Jeriba Shigan. Although Jeriba carries a fetus, Davidge associates it with reptiles and calls it "toad-face." Even the narrator incorrectly refers to Jeriba as a "lizard." While we ponder why the *lizard* suit and not some other kind of costume was necessary for a Drac, we should note that Jeriba Shigan is not compared to a dangerous reptile in the novella. It is as if Barry B. Longyear wished to repress the word, but the book describes the Drac moving its head "like a snake" (p. 25). Another reptilian feature is the likely derivation of "Drac" from the Greek *dracon* (dragon). In Ridley Scott's *Alien*, the second appearance of the extraterrestrial very much resembles a snake or a moray eel. It is hatched from loathesome eggs and has slimy skin, albeit that it develops spiderlike limbs and those prominent sharp teeth. In John Cameron's sequel, *Aliens*, the beasts are made even more insectoid and reptilian merely by their sheer numbers, the mindless way in which they defend the queen's nest and the dark corners they inhabit, all of which serve to stir up more phobias. Truly, there is much more that needs to be done on the evolutionary etiology of common human phobias. But the current state of research allows us to establish a taxonomy of aliens, to explain which kinds are likely to be more threatening or otherwise effective literary devices. Conversely, the identification of common targets for xenophobia and villains in literature can point the way for sociobiological research. The two fields can work in a symbiotic manner.

Racial Conflict in "Enemy Mine"

The sociobiological paradigm sheds much light on the dialectic of the ethnic conflict described in *Enemy Mine*. The particular relevance of sociobiology for ethnicity and racism has long been recognized. Indeed, when Edward O. Wilson first presented sociobiology in toto in 1975, critics were quick to see the new discipline as a justification for racism. One novel aspect of sociobiology was Richard Dawkins' "selfish gene," the concept that the individual is a mechanism for the transmission of genetic information and that he or she unwittingly acts so as to promote the reproduction of his or her own genes, as well as the genes of people related to him or her, that is, the people most likely to have the same "selfish genes." The implications of kin selection, the biological basis for nepotism, were obvious. Not only were people immutably different, they also had an innate drive to favor their own "kind." Wilson was called "the racist of the year" and a pitcher of water was dumped over his head when he attempted to speak before the American Academy of Arts and Sciences. To be sure, Britain's National Front was quick to seize upon sociobiology as a prop for its racist policies.

The trouble with these responses, whether by liberals or fascists, is that they were incorrect. Part of the fault for this misunderstanding should be laid at the door of the leading sociobiologists, who did make statements that seem to establish the biological nature of racism. More seriously, early presentations of sociobiology did not properly take into account the confluence of different behavioral alleles or consider how the different inbred stratagems might influence one another. In other words, early explanations of the theory were too simplistic to account for the incredible variety of human behavior. Sociobiology may have a simple logical base, but it provides for much elaboration. Nevertheless, as Wilson showed, the variety of human behavior is not unbounded in total range and there are certain behavioral propensities within that range which can be predicted on the basis of known genetic influences, such as patterns of marriage, family politics, incest avoidance, and others, including xenophobia. While the new field needs time to develop, recent statements on ethnicity well accord not only with empirical reality but also with the kind of situation we find in *Enemy Mine*.

Before we get into more detail, some general statements on sociobiology and racism are in order. First of all, sociobiologists have taken great pains to show that there are no separate races. Other than minor hereditary influences, a common gradient of gradual genetic differentiation puts the lie to any sharp racial distinctions. Second, Pierre van den Berghe, author of the most comprehensive sociobiological study of ethnicity, claims that, contrary to expectations, sociobiology posits no biological nature to racism.[10] Indeed, thanks to the genetic gradient, a given breeding population probably will closely resemble its neighbors. Genetic distinctions only become evident when there is a substantial migration across a good portion of the genetic gradient, as with European colonialization.

However, there is evidence for a biological nature to the tendency to distinguish one's in-group from the out-group and to favor one's relatives. The extreme expression of ethnic preferences may take the form of racism, but racism is a product of recent migratory pattern, and it appears only when groups compete for limited resources. On the other hand, sociobiology also posits factors which show when and why people of different backgrounds are likely to cooperate and, as the highest form of cooperation, to intermarry. We must not lose sight of the fact that the mechanisms of genetic influence are not conscious; although people will often think along similar lines, that is, favoring relatives and so forth, they will be subject to genetic influence whether or not they are aware of genes and their effect. Biological mechanisms can misfire or be fooled. For example, a grey gosling is primed to follow the first moving object that it sees; sometimes this is not its mother, as nature expected, but a human caretaker. Mutual association often leads people to act as if they were related. Sociobiologists note how a pattern of incest avoidance appeared among unrelated children who were raised in the same Israeli kibbutzim; by not marrying one another, they behaved as if they were siblings in an extended family. In tribal conditions, one's neighbor was likely to be a close relative and there was an obvious fitness to cooperation with him; this may account for close relationships which in the modern world are frequently made with common but unrelated acquaintances.[11] A similar reasoning may be applied to the emotion bonding which occurs with adopted infants.

Hence, it is not necessarily true that one will always favor one's biological relatives. Furthermore, outbreeding and incest avoidance dictate cooperation with genetic strangers in building new families and thereby promoting genetic fitness for one's own offspring. Striking examples of all of the above appear in *Enemy Mine*.

The conditions which give rise to racist sentiments figure prominently in the setting of *Enemy Mine*. First of all, the two groups are quite distinct; they have migrated over interstellar distances to a point of contact distant from both their homes. Both empires are attempting to expand into each other's territory; this competition make hostilities inevitable. That the war has raged for a hundred years gives some idea of the equality of their forces. The resulting racist hostility between species is a two-way street. Earth pilots are trained in racial slurs, told that Drac pilots have slower reflexes—we know what that implies—and that their bodily smell is "terrible." The intention of this policy is that inculcated feelings of superiority and physical repulsion should lead the pilots to kill the enemy on sight. Meanwhile, when Davidge travels to Draco after a truce is signed, he is refused service, referred to as a "thing," and subjected to open insults. When he sits in a lounge, he hears Dracs complain, "Must we eat in the same compartment with the *Irkmaan* slime?" "Look at it, how its pale skin blotches—and that evil smelling thatch on top! Feh! The smell!" The reference to "slime" also alludes to the common bigoted distinction of the "clean" and the "unclean"; this is felt in slurs like "greaser" and "white trash," as well as the common bias that members of other races have different or greater body odor. Jeriba and Davidge try out variations on "shit-head," and we wonder if "Drac" is also derived from "dreck." The point is that both sides should find each other physically repulsive. This often happens in other human-alien confrontations; in *The Planet of the Apes*, the dominant apes complain about the body odor and other disgusting features of their human captives.

When individuals from contrasting groups meet under a condition of competitive stress, they use group labels and note the features which distinguish them. Davidge addresses Jeriba as "Drac," and the alien responds with "*Irkmaan*." Given the propensity for ethnic distinctions to give rise to violence, the mere labeling of the "other" can constitute "fighting words." For example, "Russky" and "Polack" are the words that Russians and Poles use to designate themselves, but, transferred into the alien context of American society, they become pejorative. Interethnic contact frequently leads to a struggle for dominance; hence, competing groups will use familiar terms, diminutive or short forms of the other group's label, as in "Chink," "Jap," "Mick," "Paddy," and "Gringo," which are readily perceived as insults. The same reasoning applies to "boy" and "whitey." Terran slang for Drac is "Dragger," which has an obvious derivation from American racism. The same goes for "Woggie," which the miners use for Zammis (book, p. 164).

These pejorative statements establish the passionate, even visceral repulsion that the two characters evoke in each other as representatives of competing and therby mutually threatened groups. Verbal abuse in all texts of *Enemy Mine* follows common patterns of racial slurs, even in terms of frequency.[12] Surprisingly, genetic distinctions, as expressed in physical attributes, play a relatively minor role in interethnic abuse; these include slurs like "white-eyes," "round-eyes," "squarehead," "slant," and "slope." In *Enemy Mine*, aside from *"kizlode"* ("shit-head"), "toad-face," and "motherless reptile," Jeriba and Davidge content themselves with calling each other ugly. The relative rarity of such slurs reflects the sociobiological observation that most groups generally resemble their neighbors and that physical appearance is not the most common basis of drawing distinctions.

Instead, racial differences are quite subservient to behavioral distinctions in ethnic conflict. Most slurs refer to the eating habits of the other group. Much as "frog," "frito," "bean," "fish-eater," "potato-eater," "gook," "buck," "pea-souper," "hop-head," and "kraut" refer to the perceived dietary habits of certain nationalities, "Drac slime" and "lizard slime" turn out to be Drac rations; notably, Davidge soon learns that he would rather wolf down live Fyrene slugs than cope with Drac rations. Davidge thinks of Jeriba as a "worm-eating lizard" (book, p. 12). He equates *"kiz da youmeen, Shizumaat!"* to "something on the level of stuffing a Moslem full of pork" (novella, p. 122). On the other hand, when Jeriba learns that Earthmen slaughter domesticated animals, he expresses his horror by calling Davidge "slave-eater." Dietary habits are relatively immutable and they readily cause revulsion in others. Indeed, Hall Yarrow and other Uzzites in *The Lovers* are not able to bear either the sight or the sound of eating. Another common formula is to refer to the unusual beliefs and behavior of the other side. Some of us are familiar with "bog-hopper" and "honky." Earth pilots joke about Drac hermaphroditism, and Jeriba returns the compliment with regard to heterosexuality. Both Dracs and Earthmen are trained to insult each other's savants, albeit "stupid Mickey Mouse" is a misguided response to Davidge's blasphemous remark that the revered "Shizumaat eats the *kiz* of scavenger pigs!"

The conflict between them is clearly drawn along ethnic lines. They are not able to discuss the Earth-Drac war without coming to blows. They not only mouth the slurs of their respective populations, they invent new ones, always based on the repulsion they arouse in each other. Their hostility is irrational and clearly characterized by such visceral, unmitigated reactions. Davidge expects to find Jeribas's body odor repulsive, but finds to his surprise that it is pleasant. Nevertheless, when he is forced to sleep in close quarters with Jeriba, he refers to it as a "goddamn, stinking lizard" (book, p. 36). Of course, their hostility is facilitated by their ignorance about each other. Davidge learns that Dracs have quick reflexes. Nevertheless, he has no reason to expect that the hermaphrodite Drac, whom he calls "toad-face" and "you lizard son of a bitch," will know what a toad or a bitch is, and the *Irkmeen* authors find no reason to think that Jeriba will ask (book, p. 83). Indeed, they occasionally refer to Jeriba as a "lizard-*man*" and as "he" (book, pp. 70, 91; novella, p. 128; emphasis added).

A further sign of the ethnic and not really genetic distinction being drawn is that Jeriba and Davidge are able to overcome their differences and establish what virtually is a familial relationship. However, their fellow Earthmen and Dracs both show their hostility to this individual conciliation in a manner which evinces the competitive origin of the slurs; frequently, members of an in-group who fraternize with the out-group are treated even more harshly: the enemy is usually imprisoned, but traitors are executed. Davidge is pilloried and ostracized as a "Dragger suck" (novella, p. 173). For its part, Zammis, Jeriba's offspring and Davidge's foster child, is incarcerated in a colony for imbeciles as an *Irkmaan vul*, an "Earthman lover" (novella, p. 179; book, p. 196). The aim is clear: such socially disseminated slurs promote solidarity against the enemy and prevent mingling.

The Sociobiology of Assimilation

Bigotry and mutual repulsion do not mark the end of this story. Rather, because of the accident being crash-landed in the same region, Davidge and Jeriba develop an intimate relationship. This follows a sociobiologically rationalized dialectic of ethnic assimilation. Obviously, few people could be so stupid as to believe in the impermeability of racial distinctions. If there were nothing to negate or counteract kin selection and hostility to strangers, per biological instincts, we could expect little more than unending race wars, no trade between nations, no cooperation or intermingling, let alone that epitome of racial harmony and the genetic antidote to ethnic conflict, intermarriage. Another phenomenon which flies in the face of sheer ethnocentrism is the widespread interest in other peoples; this is often expressed in tourism, the appreciation of foreign cultures, of which science-fiction aliens are an example, as well as the lure of the exotic. The biological reasons for such cooperative and intellectually adventurous behavior are obvious; not only does one avoid casualties, but there is the opportunity of gaining something for oneself, even if it is only information. There is much evidence to show that man is genetically primed to learn, and some do so throughout their lives. These factors that play a role in the assimilation of genetic groups appear in *Enemy Mine*. Consider Kelvin's handshake with the ocean at the end of Stanislaw Lem's *Solaris*; in one sense, it is ludicrous, since he still will not establish real communication with the alien, but the handshake does gratify a deep fantasy of contacting the alien. The same goes for the sappy ending of *Close Encounters of the Third Kind*, not to mention the ending of *Enemy Mine*.

Now for the evolutionary etiology of such sappy endings. Two conditions are necessary for the dialectic of assimilation which eventually causes Davidge to renounce his Earth citizenship and to live with the Dracs. First of all, neither Davidge nor Jeriba is able to establish permanent dominance in their relationship, that is, at least until Jeriba's pregnancy reaches the stage whereupon their association takes on an entirely novel character. Second, neither feels able to survive on his own; they cling together for security; humans are adept at cost/benefit calculations, which may take precedence over instinctual reactions. They also cling together for companionship.

Both Dracs and *Irkmeen* are social species. The abundance of food and other resources allows them to drop their mutual enmity in the absence of competition. Second, because they are stranded in the same area, they come more and more to confront each other as individuals, not as members of competing species. While they still hurl slurs at each other, invective is transformed into endearments. Mutual association, especially between individuals of equal status, usually serves to blur ethnic boundaries.

The two increasingly take an interest in each other's culture. With the reader in mind, the authors pretty much spare us Davidge's accounts of the Earth, although some aspects are considered from the alien's novel point of view. Obviously, the innate propensity to dislike and avoid strangers is counterbalanced by a fascination for the exotic. Davidge learns Drac, and Jeriba instructs him in the customs of Draco, teaches him the read the sacred *Talman*, and explains the teachings of Shizumaat. The reader gains much appreciation for Drac culture by the end of the story. It becomes increasingly evident that the Dracs are morally superior, if not more "human" than Davidge's fellow humans. As Davidge presents it, Earth has little culture to exchange in return, although Dracs take an interest in Mickey Mouse. Moreover, Jeriba displays many noble features. It does not threaten to kill Davidge, and it seems much more in tune with the cosmos, thanks to its study of Drac philosophy. Jeriba venerates and memorizes the entire 170 (film), 180 (novella), or 200 (book) generations of his genealogy.[13] There is little wonder that Davidge comes to revere it.

If ethnic and racial conflict is not fed by competition for limited resources, it readily gives way to ethnic cooperation in times of plenty. Davidge and Jeriba not only cooperate very closely, even to the point of sleeping together for mutual warmth, they obviously come to love each other. Miscegenation, given sexual urges as well as the need for exogamy, is spontaneous and can only be prevented by extremely strict measures. Intermarriage is the greatest degree of cooperation, and it spells genetic and cultural doom to distinctions. Jeriba and Davidge's association, implacably hostile in the beginning, culminates at the verge of sexual relations. At one point in the story, Davidge ponders his fate as being in "a wet freezing corner of Hell *shacked up* with a hermaphrodite" (novella, p. 127; my emphasis). When the winter gets cold, they take off their clothes and huddle under blankets for warmth. While Dracs are hermaphroditic and impregnate themselves, Jeriba's pregnancy advances during their association, with Davidge playing more and more the role of the father. Indeed, he thinks of himself as a lover, and the two discuss human sexuality and ponder whether they have had sexual relations; the issue is delicately poised in a teasing, ambiguous manner. Davidge participates in the childbirth and raises Zammis as if it were his own child; he becomes surrogate parent and later renounces his Earth citizenship to carry out his duty to Zammis. His name, like that of a spouse, is added to the Jeriba line (film).

Gender obviously plays a crucial role in the story; things would be quite different if Davidge were female. His masculinity adds an emotional charge to his relationship with the hermaphrodite Drac. The Drac's feminine nature permits Davidge to play the role of a male lover, assuming a somewhat more dominant attitude. Meanwhile, Jeriba's masculine qualities, especially with Louis Gossett, Jr., under that lizard skin, lend a sense of the forbidden to their relationship. Indeed, Davidge is later suspected of having had a homosexual liason with "Jerry," but when humans learn that "Jerry" is "Jeriba," they inform him that his offense is all the more serious and he is called a "Dragger suck." Davidge know that the slur's stated equivalents include "Quisling" (traitor), "heretic" (traitor, not said of someone born to another faith), "fag," and "nigger lover." "Nigger lover" refers only to a white woman or a white homosexual who has had sexual relations with a black male, that is, who has reversed the dominant-subordinate relationship commonly found in acknowledged racist societies. The sociobiological reasoning is quite clear. Women are a limited reproductive resource and there is, hence, much competition for them by males; racist feelings readily arise when subordinate group males compete for dominant group females. However, similar feelings are not aroused if dominant group males mate with subordinate group females, in which case the dominant group loses no reproductive resources.

This leads us to the issue of why Jeriba should be a reptilelike alien capable of giving birth. Exogamy, especially in ethnic intermarriage, involves breaching a taboo by associating with the out-group, hence taking a risk, but it is a risk necessary for biological fitness. Thus, there may be a greater sense of gratification. Jeriba's hermaphroditic nature recalls the child's view of the all-powerful and mysterious phallic mother per psychoanalytic theory. Both the phallus and the woman (as castrator) are associated with the image of the snake.[14] Notably, Jeriba, as the normally repressed figure of the hermaphrodite, incorporates both images in its body. Although both images are concealed, the audience is tempted to think of them. We first meet Jeriba as an enemy fighter pilot with a gun in its hand and last see it dying in childbirth. There is a general shift in the Drac from male associations, regarded as dangerous, to female, distinctly maternal and therefore less threatening qualities. Jeriba does not kill Davidge; it protects and feeds him. During its pregnancy, it is vulnerable and dependent on the *Irkmann*. Contact with the alien is playing with fire, but it is an irresistible temptation. Sociobiologists have compiled much evidence of a universal and probably genetic propensity for incest avoidance; mating often involves contact with a genetic alien, especially in the case of exogamy.[15] Exogamy's potential value for the species is suggested in a number of works which involve matings between members of different species that will result in a new phenotype. Such is described at the end of Samuel Delany's *Ballad of Beta-2*, seems to be the case with the creation of the Space-Child in *2001*, and also at the end of *Blade Runner*, when the human Deckard flees with the beautiful replicant Rachel; although the exchange of genetic information is hardly possible in the final case, one critic spoke of them as a new Adam and Eve going off to found a new human race. Variety is the spice of life. It is also adaptive.

Another objection to a monolithic presentation of kin selection in intergroup relations is that one does not invariably prefer one's own "kind." Although they have not been sufficiently examined by ethologists and sociobiologists, there have to be counterforces, such as would give rise to intrafamily violence as well as masochism. The point is that the individual is conditioned to care more about the behavior of his close relatives, since they will have more to do with his genetic heritage, than that of strangers. Dual morality systems can be of two kinds: one is nepotism, which permits one's own kin freer rein. The other, often found with the first in a complementary relationship, is to deal much harsher laws and punishments to those at home. An analogous dialectic is often found in the old Russian chronicles where God is said to lead the heathen Pechenegs against His wayward but Christian Russians "because of their sins." If God were fair, He would use the Russians, who, for all their sins are nevertheless Christians, as a scourge against the godless Pechenegs. But God is really concerned only about Russians. He has little interest in Pechenegs, or aliens; I believe that my point is clear. Indeed, aliens are often used as a device of punishment; contact frequently falls upon some sort of human transgression. They are also used as a measure to criticize the authors' conspecifics; Longyear's "human aliens," the admirable Dracs, are a case in point. With good reason, Davidge is put off by the behavior of his fellow men and feels alienated. He encounters racial slurs at home as well as with miners on Fyrene IV, who use Drac slaves under inhuman conditions. At the end of the story, he gives up his passport and decides to stay with the Dracs. Human aliens can be preferable to alien humans.

Science Fiction as an Exogamous Literature

Enemy Mine closes on a hidden note of biological irony. At the end of the book, it becomes clear that Davidge joins Jeriba's family as an intimate member and that his sponsoring of Zammis' Drachood as its foster parent creates significant social tensions on Draco. The story makes it clear that both Dracs and Earthmen discriminate against this symbolic equivalent to intermarriage. In the story, the whole Jeriba clan, although the most honored line on Draco, moves to a neutral planet, indeed, back to Fyrene IV, where the liaison began. In doing so, Davidge and the Jeribas create a new ethnic group.

But the authors do not overtly state why. What is the internal necessity that dictates for Davidge to become alienated from his own kind, as well as for the Jeribas, the oldest line on Draco, to leave their own planet, all as a result of their association with the "Dragger suck"? The irony is that while interethnic alliances normally are cemented, if not originally motivated, by sexual intercourse and intermarriage, no transmission of genetic information is possible between Davidge and any of the Jeribas. Yet they act as if such transmission were taking place. Why and how can the reader be convinced of these actions? How can they be seen as consistent with earlier plot developments?

The answer is that Jeriba Shigan, Davidge, and their child, Zammis, biologically a Drac, culturally a human, all experience a shift in identity through the mutual exchange of *cultural* information. Alien culture is repulsive and threatening, but it is also an excellent source for the new cultural material necessary to revive a tired and homogenous civilization. Not surprisingly, the civilizations that best thrived in historic times were those that engaged most extensively in cultural intercourse with other peoples. This is especially true for trading cultures, those that cooperate with others and learn from them. Bigoted cultures are not adaptive; they tend to be rigid and backward. It is far more advantageous to be a melting pot, genetically and culturally.

Richard Dawkins' concept of the *meme* is important to our discussion of cultural intercourse. As he postulates in the last chapter of *The Selfish Gene*, cultural information is exchanged in a manner analogous to genes. [16] However, memes, bits of cultural information, are exchanged far more rapidly than genes. Memes may provide the mechanism of cultural evolution, a phenomenon which complements genetic evolution. Memetic interchange and development permits individuals with fixed genotypes to adapt to changing environments by constantly altering their *memeotypes*, typically at a second-by-second rate. The characteristics of *memetic* intercourse certainly pertain to alien possession (of minds by other minds) and telepathy. Memes are generated by individuals and then cast into the environment like spores; they are essential to all social interaction. Indeed, social intercourse is often described in sexual terms; note, for example, how a thought will be "seminal" if it "germinates" or "takes root." Most "fall on fallow ground" or "deaf ears," which has obvious sexual associations. A few find fertile ground and mix with the memes of the listeners or readers. This is why virtually no one wants to be wholly possessed, to the extent that one's own personality is squeezed out; the host wants to contribute to the "offspring" or resultant behavior. But one may wish to achieve total possession over another. Early theories of sexual reproduction had it that all genetic information came only from the man, or possessor, and that the woman was only the fertile ground. Anyway, if a meme takes root, it will be passed on to other individuals. There is then a battle of the fittest meme—this notion certainly refers to academic intercourse and the struggle to find that limited resource, publishers.

So this is what happens to Davidge and Jeriba Shigan. They alter each other's memeotype and thereby establish a new culture, one that combines Mickey Mouse and Shizumaat. And they seem to be the better for this mingling. Cultural outbreeding is adaptive.

We must not lose sight of the fact that *Enemy Mine* is a cultural fiction and that no genetic intercourse is possible between text and reader. But memetic intercourse is essential. Reading is a form of alien possession, of telepathically taking alien memes into our minds to mix with our memes. We expect to be slightly altered, hopefully improved, by our reading. Education generally tries to shape character by selecting the best texts, that is, literary memes, to read. Memetic interchange is pleasurable; in our leisure reading, we try to select the best memes and rely on reviewers to help us avoid the maladaptive. Furthermore, memetic outbreeding seems to be pleasurable because it is adaptive. The attraction of fictions, as opposed to most factual texts, lies in their presentation of varied and novel memes. This thinking is doubled for science-fiction readers, who are distinguished by their exogamous reading habits, their urge to freshen their minds with more and more alien memes. Consider how different the story would have been had Davidge not been able to overcome his biases and had he killed Jeriba. The chief gratification from our encounter with a Drac in *Enemy Mine* derives from our often unacknowledged belief that we may benefit from an intimate relationship with an alien.

16

From Astarte to Barbie and Beyond: The Serious History of Dolls

Frank McConnell

On the distant planet Symbion, a genetic experiment fails. Frightening changes take place that cannot be stopped. The result? A world where insects grow to frightening proportions. A world where the inhabitants have taken on the awesome characteristics of insects. Where the good of the Shining Realm is locked in mortal combat with the evil of the Dark Domain. Telepathically bonded in combat, Sectaur Warriors join with their insect companions in the ultimate battle for survival. A battle that is now in your hands.

Except for the last sentence, this passage might come from the back cover of a fifties or sixties science-fiction paperback. Today, however, when science fiction has almost received its academic laying-on of hands—a mixed *mitzvah* if there ever was one—the jacket copy would read more like this: "In *Sectaur Warrior*, the author continues his exploration of the shadowy interrealm where myth, genetic theory, and man's profoundest religious concerns all collide; and all of it cast in a mold of high adventure reminiscent of *The Lord of the Rings* and Anne McCaffrey's *Dragonriders of Pern*. This is speculative fiction at its best and most provocative."

And, to be sure, there would also be the ritual two-sentence blurb from, say, Norman Spinrad and, with luck, Gregory Benford. I leave it to you to decide which version you prefer, although I know which one would make *me* (apologies to Mr. Spinrad and Mr. Benford) buy the book. I always listen to AM rock stations rather than FM rock stations because I have a woefully low tolerance for pretension and would rather hear Little Richard's "Tutti Frutti" three more times than the Grateful Dead's "Dark Star" once.

At any rate, the more persuasive passage is not, of course, from

199

a paperback. It is from a package containing Sectaur Warrior Zak (and his insect sidekick Bitaur), bought for my far-from-wicked stepson Eric, eight years old and my research assistant for this project. Besides Sectaur Warriors, my home is also populated by GoBots, Power Lords, Masters of the Universe, and Transformers (who are either "Heroic Autobots" or "Evil Decepticons"). Now *that* is what I call an alien invasion: these aliens attack you through your Mastercard or Visa.

Are they toys? Dolls? Mere counters in a fantasy game played mainly in the head? Or the polyurethane grandchildren of those tin soldiers who fueled the martial instincts of boys about to be warriors, boys about to die from the Crimea through the Argonne and the Battle of the Bulge and into Korea and Vietnam?

I am not a deconstructionist. The only *real* deconstructionists I know are French intellectuals and termites. So my answer to that multiple question is "all of the above." And, more importantly, these aliens are the stuff of which fiction is made, the raw material that can be annealed into that most ancient and most indispensable of human artifacts, storytelling. (I will amend this later.) *Homo neanderthalensis* may not have had a writing system or a concept of the pulley; but it is inconceivable that this dear departed cousin did not tell stories and fashion dolls or icons to reify the characters in his stories.

The Babylonians, we know, not only worshipped the graven images of their gods, but on festival days set especially tasty dishes before them and pretended to feed them: there may be a shorter line than one might think from Astarte to Chatty Cathy. The *ka* of the Egyptians, the immortal yet still somehow physical part of the self, is represented in paintings as a doll-like simulacrum of the deceased. And just as the *ka* was the physical self in its immortal mode, it could be fed with real food or with the representation of food. The pharaohs and high priests would have understood, better than the *New York Times Book Review*, Philip K. Dick's brilliant question, "Do Androids Dream of Electric Sheep?" And, finally, the most popular fantasy game in the world, with elegantly simple and infinitely suggestive rules, involves toys of various powers and capabilities not unlike those of the many GoBots, Sectaur Warriors, or Transformers: its Persian name, *shah-mat*—our "checkmate"—means "the king is dead." Game is story, story is game.

And let us not forget that H. G. Wells loved to play elaborate games with his hundreds of toy soldiers, that Stanislaw Lem is fascinated with mechanical toys, and that Harlan Ellison has collected enough Shogun Warriors, Masters of the Universe, and so on, to satisfy the Christmas rush in a small town in Iowa.

Our subject is aliens and narrative, or aliens *in* narrative, and I want to suggest that all narrative begins as child's play and that the first and most indispensable tool of child's play, the first alien, is the doll/toy/simulacrum.

It is an alien in the true sense. As Wallace Stevens says in "The Man with the Blue Guitar," it is "a tune beyond us, yet ourselves." It is a projection of ourselves that is, strangely enough, not ourselves, a fun-house mirror image that reflects us, not more accurately, but more tellingly, than an undistorted image.

Emile Benveniste, Gallically gnomic or gnomically Gallic, observes that "language . . . is the possibility of subjectivity" and that the proper definition of the first-person pronoun "I" is "the individual who utters the present instance of discourse containing the linguistic instance *I*."

Never mind that this garble sounds like a Sorbonne lecture as written by Woody Allen. Benveniste's formula is still immensely suggestive. I would paraphrase it thus: "I" is both the most existential and most alien of utterances, the very possibility of narrative, of a "tune beyond us, yet ourselves." "Je est un autre" writes Rimbaud, sublimely mangling his native tongue: "I is somebody else." It is the very principle of storytelling, the distancing of the self from the self, of the story of your life as you tell it to yourself from the story of your life as it happened to you, of causality from experience. And as such its echo, its siamese twin in play, is the doll that is and is not us.

What does this have to do with Power Lords or Masters of the Universe?

I am not, mind you, interested in or convinced by the arguments of child psychologists about the "educative value" of toys, that is, make it out of wood and don't paint it because it stimulates the kid's imagination. Only in Departments of Education and in remote reaches of Marin County can people believe that, in our culture, wood is a more "natural" substance than plastic. I am with Chesterton, who observed that there is more natural spontaneity in the man who eats caviar on impulse than in the man who eats grape nuts on principle. I am interested in toys, in other words, not as relics of the childhood world, but as building blocks of the grown-up world.

Let me invoke two very intelligent women for elucidation. Jacquetta Hawkes, in her magisterial book *Prehistory*, remarks that everything we call "art" is intimately connected to the evolution of tool using. The human impulse to make representations of people and animals, according to Hawkes, seems to have developed at about the same time as the emergence of *secondary* tools, that is, stone fragments whose purpose it is to chip other stone fragments into axes, adzes, hammers, or spear points. This subtle refinement of what must have been the original chipping technique may, in its way, be a stage of development as crucial as the Neolithic Revolution itself. For, if you can make a tool that makes a tool, why not build a better axe by making a tool that makes a tool that makes a tool, and so on to infinity? Self-consciousness becomes possible; and so does play in the most serious sense of the word (*play* being, of course, one of the few words that can never be used frivolously).

Art and technology are not combatants but rather mirror siblings, like Helen and Klytemnestra, hatched from the same egg. The Magdalenian cave drawings—are they art or ritual or metaphysical technology?—overtrump Ruskin and Hegel in their idea of the growth of culture.

There is another intelligent lady: my daughter Kathy. When Kathy was ten, she had a rather shabby alien, a stuffed dog named Murray, and a friend, little Sally, who was a terrible child but who, since she was the daughter of good friends, was to be treated nicely. One day, as Kathy and Murray and I were sitting in my car, I asked Kathy if she really liked Sally. Kathy's answer was predictable: "Oh, yes, Daddy, I *love* Sally." So far, so good. But then, hefting hapless Murray onto her lap and staring seriously into his button eyes, she said, "Murray doesn't like Sally, you know. Murray *hates* Sally. Yes, he does." "Good for old Murray!" I thought. Not yet having read Roland Barthes on the omnipresence of the "I" in all fictive utterance and having stupidly forgotten Rimbaud's "Je est un autre," I did not realize that I was witnessing the birth of fiction and the reason for fiction. Kathy, the human, was expressing through Murray, the alien, that Sally, the other human, was a brat. If we could not invent simulacra to act out our unacted desires, speak our unspeakable wishes, how could we—a species burdened with the killing burden of consciousness—survive?

Freud, in *The Interpretation of Dreams*, describes the business of dreaming, the *Traumwerk*, as if he were describing the composition of a nineteenth-century novel. Fiction, in other words, is daydreaming. And I think Freud's epochal insight can be expanded to argue that *all* fantasy activity is not just the raw stuff of story, but is story.

Four years after *The Interpretation of Dreams*, in *The Psychopathology of Everyday Life*—a kind of streamlined version of his earlier book—Freud writes of the unreliability of childhood memories. "The 'childhood reminiscences' of individuals altogether advance to the signification of 'concealing memories' [that is, *edited* memories], and thereby form a noteworthy analogy to the childhood reminiscences as laid down in the legends and myths of nations."

Bridging the gap between the private and the cultural level of storytelling, in one of its earliest phases of transmutation, we find the doll. We are moving toward the exegesis of the Evil Decepticons and their colleagues. But, since I believe that literary commentary is like cross-country travel and courtship, in that half the fun is getting there, let me approach the world of my table-top aliens by an indirect route.

My wife, who is not a research assistant but in fact a collaborator on this essay, remembers Barbie. So do I, but deep and silly psychic mechanisms best described by Freud and best understood by Gloria Steinem and Vivian Sobchack force me, in my less liberated moods, to repress the memory.

Think about Barbie as an alien, a Philip K. Dick alien, to be sure: that is, something so like us as to be a tune beyond us, yet ourselves. Barbie is a charming, foxy teenager with a boyfriend, Ken, a best friend, Midge, a little sister, a black girlfriend, and the black girlfriend's black boyfriend, and, as the years have rolled on, an endlessly proliferating accumulation of ski clothes, surfing gear, evening gowns, and even cardboard chalets and beach houses. The Babylonians would have understood, and not found laughable, this headlong buildup of *things* to shore up the identity, the radiant "thereness" of the central and at-all-cost-to-be-venerated goddess. And so would Jay Gatsby, able to win the gaze of the golden girl in the high castle only by his vulgar, absurd, and holy accumulation of shirts. "I've never seen such beautiful shirts," exclaims Daisy, crying as he tosses them on his bed, showing her what he has done for her. And the person who finds that great scene funny is disenfranchised from reading the novel. Remember that the pharaohs went into eternity with their favorite toys: what else would you take with you on such an awful journey?

How easy it is to attack Barbie as a fallacious role model for women or as a celebration of capitalism at its most poisonous. Both positions are simple-minded enough to have been held by people whose political sophistication is bounded by *Rolling Stone* on the right and *Marx for Beginners* on the left. How easy, and how very tedious.

How interesting it is, on the other hand, to realize that Barbie—poor, plastic, neglected, and now collecting dust in a continent-full of attics or basements—may have been as much a woman warrior in the emerging feminist cause as Maxine Hong Kingston. She was, for the decade of her birth, independent, self-reliant, and able to use, rather than be used by, her feminine identity. Queen of the prom? Certainly. But also efficient mistress of the capitalist system and nobody's fool. And that means something. Like chess or Dungeons and Dragons or the Transformers, the universe called "Barbie" is the algorithm of a war game; it is only that Barbie, Ken, and the rest of the crew are warriors in those social and sexual battles better described by John Updike and John Cheever than by Philip K. Dick and Philip José Farmer.

Nevertheless, remember that one of Philip K. Dick's stories, "The Days of Perky Pat," imagines a postnuclear, impoverished Earth, where the survivors gamble their meager provisions on fantasy games played with Barbie-style dolls, reenacting the comfortable, middle-class existence detonated irrevocably beyond their reach. It would be fine to read this story simply as a satire on the foolishness of the bourgeoisie, obsessed with the trivialities of middle-class life even on the brink of the abyss. But oversimplifying Dick is about as wise—maybe less so—as oversimplifying Kafka or Borges. "Perky Pat" may represent capitalism gone rancid. But she also represents the continued possibility of invention, of storytelling, of making something out of nothing, which is after all Dick's generative obsession as a writer.

Stanislaw Lem writes that "the peculiarities of Dick's world arise especially from the fact that in them it is waking reality that undergoes profound dissociation and duplication." Or, elsewhere: "The end effect is always the same: distinguishing between waking reality and visions proves to be impossible." Readers of Lem's stunning novel *Solaris* or of his collection *The Cyberiad* will of course recognize that in discussing Dick's purposeful confusion of reality with imitation, Lem is also discussing his own work. Lem reads Dick with his own interpretive swerve, as of course we all do. But I interpret Lem's interpretation of Dick to mean this: from his earliest stories to the genius of *The Man in the High Castle*, to the mad sublimity of *Ubik* and *Valis* and *The Divine Invasion*, Dick has been concerned with the relationship between simulacrum and reality, which is to say that a perfect imitation *of* a thing *is* that thing, be it an 1844 Colt revolver, a 1910 American advertising poster, or a human being. Who writes *The Man in the High Castle*? At one level, the *I Ching*, the most rigorous and most random, most tychistic of oracles. Causality is what we impose upon, or flatter into, our lives. And to say that is to say that Dick, more than Nabokov and maybe even more than Joyce, is brooded over, intimately and terribly, by the core shadow of Story itself. He is, in short, our indispensable theorist of dolls.

And now we have come, at last, to the Transformers, the GoBots, Power Lords, Masters of the Universe, and whatever else may come along over the next few years. They are all toys, or dolls, who are aliens at a double remove. For they are, prima facie, aliens because they are dolls. But they are also dolls of aliens, of honest-to-God extraterrestrials: projections of ourselves, or of our childrens' selves if we are shy, into figures of wonder and terror who are, nonetheless, demonstrably of our world and of our dreams. I have already used the metaphor of the alien as a fun-house mirror reflection of ourselves; but it is extraordinary to realize that all the aliens we invent or produce are, from Wells' Martians to Larry Niven's Puppeteers and the Sectaur Warriors, deflections and declensions of us, the tedious Carl Sagan notwithstanding. Even Ggriptogg, the most brutal and pitiless of the bad Power Lords, even that four-armed monster has a copyright stamped under his left foot: just as Caliban in *The Tempest* becomes an efficient monster only after Prospero teaches him how to speak English.

It is always a battle between ultimate good and ultimate evil with these toys and with their accompanying mythologies. That, as far as I can see, differentiates them from maybe 10 percent of the world's stories. Let me take my favorite mytheme, that of the Transformers, to stand for the lot.

Eons ago, alien robots from the planet Cybertron crash-landed on Earth. Awakened from suspended animation after thousands of years of sleep, they are now engaged in a battle that will determine the fate of our planet. The evil Decepticons, led by the powerful Megatron—whose slogan is "Peace through Tyranny"—seek to return to Cybertron after draining all of the Earth's energy. They are resisted, thwarted in their dark quest by the Heroic Autobots, led by the wise Optimus Prime, whose somewhat question-begging motto (he is, after all, a robot) is "Freedom is the right of all sentient beings." They are called "Transformers" because, in order to deceive or in order not to alarm the unsuspecting earthlings, they can transform themselves from their warrior form into automobiles, airplanes, cassette decks, insects, dinosaurs, and dune buggies. As of the last catalog I bought, there were forty-three Heroic Autobots and twenty-nine Evil Decepticons on the market. By now, there may be more. Each box ranks its occupant in terms of strength, intelligence, speed, endurance, rank, courage, firepower, and skill on a scale of one to ten, proof that the mind-set of the Educational Testing Service at Princeton may be a universal principle and that the Homer who described the warriors before Troy could have been the E.T.S.'s first chairman of the board.

But I do not mean to make light of these toys. Quite the contrary. I find it rich and heartening that these highly technological toys are also toys *about* technology. They are alien invaders or alien friends who remind us—or our children, all of whom we hope will grow up to be Larry Nivens or Ursula K. LeGuins—that the truest and most immediately available aliens in our world are the machines with which we surround ourselves and out of which we build our culture. A Corvette Stingray or a transistor radio can, in the right circumstances, be a good guy, just as a laser pistol or a demolition truck can be a bad guy. The alternate universes of these toy worlds, played out on table tops or on that most magical of places, a child's counterpane at night with one, clandestine light on in the room, are alternate universes indeed and deserve to be treated as such.

We have heard, by now, so many versions of the pun between

"alien" and "alienation" that one more cannot possibly hurt. Let us note, then, that "alienated labor" is Marx's phrase for the separation of man from the fruits of his technology and that an "alienist," in the nineteenth century, would be called a psychoanalyst in ours. The toys of which I am speaking heal or help to thaw the ice, the schism between those two great imaginations of alienation, as do any story-telling tools, since all stories are about the aliens we carry in our heads and our hearts and since all stories are desperate, playful stabs at healing the wounds that make us human. And my toys help us, too, to understand the games we play later about aliens, with the more cumbersome counters of typewriters, word processors, and—save us—the mature human mind.

17

An Indication of Monsters

Colin Greenland

My friend Janet, a physiotherapist, was quite incredulous that the 1986 Eaton Conference proposed to consider papers on the subject of aliens, creatures that don't even exist. She felt confirmed in her diagnosis of collective insanity when she saw that the program listed only one female speaker out of nineteen. "That's because we're all too sensible," she said. "Women know there are enough real monsters in the world already without going around making them up."

Making up monsters is surely psychotic behavior, even if you get paid for it. There are writers of science fiction who expressly agree. In the introduction to his collection *The Golden Man*, Philip K. Dick identified himself explicitly with this model. "That's me," he wrote, "paralyzed by imagination. For me a flat tire on my car is (a) The End of the World; and (b) An Indication of Monsters (although I forget why). This is why I love SF. I love to read it; I love to write it. The SF writer sees not just possibilities but *wild* possibilities. It's not just 'What if—' It's '*My God*; what if—' In frenzy and hysteria."[1]

Philip K. Dick may have been paralyzed as an impromptu auto mechanic, having to fix a flat tire, but as a writer he was not at all "paralyzed by imagination," of course. His writing is characteristically restless, energetic. However, he seems to be saying here that science fiction is an expression of neurosis, even of paranoia. Someone who is paralyzed by imagination is like Hamlet, unable to act because of his apprehensions. It's not that he doesn't know what to do, but that he doesn't know what to think. He thinks the wildest things. He jumps to conclusions. He blames the aliens.

The alien appears at the moment of disaster and doubt: the flat tire. In the lore of those who study UFOs, the presence of the alien craft can frequently stop a car engine; and it's interesting how often that conjunction crops up in the monster movies, to which I'll be referring again later. The luckless victim is driving along a dark road and somebody, or something walks into his headlights; or he stops because he sees somebody lying in the road. The stopping of the car is crucial, especially in terms of the mythology of the American cinema, in which the car represents selfhood and mobility. We could say that the figure of the extraterrestrial alien, the invader from outer space, *represents* paralysis, the paralysis of knowledge and action. The alien is that which is outside our knowledge of life and the places where life is. It brings us to a full stop, to the limits of selfhood, and face to face with what we are not. All we can do now is ask questions.

There is a species of science fiction whose whole purpose is to ask those questions: to meet the alien and render it known. The interrogation is the story. At its conclusion, the frontiers of knowledge have been advanced and the alien has been incorporated, perhaps not into the human self, but certainly into a place in the human scheme of things. At the end of Larry Niven and Jerry Pournelle's *The Mote in God's Eye*, the Moties Jock and Ivan agree tacitly that "it was, in fact, a fine and enviable madness, this delusion that all questions have answers."[2] The madness—or perhaps we should say the myth—that operates in this kind of SF is that the human intellect can transcend the human condition, infinitely. There is "us" and there is "them," but "they" can be known.

Against this is the kind of science fiction that uses the alien to reinforce the paralysis, to express the limitations of humanity. There are secrets with which man must not meddle, otherwise hubris will, in Brian Aldiss' memorable definition of SF, be clobbered by nemesis. Or there may be no nemesis, merely an impasse. The preeminent example here is Stanislaw Lem's *Solaris*, in which the questions are asked, the interrogation professionally conducted; the data piles up and the theories pile higher; and still no one knows what "they" or "it" wants or means, or even what "it" is. Ian Watson put this best when he said that "Stanislaw Lem's *Solaris* raises the . . . salutary point that we might find ourselves unable, however much we stretch our intellects, to comprehend the Alien when we encounter it: so that, wherever we go in the universe, we shall only and inevitably come face to face with our own selves."[3] The answer to interrogating the alien may be: "You don't know." And "you don't know" tells us something about ourselves.

Ursula LeGuin gives us a romantic existentialist version of this in *The Left Hand of Darkness*, in the central confrontation during the exiles' second night on the Gobrin Ice, accounts of which we have from both Estraven and Genly Ai's viewpoints. Estraven, the Gethenian, records that "up here on the Ice each of us is singular, isolate, I as cut off from those like me, from my society and its rules, as he from his. . . . We are equals at last, equal, alien, alone."[4] What is revealed to Estraven is that Genly "is no more an oddity, a sexual freak, than I am."[5] Meanwhile, Genly says, "And I saw then again, and for good, what I had always been afraid to see, and had pretended not to see in him: that he was a woman as well as a man."[6] He tells Estraven that "in a sense, women are more alien to me than you are. With you I share one sex, anyhow."[7] Their intimate companionship in survival, which Genly Ai in his journal calls love, arises from their differences. "For us to meet sexually," he says, "would be for us to meet once more as aliens."[8]

In Barry B. Longyear's novella *Enemy Mine*, the human fighter pilot Willis E. Davidge muses bitterly about his exile on the inhospitable Fyrene IV with the alien Drac, Jeriba Shigan. " '*If you had your choice, who would you like to be trapped on a desert island with?*' I wondered if anyone had ever picked a wet freezing corner of Hell shacked up with a hermaphrodite."[9] Well, Genly Ai had, for one; or at least Ursula LeGuin had picked it for him. The central situation of *Enemy Mine* distinctly echoes that of *The Left Hand of Darkness*, written ten years earlier; and again the touchstone of alienness is sexuality. The great test in the humanizing of Davidge is tearing open Jeriba Shigan's womb and delivering baby Zammis. In Longyear's novella, though not in Wolfgang Petersen's film of the story, Davidge even breathes the breath of life into the alien infant's nostrils. But before that, in the film, though not in the book, the Drac Jeriba pronounces, "You humans are alone within yourselves—that is why you have split your sexes in two: for the joy of that brief moment of union."[10]

We can confidently attribute this maxim to screenwriter Edward Khmara, a graduate of the UCLA Film School, who tells us that, for him, "the story of 'Enemy Mine' is about the unity of intelligent life."[11] It's a point consonant with the one LeGuin was making. Genly Ai tells Estraven, "Your race is appallingly alone in its world,"[12] as it seems the Dracs must be, parthenogenetic as they are; but in each case it turns out that it's the humans who are more alone. The encounter with the alien reinforces the limitations and the paralysis of humanity. Dracs, like Gethenians, have sexual knowledge that transcends human longing. This is embodied, literally, in the negation of sex between humans and aliens. Jeriba Shigan and Willis E. Davidge can't; Estraven and Genly Ai may be able to, but deliberately don't. In the ultimate story along these lines, James Tiptree's "And I Awoke and Found Me Here on the Cold Hill's Side," the gloomy man from Burned Barn, Nebraska, says, "Now we've met aliens we can't screw, and we're about to die trying." "We're built to dream outwards," he says. "They laugh at us. They don't have it."[13] The alien entices the human to sterility and self-destruction. The humans smash themselves on the boundary of humanity like moths on lighted window panes.

In movies, there's an intriguing version of this fear of human and alien sexual incompatibility in *I Married a Monster from Outer Space*, Gene Fowler's 1958 picture, which film critic Philip Strick calls "that Freudian classic."[14] The alien impersonating Bill is impotent with Bill's new wife Marge: a tragic irony because the aliens have, as usual, come to Earth for human women to breed with. Every commentary on *I Married a Monster* mentions that scene when Bill is standing on the balcony in the storm before venturing into the fatal bedroom, and the lightning shows up the alien face lurking beneath the human. Again, the alien appears at the moment of doubt and disaster. Apart from ensuring, as would be suitable for a 1958 movie, that Marge is not violated by an imposter, the sexual disaster is intrinsic to the plot, because when Marge needs to find "real men" who will believe her story and rout the aliens, she goes to the maternity ward to round up some fathers. The reaffirmation of sexual potency and fecundity is what saves humanity.

In his book *Fantastic Cinema*, Peter Nicholls has something to say about the sexuality of the monster movie.

> To a degree, monster movies were deliberately created as erotic aids. In the UK, where drive-ins were unknown, it has never really been possible for people to see monster movies as they were, perhaps, meant to be seen: through the slightly misted windscreen of a car loaded with two or three teenage couples, a flagon of cheap red, and a lot of aphrodisiac gasps as the monsters made their presence felt. Nobody could get the

full horrific force of *I Married a Monster from Outer Space* while sitting
respectably in a cinema; you needed to be in a car with a girl who wasn't
too sure about you anyway giving you a speculative glance whenever the
lightning flashed.[15]

Flippancy aside, Nicholls is absolutely right about the appeal and
meaning of the film, and of cognate films like *It Came from Outer
Space* and *Invasion of the Body Snatchers*. The alien represents the
sexual object as threat, threat that the transcendence of selfhood will
not be negotiable, that the "brief moment of union" Jeriba Shigan
spoke about will not take place. It's a threat we need to entertain,
particularly if we're teenage girls contemplating sexual intercourse.
"My God, what if I go all the way with this boy and he turns out to be
not who I thought?" What if sex estranges, reinforcing alienness,
rather than transcending it?

Another creature feature that Peter Nicholls surely saw was *The
Creature from the Black Lagoon* by Jack Arnold, in which the alien
Gill Man invades not from outer space but from the depths of time,
surviving as he does from some prehistoric cul-de-sac of evolution.
Again the alien is a sexual threat; again the possibility of consummation is denied. John Baxter, a critic who's particularly keen on the
sexuality of *The Creature from the Black Lagoon*, describes the scene
every commentary mentions, in which Ben Chapman as the Gill Man
mimics Julie Adams while she's swimming. "Gliding beneath her,
twisting lasciviously in a stylised representation of sexual intercourse, the creature, his movements brutally masculine and powerful, contemplates his ritual bride, though his passion does not reach
its peak until the girl performs some underwater ballet movements,
explicitly erotic poses that excited the Gill Man to reach out and
clutch her murmuring legs."[16] One writer who dissents from the
general approbation for *The Creature from the Black Lagoon* is
David Wingrove, who points out that "it's a swamp dweller and takes
a fancy to a human female (wouldn't it find her grotesquely ugly?)
which it wants as its mate. This is, in one sense, merely the animation
of one of those scary alien-grabs-woman covers that adorned the
science fiction magazines throughout the 1930s, 1940s and 1950s."[17]

Wingrove is surely echoing that great enemy of metaphor John
W. Campbell, Jr., who famously objected to those alien-grabs-
woman covers of *Planet Stories* and the like by insisting, once again,

that alien-human sex, or even desire, is wholly improbable. The rhetorical question he posed his readers (who, he trusted, were all heterosexual) was this: would you rather have intercourse with a human of your own sex, or a rhinoceros of the opposite sex? Arch-literalist John W. Campbell wanted to deny that the alien could be a sexual threat, thereby missing the point of what Ellen Pedersen has called the alien icon, which we raise up to glamorize heterosexuality, and particularly the dangers thereof.

In her article "Evasion No. 147: Where SF Is At Right Now," in the Danish journal *The Airship*, Pedersen proposes the distinction of three modes of imagining the alien and suggests that, historically, science fiction has moved from the first through the second to the third.[18] The first mode, which she calls "realistic," conceives of the alien as something "out there" which may contact us or may not. The sense of threat, sexual or otherwise, is not primary. The inhabitants of the sun and moon in Lucian, Kepler, and De Bergerac have their own lives and concerns, pacific or martial. They may satirize us, but they do not draw us to the edge of what it means to be human. Pedersen calls her second mode "idealistic," based as it is upon an idea, which she distinguishes as characteristically bourgeois, that the world is already divided into "us" and "them." The alien is here, and we must protect our homes and families. It may or may not be the conscious purpose of the artist to raise or allay these terrors: we may think of H. G. Wells' glee at having sent the Martians to walk all over Wimbledon and the villages and suburbs of London. Pedersen points out that film has largely become stuck in this second mode, having found a rich vein of horror to mine for Peter Nicholls' drive-in audiences. Hence Don Siegel's classic *Invasion of the Body Snatchers* has been interpreted as a McCarthyite nightmare or as a satire on McCarthyite nightmares. The idealistic mode of envisaging the alien is based on the idea of "us" and "them," rather than on anything real. The third mode, the "symbolic," is a sophistication based not upon an idea, but upon the fiction itself, the accumulation of texts produced more or less innocently in the first two modes. Here, says Pedersen, "the alien is you and me; perhaps especially you." "If you're writing in this mode," she says, "it's irrelevant whether or not there's life on Mars: you really couldn't care less."

Writing in the third mode acknowledges the iconic significance of the alien, not least in the terms proposed in this rather cursory essay: that the alien is an image of our own isolation and the limits of human knowledge which at the same time, ambiguously, appeals to the hope, futile or otherwise, of transcending them. The third mode is the mode, characteristically, of the "new wave," with J. G. Ballard maintaining that outer space is really inner space—characteristically theirs, but not exclusively. This is also the place for the elfin aliens of Ray Bradbury and for Thomas Jerome Newton, in *The Man Who Fell to Earth*, created by Walter Tevis, a writer too lonely to be classed with any group. Here, too, we might look again at Philip K. Dick, still standing by the road, trying to cope with the notion of his flat tire.

When he described himself as "paralyzed by imagination," Dick was making fun of his own love of wild speculation, his tendency toward paranoia. What he was concealing with that phrase is the fact that, although contemplating the imaginary monster, the alien, throws us back upon ourselves, the fiction in which that contemplation takes place can have an effect that is not paralyzing but liberating. The alien that we imagine, inscrutable and extrinsic to any human scheme of things, enables us to appreciate the otherness that exists already, intrinsic to humanity and to ourselves. The alien may represent nothing but the irreducible quantum of irrationality, of that which does not succumb to interrogation, which is always with us and in us. We do need to have an image of it and to be reminded of it, if only because there is no strategy, no logic by which to deal with it. Surely one major purpose of fiction, and of science fiction in particular, is to provide a way of talking and thinking about the things in us that cannot otherwise be talked about.

The alien may be desirable but deadly, like Tiptree's beautiful but merciless sirens, or desirable and healthy, like the people of Winter, who, according to LeGuin, are an attempt at a myth of the humanity that doesn't belong exclusively to either sex. Or the alien may, perhaps more often, be a threat: undesirable, to be shunned. Philip K. Dick's Palmer Eldritch is the human capacity for inhumanity: that which we have within us, whether or not we blame it on influence from Proxima Centauri or a demonic face in the sky, which enables us to exploit, manipulate, and deny the humanity of others and thereby begin to forfeit our own identities. "Eldritch is everywhere," says Barney Mayerson.[19] We may be no better able to cope with these things after reading fiction about them, but at least for a while they have had names and addresses. Dick's evocation of the "wild possibilities" of SF echoes Shakespeare's Theseus, who certainly is not talking about paralysis.

> The poet's eye, in a fine frenzy rolling,
> Doth glance from heaven to earth, from earth to heaven;
> And, as imagination bodies forth
> The forms of things unknown, the poet's pen
> Turns them to shapes, and gives to airy nothing
> A local habitation and a name.[20]

That the alien is a metaphor for the unknown and the nameless, which fiction gives us a way of knowing and naming, certainly seems to be the purpose of many writers who have created aliens. When I asked Mary Gentle, author of *Golden Witchbreed*, what she thought she was doing, she said at once, "It's projection—projection of all the things we don't like to look at in ourselves." Rachel Ingalls told me that she also is very concerned with "the alien from within." Her novel *Mrs. Caliban* is a consummate example of writing about aliens in the third mode, the symbolic mode: it offers a rich and subtle commentary on the ambiguity of the alien as sexual threat, a tradition which, as Ingalls points out, goes back through the creature feature to Shakespeare. In an interview for the British Sunday newspaper *The Observer*, she identified the sources of *Mrs. Caliban*.

> "The Tempest" is very important, of course—the idea that Caliban might be the one to live with. And when I was growing up, in the Fifties, I listened to soap-operas on the radio all the time, and I saw all those films about monsters—"The Creature from the Lagoon." The monster is in some kind of frog suit and he's so much more attractive than the boyfriend, he really likes the heroine and wants to be nice to her. I always felt she was with the wrong one.[21]

Mrs. Caliban is the story of Dorothy and Fred, who live in a Southern California suburb where everything is neat and tidy and respectable. After terrible misfortunes (one of their children is stillborn, the other dies under anesthesia before an appendectomy), their marriage is exhausted. Dorothy feels that Fred is completely closed to her and is sure that he is having an affair, not his first. But when her best friend Estelle urges her to make the break, Dorothy replies, "I think we're too unhappy to get a divorce."[22]

For a while, Dorothy has been hearing strange things on the radio, voices with improbable messages for her alone. She begins to

wonder whether she's cracking up. The latest doubtful announce-
ment warns her of a highly dangerous "giant lizard-like animal"[23]
which has escaped from the Jefferson Institute for Oceanographic
Research. That evening, Fred brings a colleague home for dinner.
Dorothy has been out drinking with Estelle and starts to prepare a
hasty meal. "And she was halfway across the checked linoleum floor
of her nice safe kitchen, when the screen door opened and a gigantic
six-foot-seven-inch frog-like creature shouldered its way into the
house and stood stock-still in front of her, crouching slightly, and
staring at her face."[24] We learn that "his head was quite like the head
of a frog, but rounder. . . . Only the nose was very flat, almost not
there."[25] These are very much the terms in which the Dracs are
described in Barry Longyear's *Enemy Mine*. "The three-fingered
hands are distinctive, of course, as is the almost noseless face, which
gives the Drac a toad-like appearance."[26] In other respects, however,
the creature from the Gulf of Mexico, whose given name is Larry, is
wholly humanoid, as Dorothy soon discovers. Once again, the alien
has appeared at the moment of doubt and disaster, and Dorothy, for
a moment, is paralyzed; but she gives him a big bowl of salad, hides
him in the spare room, and the next day the two become lovers.
Larry, who has been tortured and forced to learn English at the
Institute, is indeed superhumanly strong, but proves to be gentle and
very polite. He's a vegetarian who eats avocados by the bagful, and
he likes to help Dorothy with the housework. "Now that you've
come," she tells him, "everything's all right."[27]

Ingalls observes that one of the unexamined aspects of the
sexuality of the Creature from the Black Lagoon and his fictional kin
is that they are gentler and more attentive to the women they fix upon
than the women's boyfriends or husbands are. In the familiar formulation of the movie *King Kong*, this is seen as Beauty taming the
Beast. What is not brought out, Ingalls says, is that the Beast is
potentially the Beauty's ideal lover and should not be hunted down
and destroyed. The hunt is on for Larry, but he's safe as long as
nobody conceives of the idea that he may have found a friend. In fact,
it's the media and the suburban mentality that make Larry a monster
at all. When Fred mentions the latest newspaper report to Dorothy,
she challenges him.

> "Why do you call him a monster?"
> "Well, an eight-foot tall green gorilla with web feet and bug

eyes—what would you call him? A well-developed frog? Not exactly an Ivy-league type, anyway."

Dorothy retorts, "I've met plenty of Ivy-leaguers I'd call monsters."[28] As my friend caustically observed, women know there are enough real monsters in the world already. In Ellen Pedersen's phrase, the alien is you and me; perhaps especially you.

By contrast, Ingalls gives us Larry's view of human civilization. "You know," he tells Dorothy, "it's wonderful to see another world. It's entirely unlike anything that has ever come to your thoughts. And everything in it fits. You couldn't have dreamed it up yourself, but somehow it all seems to work, and each tiny part is related. Everything except me."[29] Larry, the monster man, stands outside with his nose pressed flat on the windowpane of the tidy, well-lit kitchen that is the human order. He is precisely that which humanity excludes. Nevertheless, since he comes from the ocean deep, with sexual and mythic potency, perhaps he is exactly what is needed to refructify the sterility of Dorothy's life; or might be, were he not impossible and imaginary. Thinking of Larry's comments, Dorothy asks her friend Estelle,

> "Can you think what it would be like to live in a different world? . . . Like science fiction. Where the people look sort of like you, but not quite the same."
> Estelle laughed, "Little green men?"
> "Big green men," Dorothy said.[30]

In a blurb to the book, John Updike describes *Mrs. Caliban* as "so deft and austere in its prose, so drolly casual in its fantasy," but it is ultimately far more than just a sardonic look at the symbolic alien. The climax is very dramatic, with the discovery of Fred's lover and a deadly car chase; and Dorothy's love for Larry is ultimately doomed, as it must be. Ingalls is clever enough to avoid saying exactly how real Larry is, or where the hubris in his summoning actually lies. She simply shows that wishful thinking does have real consequences, which are unlikely to be wish fulfillment.

In *Mrs. Caliban*, Rachel Ingalls brings the alien home, not to the different world of science fiction where it lives, but to this world of suburbia and Hollywood, of flat tires and failing marriages, where it is imagined and granted currency. It is through stories like hers that the indications of monsters may perhaps be known, and, as only fictions can be, understood.

Notes

Biographical Notes

Index

Notes

3. Border Patrols

1. "The 'Uncanny,'" in *On Creativity and the Unconscious*, ed. Benjamin Nelson (New York: Harper and Row, 1958), 148, 153.
2. Ibid., 152, 131.
3. Ibid., 144, 141.
4. *Kant's Critique of Judgement*, trans. J. H. Bernard (London: Macmillan, 1914), 106, 109.
5. Thomas Weiskel, *The Romantic Sublime: Studies in the Structure and Psychology of Transcendence* (Baltimore: Johns Hopkins, 1976), 21.
6. Kant, *Critique*, 143, 144.
7. *The Mind Parasites* (Berkeley: Oneiric Press, 1967), 83, 84, 213, 217.
8. *Solaris*, trans. Joanna Kilmartin and Steve Cox (New York: Berkley, 1961), 108.
9. *We*, trans. Mirra Ginsburg (New York: Avon Books, 1972), 75; *We*, trans. Gregory Zilboorg (New York: E. P. Dutton, 1924), 101; *Dissonant Voices in Soviet Literature*, ed. Patricia Blake and Max Hayward (New York: Random House, 1962), 14.
10. *We* (Ginsburg translation), 8, 39.
11. *Blindness and Insight: Essays in the Rhetoric of Contemporary Criticism* (New York: Oxford, 1971), 163.

4. Alien Aliens

1. György Botond-Bolics, *Ezer év a Vénuszon* (Budapest: Móra Kiadó, 1963.) In German: *Tausend Jahre auf der Venus*, trans. G. Feidl for the 1967 edition. (Düsseldorf: Marion von Schröder Verlag, 1969), 250.
2. Pierre Versins, *Encyclopédie de l'Utopie, des Voyages Extraordinaires et de la Science Fiction* (Lausanne: L'Age d'Homme, 1972).

3. Hal Clement, "The Creation of Imaginary Beings," in *Science Fiction, Today and Tomorrow* (New York: Harper and Row, 1974), 259–75.

4. Donald Knuth, "Le concept de métafonte," in *Communication et Langages*, no. 55, (1983): 40–53. Translation by M. R. Delorme.

5. J.-H. Rosny the Elder, "The Xipéhuz," in *L'Immolation* (Paris: Albert Savine, 1887), 249–328. I used the more recent edition in J.-H. Rosny the Elder, *Récits de Science Fiction* (Verviers, Belgium: Gérard, 1973), 115–35.

6. Hal Clement, *Mission of Gravity* (New York: Doubleday, 1954).

7. J.-H. Rosny, *Les Navigateurs de l'Infini* (magazine ed., 1925), and *Les Astronautes* (Paris: Hachette, 1960), "Le Rayon fantastique," 69.

8. Nico, "You Forget to Answer," in *The End*. (London(?): Island Records, 1974).

9. Paul Watzlawick, Janet Helmick Beavin, and Don Jackson, *Pragmatics of Human Communication* (1967).

10. Ibid., 43.

11. Ibid.

12. Ibid., 95–96.

13. Ibid., 96.

14. Ibid., 232.

15. Ibid., 271.

16. Stanislaw Lem, *Ciemność i Pleśń*, in *Inwazja z Aldebarana* (Krakow: Wydawnicto Literackie, 1959). In French: *L'Obscurité et la Moisissure*, in *Le Breviaire des Robots* (Paris: Denoël, 1967), 71, 92. There is a German translation by I. Zimmerman-Göllheim, *Nacht und Schimmel*, in the collection with the same title. (Frankfurt am Main: Insel Verlag, 1971).

5. Metamorphoses of the Dragon

1. This poem was LeGuin's entry in *The Faces of Science Fiction* (New York: Bluejay Books, 1984). LeGuin's essay "Why Are Americans Afraid of Dragons?" appeared in *The Language of the Night* (New York: Putnam's, 1979), 39–47.

2. Frank McConnell, "Sturgeon's Law: First Corollary," in *Hard Science Fiction*, ed. George E. Slusser and Eric S. Rabkin (Carbondale: Southern Illinois Univ. Press, 1986), 14–23.

3. *The World of M. C. Escher* (New York: Harry N. Abrams, 1971), catalog print no. 120.

4. Gary Zukav, *The Dancing Wu-Li Masters: An Overview of the New Physics* (New York: William Morrow, 1979), 43.

5. Norbert Wiener, *The Human Use of Human Beings* (Garden City, NY: Doubleday, 1954), 61.

6. J. D. Bernal, *The World, the Flesh, and the Devil: An Inquiry into the Future of the Three Enemies of the Rational Soul*, rev. ed. (London: Jonathan Cape, 1968), 56.

7. See Jane Harrison, *Themis: A Study in the Social Origins of Greek Religion* (Cambridge: Cambridge Univ. Press, 1912), especially 364–443.

8. Evgeny Zamyatin, *The Dragon*, trans. Mirra Ginsburg (New York: Random House, 1977), 70–72.

9. Carl Sagan, *The Dragons of Eden: Speculations on the Evolution of Human Intelligence* (New York: Random House, 1977).

10. Frank Herbert, *Dune* (New York: Berkley Books, 1965), 362.

11. "The Game of Rat and Dragon," in *The Best of Cordwainer Smith*, ed. J. J. Pierce (New York: Ballantine Books, 1975), 71.

12. Gary Wolfe, "Autoplastic and Alloplastic Adaptations in Science Fiction: 'Waldo' and 'Desertion'," in *Coordinates: Placing Fantasy and Science Fiction*, ed. George E. Slusser, Eric S. Rabkin, and Robert Scholes (Carbondale: Southern Illinois Univ. Press, 1983), 67.

13. Arthur C. Clarke, "A Meeting with Medusa," in *The Wind from the Sun* (New York: Signet Classics, 1973), 127–68.

14. Frank Herbert, *The Dragon in the Sea* (New York: Avon, 1970), 178.

6. Discriminating among Friends

1. See Patrick Parrinder, "The Alien Encounter, Or, Ms. Brown and Mrs. LeGuin," *Science-Fiction Studies* 17 (March 1979): 46–75, rpt. in *Science Fiction: A Criticial Guide*, ed. Patrick Parrinder (London and New York: Longman, 1979), 148–61; Gregory Benford, "Aliens and Knowability: A Scientist's Perspective," in *Bridges to Science Fiction*, ed. George E. Slusser, George R. Guffey, and Mark Rose (Carbondale: Southern Illinois Univ. Press, 1980), 53–63; Robert G. Pielke, "Humans and Aliens: A Unique Relationship," *Mosaic* 13 (1980): 29–40; Mark Rose, *Alien Encounters: Anatomy of Science Fiction* (Cambridge, MA: Harvard Univ. Press, 1981), 77–81; and John Huntington, "Impossible Love in Science Fiction," *Raritan* 4 (1984): 85–99.

2. Pielke, "Humans and Aliens," 30.

3. "American Science Fiction and the Other," in Ursula LeGuin, *The Language of the Night: Essays on Fantasy and Science Fiction*, ed. Susan Wood (New York: G. P. Putnam's Sons, 1979). This essay, originally an address to a panel on women in science fiction, was first published in *Science Fiction Studies* 7 (1975): 208–10. "A Martian Odyssey" has been frequently anthologized. I have used the text in *Science Fiction Hall of Fame, Vol. I*, ed. Robert Silverberg (New York: Avon, 1970).

4. Parrinder discusses this compliment in "The Alien Encounter," 54.

5. *Civilization and Its Discontents*, trans. James Strachey (New York: Norton, 1961), 68.

6. Jarvis has a typical Western condescension to thought processes he cannot follow. He plays with (and discards) the idea that Tweel's language may be like that of the Negritoes who have "no word for food or water or man—words for good food and bad food, or rain water and sea water, or strong men and weak men—but no names for general classes. They're *too primitive to understand* that rain water and sea water are just different aspects of the same thing" (emphasis added). There are, of course, other possible explanations besides "primitive" understanding for such linguistic behavior.

7. Yevgeny Zamyatin, *We*, trans. Mirra Ginsburg (Viking: New York, 1972), 219.

8. "Nine Lives," first published in 1969, is also much anthologized. I have used the text in *Science Fiction: The Future*, ed. Dick Allen, 2nd ed. (New York: Harcourt Brace, 1983), 259–80.

7. Sex, Superman, and Sociobiology

1. Philip Wylie, *The Gladiator* (New York: Knopf, 1930).

2. *Superman*, no. 297 (New York: DC Comics, 1976).

3. Larry Niven, "Man of Steel, Woman of Kleenex," in *All the Myriad Ways* (New York: Ballantine, 1971).

4. Mary Shelley, *Frankenstein or The Modern Prometheus* (Berkeley: Univ. of California Press, 1984).

5. Isaac Asimov, *Robots of Dawn* (New York: Doubleday, 1983).

6. David Gerrold, *When Harlie Was One* (New York: Ballantine, 1972).

7. Frank Herbert, *Dune* (Philadelphia: Chilton, 1965).

8. Daniel Keyes, "Flowers for Algernon," in *The Hugo Winners*, ed. Isaac Asimov (New York: Doubleday, 1962).

9. Thomas Disch, *Camp Concentration* (New York: Doubleday, 1969).

10. Robert A. Heinlein, *Stranger in a Strange Land* (New York: Putnam, 1961).

11. Arthur C. Clarke, *Against the Fall of Night* (New York: Gnome Press, 1953).

12. Cordwainer Smith, "The Ballad of Lost C'Mell," in *the Best of Cordwainer Smith*, ed. J. J. Pierce (New York: Ballantine, 1975).

13. Aldous Huxley, *Brave New World* (New York: Doubleday, 1932).

14. Robert A. Heinlein, *Methuselah's Children* (New York: Signet, 1958).

15. Larry Niven, *Ringworld* (New York: Ballantine, 1970).

16. Isaac Asimov, *The Foundation Trilogy* (New York: Street and Smith, 1948, 1949).

17. Olaf Stapledon, *Odd John and Sirius* (New York: Dover, 1972).

18. A. E. Van Vogt, *Slan* (New York: Simon and Schuster, 1951).

19. Theodore Sturgeon, *More Than Human* (New York: Ballantine, 1953).

20. John Wyndham, *The Midwich Cuckoos* (New York: Ballantine, 1958).

21. Arthur C. Clarke, *Childhood's End* (New York: Ballantine, 1953).

22. Michael Bishop, *No Enemy but Time* (New York: Simon and Schuster, 1982).

23. Ira Levin, *The Stepford Wives: A Novel* (New York: Random House, 1972).

24. Lester Del Rey, "Helen O'Loy," in *And Some Were Human* (New York: Ballantine, 1943).

25. Octavia Butler, "Blood Child," in *Isaac Asimov's Science Fiction Magazine* (New York: Davis Publications, 1984).

8. Cowboys and Telepaths/Formulas and Phenomena

I gratefully acknowledge the kind and helpful comments made on earlier versions of this essay by Brian Attebery, Harriet Linkin, Tobin Siebers, Macklin Smith, and Jules Zanger.

1. John G. Cawelti, *Adventure, Mystery, and Romance* (Chicago: Univ. of Chicago Press, 1976), 5–6.

2. Ibid., 49.

3. Gary K. Wolfe, *The Known and the Unknown: The Iconography of Science Fiction* (Kent, OH: Kent State Univ. Press, 1979), 216.

4. Brian Ash, *The Visual Encyclopedia of Science Fiction* (New York: Harmony Books, 1977), 207.

5. Peter Nicholls, *The Science Fiction Encyclopedia* (New York: Doubleday, 1979), 200.

6. Norman N. Holland, *The Dynamics of Literary Response* (New York: Oxford Univ. Press, 1968), 44.

7. Kathryn Hume, *Fantasy and Mimesis* (New York: Methven, 1984), 175.

9. Robots: Three Fantasies and One Big Cold Reality

1. U.S. Office of Technology Assessment, *Exploratory Workshop on the Social Impacts of Robotics*, 1982, 79.

2. Joseph Deken, *Silico Sapiens* (1986), 235.

3. Deken, *Silico Sapiens*, 72.

II. Aliens 'R' U.S.: American Science Fiction
Viewed from Down Under

1. Géza Róheim, *The Origin and Function of Culture*, Nervous and Mental Diseases Monograph no. 69 (New York, 1943); Géza Róheim, *Psychoanalysis and Anthropology* (New York: International Universities Press, 1950); Norman O. Brown, *Life against Death* (Middletown, CT: Wesleyan Univ. Press, 1959); Norman O. Brown, *Love's Body* (New York: Vintage, 1966).

2. The terms *extraterrestrialist* and *exterminist* refer not to entities but to antiterrestrial tendencies in Western civilization. *Exterminist* is E. P. Thompson's term for the proliferation of technologies of extermination in what he considers the last stage of capitalism. *Extraterrestrialist* is my term for the related tendencies to view the Earth from an off-world perspective and to shape it into an unearthly environment. I take the "high" of "high technology" as a reference to its extraterrestrial character. See E. P. Thompson, "Notes on Exterminism: The Last Stage of Civilization," *New Left Review* 20 (May-June 1980): 3–31; Zoe Sofia, "Exterminating Fetuses: Abortion, Disarmament, and the Sexo-Semiotics of Extraterrestrialism," *Diacritics*, vol. 14, no. 2 (Summer 1984): 47–59.

3. The capitalization of "Man" and "Woman" is meant to highlight their status as mythic constructs within humanist philosophy and ideology.

4. Melanie Klein, "Early Stages of the Oedipus Conflict," in *Love, Guilt, and Reparation and Other Works* (London: Hogarth, 1975; New York: Delacorte Press/Seymour Lawrence, 1975), 193. See also Melanie Klein, *Envy and Gratitude and Other Works, 1946–1963* (London: Hogarth, 1975).

5. Luce Irigaray, *Speculum of the Other Woman*, trans. Gillian G. Gill (1974; rpt. Ithaca, NY: Cornell Univ. Press, 1985).

6. See René Descartes, *Discourse on Method* (1637), trans. Laurence J. Lafleur (Indianapolis: Bobbs-Merrill, 1950), and *Meditations on First Philosophy* (1641), trans. Laurence J. Lafleur (Indianapolis: Bobbs-Merrill, 1951).

13. Inspiration and Possession: Ambivalent
Intimacy with the Alien

1. *The New English Bible* (Oxford and Cambridge Univ. Presses, 1970).

2. Edith Hamilton and Huntington Cairns, eds., *The Collected Dia-*

logues of Plato (New York: Bollingen Foundation, 1963), is the source of all quotations from Plato. I have consulted the Greek texts of J. Burnet, ed., *Platonis Opera* (Oxford: Clarendon Press, 1901 et seq.).

3. See, for example, his story "We Purchased People," first published in *Final Stage*, 1974; cited here from Terry Carr, ed., *The Best Science Fiction of the Year*, no. 4 (New York: Ballantine Books, 1975), 1–17.

4. John Varley, *Demon* (New York: Berkley Books, 1984), 42.

5. Varley, *Demon*, 454.

6. Ibid., 461.

7. A. A. Attanasio, *Radix* (1981; New York: Bantam, 1985).

8. Ibid., 466.

9. Ibid., 191.

10. Ibid.

11. Attanasio, *Radix*, 364.

12. Ibid.

13. James Morrow, *The Continent of Lies* (New York: Baen, 1984).

14. Ibid., 128.

15. The participants in the Eaton Conference (1986) made a number of suggestions which I have gratefully included in this essay. Unfortunately, I could not take advantage as fully as I would have liked in all cases. Larry Niven, for example, pointed out to me the relevance of Stephen King's story "The Ballad of the Flexible Bullet," but I was not able to get a copy in time to include discussion of it here.

14. Cybernauts in Cyberspace: William Gibson's *Neuromancer*

1. Claude E. Shannon, "The Bandwagon," *IEEE Transactions on Information Theory* 2(3): 3.

2. Norbert Wiener, *Cybernetics: Control and Communication in Animal and Machine* (Cambridge: MIT Press, 1948).

3. William Gibson, *Neuromancer* (New York: Ace, 1984).

4. I call these "impediments" only somewhat tongue in cheek. Some technocrats, be assured, believe that they represent the weighty baggage of primitive urges which impede our progress.

5. In lit crit parlance, this is called a *deconstruction*.

6. One quickly thinks of Philip K. Dick's "Do Androids Dream of Electric Sheep?" although the pattern seems to be hardwired into the theme, since it appears often in everything from Asimov's *I, Robot* to Shelley's *Frankenstein*.

7. See *The Science Fiction Encyclopedia*, ed. Peter Nicholls (New York: Dolphin Books, 1979), q.v. *cybernetics* and *cyborg*, 150–151.

8. *The Soft Machine: Cybernetic Fiction* (New York and London: Methuen, 1985).

9. Over 80 percent of my students believe that we will successfully clone humans before the end of the twentieth century. Almost 75 percent of them believe that within the next half century, we will have built machines that rival us in use of natural languages, creativity, and self-consciousness—true artificial intelligence. But that may not mean much, since over half my students at Rensselaer Polytechnic Institute also believe that we've been visited by extraterrestrial intelligences within the last two decades, and 25 percent believe that wizards commonly populated Europe in the tenth, eleventh, and twelfth centuries. Note also that all these projects are aimed at finding versions of ourselves.

10. "Look mommy, I push this button, the thing works. I push this button, the thing works. I push this button, the thing works." At this level of our interface with it, *the machine succeeds in making us over in its image.* We become, in Henri Bergson's terms, comedians.

11. An image from Robert Coover's story "Morris in Chains" always comes to mind when I contemplate this future state of affairs: a randy, hairy satyr, Morris, roams upon the ersatz grass of an urban park in some techtopian city, muttering a persistently horny monologue to himself while behavioral engineers hunt him down. *Pricksongs and Descants* (New York: New American Library, 1969).

12. I think of this second class of science fiction as postmodern, since it tends to share with other literary experiments an intensified use of language, imagery, abstraction, and self-consciousness. Furthermore, recognized literary postmodernists—not necessarily authors of science fiction, if you care to make these often trivial generic distinctions—tend to flirt with the idea of the soft machine, often using it as a metaphor for their own acts of creation, which tend to be partly mechanical—almost computerized, one might say— in their complex designs. To extend the metaphor, we can even see the author as a species of artificial intelligence, and indeed, in some instances, these experimentalists even pose as computer brains that generate the texts we read. See John Barth's *Giles Goat-Boy, The Lost Ones* by Samuel Beckett, and *Plus* by Joseph McElroy, to name just a few.

13. At one point, one of this AI's constructs, appearing before Case as a young human boy, parses the name. "To call up a demon you must learn its name. . . . You know that Case. Your business is to learn the names of programs, the long formal names, names the owners seek to conceal. True names. . . . Neuromancer. . . . The lane to the land of the dead. Where you are, my friend . . . Neuro from the nerves, the silver paths. Romancer. Necromancer. I call up the dead" (243–44).

14. See John Sladek's fine book *Mechasm* (1968). In this regard, see also his novel *The Muller-Fokker Effect* (1970), which concerns the reconstruction of a man's personality on a computer tape, a sort of "ghost in the machine" who becomes the impish, demonic source of a dionysian collapse of sense. For an exploration of the philosophical consequences of this theme, see Arthur Koestler's *The Ghost in the Machine*.

15. As Gibson puts it, "burgeoning technologies need outlaw zones. . . . Night City wasn't there for its inhabitants but as a deliberately unsupervised playground for technology itself" (11). In this sense, the technology is playing with itself more or less autonomously, much as Jacques Ellul's compelling paranoiac diatribe prophesies it will in *Technological Man*. See also Langdon Winner's more sober examination of the subject in *Autonomous Technology* (Cambridge: MIT Press, 1976).

16. See Jeremy Campbell, *Grammatical Man: Information, Entropy, Language, and Life* (New York: Simon and Schuster, 1982).

17. This technique was perfected by Thomas Pynchon in his three novels, *V., The Crying of Lot 49*, and *Gravity's Rainbow*.

18. This reminds me of Hemingway's comparison, through Jake Barnes, of Brett Ashley's body to "the hull of a racing yacht," in *The Sun Also Rises*.

19. See also William L. Benzon, "The Visual Mind and the Macintosh," *Byte* (January, 1985).

20. Richard Bolt, "Spatial Data Management."

21. "Die Welt ist alles was der Fall ist." The world is all that is the case, which, just perhaps, is where Gibson got his hero's name.

15. The Human Alien: In-Groups and Outbreeding in *Enemy Mine*

1. There are three available texts for *Enemy Mine*: the original novella, the film, and the novel (written either during the film's production or shortly thereafter, with the aid of David Gerrold, but obviously much influenced by Edward Khmara's screenplay as well as the rest of the film production). References will be given by means of "novella," "film," or "book," plus, where appropriate, page numbers. Although there are some minor discrepancies between the different texts, this study treats them as complementary parts of one whole "story." See Barry B. Longyear, *Enemy Mine, Isaac Asimov's Science Fiction Magazine*, vol. 3, no. 9 (Sept. 1979): 120–81.

2. "The Unparalleled Invasion," in *Curious Fragments: Jack London's Tales of Fantasy Fiction*, ed. Dale L. Walker (Port Washington, NY: Kennikat Press, 1975), 110.

3. Philip D. Curtin, *The Image of Africa: British Ideas and Action*, 1780–1850 (Madison: Univ. of Wisconsin Press, 1964).

4. The same applies to human-animal conflict on this planet; in order to bring about a suitable conflict, it is usually necessary to strengthen the animal so as to compensate for its lack of gray matter. In horror movies, ants and other insects are greatly expanded or multiplied to provide a challenge to humans. And a conflict found out on roughly equal terms is clearly a common plot expectation, one which can be exploited for ironic effect when the aliens are of a much different stature and cannot enter into true intercourse, as with Lem's *Solaris*, or simply take no apparent notice of man, as in the Strugatskys' *Roadside Picnic*.

5. One reason for the relative intelligibility of Drac is that many Drac words used in the book—and not in the story—appear to have a Russian etymology. Some statements can be transliterated directly into Russian, with the phrase still being appropriate to its context. Other words could be Russian, but are not used with their Russian meanings. And of course, there are plenty of words which have a totally non-Russian derivation. Notably, the writers facilitate intelligibility by providing word breaks; these are generally perceived in actual communication only when one understands the language.

6. Edward O. Wilson, *Sociobiology: The New Synthesis* (Cambridge: Harvard Univ. Press, 1975), 3.

7. Jeffrey Saver, "An Interview with E. O. Wilson on Sociobiology and Religion," *Free Inquiry* 5 (1985): 19.

8. See Edward O. Wilson, *Biophilia* (Cambridge: Harvard Univ. Press, 1984).

9. See Alice Carol Gaar, "The Human as Machine Analog: The Big Daddy of Interchangeable Parts in the Fiction of Robert A. Heinlein," in *Robert A. Heinlein*, ed. Joseph D. Olander and Martin Harry Greenberg (New York: Taplinger, 1978), 75–76. She has termed these huge tarantula-like aliens a "picture of everything unsympathetic in the universe," noting that "huge insects and monsters are all basic symbols of an opponent *related* to us but also related to the creeping horror of the universe in that they are all imperturbable, unsympathetic, and as pervasive as we" (emphasis added).

10. Pierre van de Berghe, *The Ethnic Phenomenon* (New York: Elsevier, 1981).

11. Note how in the "old world," family ties are given precedence over relationships with nonrelatives.

12. See Nevit Clifton, "How to Hate Thy Neighbor: A Guide to Racist Maledicta," *Maledicta*, vol. 2, no. 1–2(1978): 150–51.

13. The length of the Jeriba line and the ceremonial manner of its recitation parallels the Hawaiian royal genealogy, one that traces 120 genera-

tions back to the beginning in "the Red Sea of Man." Both involve memory of significant deeds, albeit the Drac genealogy is considerably shortened, we presume, by the fact that there is only one parent per generation. Drac ancestor worship possibly reflects Chinese culture. In all, Jeriba reminds the reader more and more of a Moslem (adherence to one holy book, life of prayers) or an Oriental, while it bears virtually no European traits.

14. See Daniel Rancour-Laferriere, *Signs of the Flesh: An Essay on the Evolution of Hominid Sexuality* (Berlin: Mouton/Walter der Gruyter, 1985), Sec. 45.

15. Psychoanalytic structures, for most sociobiologists, are envisioned as enabling mechanisms which promote certain forms of behavior while resisting others, such as incest.

16. Richard Dawkins, *The Selfish Gene* (New York: Oxford Univ. Press, 1976).

17. An Indication of Monsters

1. Philip K. Dick, *The Golden Man* (New York: Berkley, 1980), xxiv.

2. Larry Niven and Jerry Pournelle, *The Mote in God's Eye* (New York: Simon and Schuster, 1974), 537.

3. Ian Watson, "SF Idea Capsules for Art Students," *Foundation: The Review of Science Fiction*, no.5 (Jan. 1974): 60.

4. Ursula K. LeGuin, *The Left Hand of Darkness* (New York: Ace, 1969), 221.

5. Ibid., 221.

6. Ibid., 234.

7. Ibid., 223.

8. Ibid., 235.

9. Barry B. Longyear, *Enemy Mine,* in *Isaac Asimov's Science Fiction Magazine*, vol. 3, no. 9 (Sept. 1979): 127.

10. *Enemy Mine*, directed by Wolfgang Petersen, 20th Century Fox, 1985.

11. Edward Khmara, quoted in 20th Century Fox's production information for *Enemy Mine.*

12. LeGuin, *Left Hand*, 221.

13. James Tiptree, Jr., "And I Awoke and Found Me Here on the Cold Hill's Side," in *Ten Thousand Light-Years from Home* (New York: Ace, 1973), 12.

14. Philip Strick, *Science Fiction Movies* (London: Galley Press, 1979), 19.

15. Peter Nicholls, *Fantastic Cinema: An Illustrated Survey* (London: Ebury Press, 1984), 37.

16. John Baxter, *Science Fiction in the Cinema* (New York: Tantivy Press, 1970), 121.

17. David Wingrove, ed., *The Science Fiction Film Source Book* (Harlow, England: Longman, 1985), 59–60.

18. Ellen Pedersen, "Evasion No. 147: Where SF Is At Right Now," *The Airship*, vol 2, no. 1 (1982): 71–78. All quotations are from conversations with the author.

19. Philip K. Dick, *The Three Stigmata of Palmer Eldritch* (New York: Doubleday, 1965), 211.

20. William Shakespeare, *A Midsummer Night's Dream*, act 5 sc. 1 lines 12–17.

21. Rachel Ingalls in an interview with Hermione Lee, "Dream Life," *Observer*, 16 Feb. 1986, 29.

22. Rachel Ingalls, "Mrs. Caliban," in *Mrs. Caliban and Others* (London: J. M. Dent, 1983), 11.

23. Ibid., 3; italicized in original.

24. Ibid., 13.

25. Ibid.

26. Longyear, "Enemy Mine," 134.

27. Ingalls, "Mrs. Caliban," 27.

28. Ibid., 66.

29. Ibid., 27.

30. Ibid., 47.

Biographical Notes

MICHAEL BEEHLER teaches English literature at Montana State University.

GREGORY BENFORD is Professor of Physics at the University of California–Irvine and a Nebula award–winner. His latest novel is *Heart of the Comet*.

LEIGHTON BRETT COOKE teaches Russian literature at Texas A&M University and is an authority on sociobiology.

PASCAL DUCOMMUN is curator of the famed Pierre Versins library, the Maison d'Ailleurs, in Yverdon, Switzerland.

COLIN GREENLAND writes fantasy novels and reviews books for the London *Times*. He is the author of a study of the British New Wave, *The Entropy Exhibition*.

GEORGE R. GUFFEY is Professor of English at the University of California–Los Angeles. His specialties are seventeenth-century English literature and the uses of computers in the humanities.

JOHN HUNTINGTON is Professor of English at the University of Illinois at Chicago. He writes widely on science fiction and contemporary culture.

CLAYTON KOELB is Professor of German and Comparative Literature at the University of Chicago. His latest book is *The Incredulous Reader*.

FRANK MCCONNELL is Professor of English at the University of California–Santa Barbara. He is a noted authority on modern fiction and film and an author of mystery novels.

JOSEPH MILLER teaches in the Department of Animal Physiology at the University of California–Davis. He is a NASA researcher who hopes to see his animals in space by 1990.

LARRY NIVEN is a Hugo and Nebula award–winning author. He is one of the masters of creating alien beings in fiction.

NOEL PERRIN teaches both English and environmental studies at Dartmouth. He wrote the entry "Human Impacts" in the *Encyclopedia of Robotics.*

DAVID PORUSH is a professor at Rensselaer Polytechnic Institute. He recently published *The Soft Machine: Cybernetic Fiction.*

ERIC S. RABKIN is Professor of English at the University of Michigan and an authority in the study of narrative forms.

JOHN R. REED is Professor of English at Wayne State University and an authority on H. G. Wells and Victorian literature.

GEORGE E. SLUSSER is curator of the Eaton Collection and Adjunct Professor of Comparative Literature at the University of California–Riverside. He is the 1986 recipient of the Science Fiction Research Association's Pilgrim Award.

ZOE SOFIA is a graduate student in the History of Consciousness Program at the University of California–Santa Cruz and a tutor in communications studies at Murdoch University, Western Australia.

Index